The Great
Peking to Paris
Expedition

The Great
Peking to Paris
Expedition

Warren Brown
Mick Matheson
Lang Kidby

PHOTOGRAPHS BY
Bob Barker

HarperCollins*Publishers*

HarperCollins_Publishers_

First published in Australia in 2005
by HarperCollins*Publishers* Pty Limited
ABN 36 009 913 517
A member of the HarperCollins*Publishers* (Australia) Pty Limited Group

www.harpercollins.com.au

HarperCollins_Publishers_
25 Ryde Road, Pymble, Sydney, NSW 2073, Australia
31 View Road, Glenfield, Auckland 10, New Zealand
77–85 Fulham Palace Road, London W6 8JB, United Kingdom
2 Bloor Street East, 20th floor, Toronto, Ontario M4W 1A8, Canada
10 East 53rd Street, New York NY 10022, USA

National Library of Australia Cataloguing-in-Publication data:
Brown, Warren.
The Great Peking to Paris Expedition.
ISBN 0 7322 8253 5.
1. Peking to Paris Motor Challenge (1st : 1907). 2.
Automobile racing – History. 3. Antique and classic cars –
History. 4. Asia – Description and travel. 5. Europe –
Description and travel. I. Matheson, Mick. II. Kidby,
Lang. III. Barker, Bob. IV. Title.
796.72

Cover design by Helen Biles and Sharyn Raggett, HarperCollins Design Studio
Internal design by Melanie Young, Inhouse Graphic Design
Internal layout by Judi Rowe
Colour reproduction by Graphic Print Group, Adelaide
Produced in China through Phoenix Offset on 128gsm Matt Art

Photographs on pages 12, 17, 27, 30 and 198 (top left) by Luigi Barzini
Photographs on pages 47, 69, 78, 81, 97 by Scott Cameron
Photographs on pages 127, 132 and 133 from the collections of the drivers
Peking to Paris map reproduced by permission of the Australian Broadcasting Corporation and
ABC Online. © 2005 ABC. All rights reserved. The program website is available online at:
http://www.abc.net.au/tv/pekingtoparis/default.htm
6 5 4 3 2 1   05 06 07 08

I DEDICATE THIS TALE TO MY DAUGHTER, ARIEL,
WHO HAS A WHOLE WORLD WAITING FOR HER.
I KNOW SHE'LL MAKE THE MOST OF IT.
– MICK MATHESON

I WOULD LIKE TO DEDICATE THIS BOOK TO
THOSE FEARLESS MEN OF THE ORIGINAL 1907 RAID –
TO BORGHESE, CORMIER, COLLIGNON, PONS,
GODARD, DU TAILLIS, LONGONI, GUIZZARDI, BIZAC,
BARZINI AND FOUCAULT. THEY WERE TRUE HEROES.
FOR US, WE HAD OUR OWN HEROES AND
MY DEDICATION IS FOR YOU AS WELL.
– WARREN BROWN

Peking to Paris 2005
Cast of Characters

IN THE CARS

Warren Brown — driver, Itala
Lang Kidby — driver, Itala
Mick Matheson — driver, Contal

Chris Boyle — driver, Contal
Keith Brodie — driver, yellow De Dion Bouton
Louise Brodie — driver, yellow De Dion Bouton (Beijing to Moscow)
Peter Brown — driver, yellow De Dion Bouton (Moscow to Paris)
John Matheson — driver, blue De Dion Bouton
Stijnus Schotte — driver, Spyker
Andrew Snelling — driver, blue De Dion Bouton
Rob Spyker — driver, Spyker

OTHER CREW

Bob Barker — photographer
Brian Boyle — co-driver
Anthony Eden — mechanic and driver
Mark Jackson — driver, Europe
Bev Kidby — fixer
Sergei Maslyankov — fixer/translator, Russia
Henry Pang — driver, back-up truck
Robert Rosenberger — driver, back-up truck
Mark and Peter Tombs — drivers, Europe
David Wyvell — fixer/translator, China

FROM THE ABC

Peter George — series producer, *The Great Peking to Paris Expedition*
Paul Costello — director/camera
Kate McCure — sound
Bruce Permezel — director/camera
Lynne Shaw — publicist
Kim Traill — associate producer
Graham Wyse — sound

Contents

ACKNOWLEDGMENTS ~ IX

INTRODUCTION ~ 2

MAP OF THE EXPEDITION ~ 6

PEKING TO PARIS 1907...8

THE CARS, THE DRIVERS...20

Itala...22

De Dion Bouton...50

Contal...82

Spyker...100

ALMOST ON THE ROAD...120

ON THE ROAD TO PARIS...138

Acknowledgments

WARREN BROWN

Sitting here in my hotel room in Paris, the realisation of what we have achieved has only just hit me. That we have driven the same route from Peking to Paris as those lunatic motorists of 1907 in five 100-year-old cars of the original make is astonishing. Maybe we're crazier than they were — their cars were still under warranty. Quite often, there was an eerie feeling as we retraced their steps, particularly when we saw and experienced the same things they did almost 100 years ago.

There are so many people who threw their weight behind this extraordinary Expedition to make it actually succeed that I'm in grave danger of not thanking you all. There are those I will no doubt forget to thank, so I'm leaving a space for you to fill in your name when the inevitable happens and you find I've inadvertently left you out. Your name here: _____ .

Firstly, I'd like to thank Lang and Bev Kidby for their determination in seeing this crazy job through. The project became a bit a of Frankenstein's monster, and as it grew nearly out of control (over a remarkably short time, I might add) they both rolled with the punches and kept everything going. Lang prepared the Itala for this incredible drive in no time flat — no mean feat when you realise that the entire project from conception to completion took only a year. On top of that, during this time Lang also accompanied the ABC on the reconnaissance journey and was there in Beijing to unload the cars. Bev, the other half of this remarkable couple, carried on unfazed, as apparently she always does during their wild adventures around the world, and was indispensable in her role as administration officer during our race across two continents.

To the drivers, all exceptional people. To John Matheson, who had the vision and just enough maverick in him to build the Contal and drive the blue De Dion to make the dream of rallying the five original types of cars from Peking to Paris possible. To Mick Matheson, a co-author of this book, who piloted the Contal with Chris Boyle, both of whom had no idea how safe, stable or reliable the ridiculous machine would be. To crazy Stijnus Schotte, who was prepared to gamble with a near-priceless motorcar and, in doing so, nearly lost the thing in a ditch in the Urals and then pressed on. To the always cheery Rob Spyker, a descendant of the clan that made the great Dutch car in the first place. An extra special thanks to Keith Brodie, who, with wife Louise and later Peter Brown, fearlessly battled on with the yellow De Dion despite all sorts of catastrophic breakdowns. Keith's contribution in organising many of the sponsors made the Expedition feasible — no shadow of a doubt. For this, his great humour and his unflagging spirit, I dips me lid.

And to two great characters, the hairy fixit men who kept us on the road: the wild Andrew Snelling and even wilder-looking Anthony Eden, an old mate who just downed tools from fixing tractors on a winery in Margaret River to haul broken-down cars around in Mongolia. Two finer blokes you couldn't meet — serious heroes.

Our sponsors looked after us all like you wouldn't believe. Many thanks to the remarkable Helen Wong from Helen Wong Tours in Sydney, and Air China, who embraced this crazy idea and saved the day with air travel for the entire Expedition. Thanks also to P&O Nedlloyd for freighting the cars from Australia to China and back to Australia again. To KLM, who slid in to airlift the Spyker from Rotterdam to Beijing. To Marsh Insurance and Ace, who gave us incredible insurance coverage. To RM Williams Bushmen's Outfitters, who fitted us all out in oilskins, boots, hats and shirts that helped to create the whole 1907 period-piece idea. Thanks also to Cellhire for the use of their invaluable satellite phones, which more than saved the day on many occasions. To Motorworks in Botany, which allowed us to store the cars in Sydney before departure. An old mate, Jason Li, and his staff at CAA made our send-off from Beijing better than we ever expected. The magnificent Kempinski Hotel in Beijing and the wonderful Castille Hotel in Paris made our adventure beyond perfect — at the start and at a very welcome finish. Thanks also to those involved in our Sydney launch: Dr Meredith Burgmanns, NSW Premier Bob Carr, NSW Art Gallery Director Edmund Capon, Pages Event Hire, Malt Shovel Breweries and Nightingale Wines.

Faith from those at News Limited and News Corporation made so many things possible. News CEO John Hartigan, who had the vision to realise what a remarkable adventure this would be; the wonderful Janet Fife-Yeomans and the not nearly so attractive Bruce Loudon. Special thanks go to my mates from the *Daily Telegraph*. who thought this crazy idea just might work: Campbell Reid, who has gone from editor to senior News Limited executive; Editor David Penberthy, Editorial Manager Roger Coombs; and a great mate, Paul Leigh. But most of all, a most special thanks goes to the evil genius of the universe, Lana Hurst, whose experience in the world of freight produced miracles — a truly astonishingly, brilliant effort. I'll never forget her wild, grinning face at the Eiffel Tower as she handed me a glass of Champagne.

Much of this Boys' Own Adventure was made possible by the Australian Broadcasting Corporation. In the pages that follow, I deliberately haven't listed the remarkable things they organised, as the story would be a never-ending stop–start of accreditation. So here is the place to do it. Many thanks go to Sandra Levy, Director of Television, and Denise Eriksen, the ABC's Head of Factual, who became intrigued with the concept after a chance meeting in a pub in Ultimo in Sydney. Sandra and Denise, after careful consideration, took a punt to turn our adventure into a documentary television series. Peter George, with whom I had worked on the ABC TV series *Rewind*, was given the task of putting together a proposal, the $5 steak-eating Tim Clark was placed in charge as Executive Producer and the furious process of making heads and tails of a wonderful international story no one in Australia had ever heard of was under way. The amazing re-creation of various events from Beijing to Paris — the hill climb and lifting the Itala, among other fantastic scenes — were painstakingly organised from the ABC's Mission Control in Sydney, where a remarkable team was assembled to make it all work. Many thanks to Tim Clark, Sue Brandt and Belinda Gibbon, who, through the ABC's international tentacles, made all sorts of things possible.

Peter George had the task of producing what would have to be one of the most audacious TV docos ever made: two months, 24 hours a day, in some of the world's most inhospitable locations. Peter and his two crews suffered every inch of the drive with us and despite every person getting 'cabin fever' at some time or other, we all hit if off so well. The TV crew that travelled with us was every bit a part of the Expedition as the drivers themselves: Kim Traill, Paul Costello, Graham Wyse, Broooce Permezel and Katy McCure. All these guys helped make this occasional road-going nightmare fun.

But on top of this, a special thanks to a great mate: the ABC's Lynne Shaw, who right from the word go was always going to participate on the journey, and she brilliantly maintained the website and conducted regular radio interviews all over Australia, her great humour and observation creating a wide following.

And to the amazing people at HarperCollins, who have made this wonderful book you're holding possible. They have put together an exquisite book under the most pressing conditions, relying on stories written between breakdowns in the field and receiving Bob Barker's breathtaking photographs, sent via satellite equipment perched on top of trucks in Lithuania, held out of windows in China and laid out in the desert sands of the Gobi. Many thanks to Shona Martyn and Alison Urquhart, and to the ever-patient and enthusiastic Sophie Hamley, who somehow managed to wrangle all this together, produce a beautiful book and still offer to take all us authors out to lunch when we get back.

Warren Brown, Room 111, The Castille Hotel, Rue Cambon, Paris, July 2005

MICK MATHESON

No one can succeed in making a journey like this and writing a book about it without some exceptional support, and I'm so grateful to so many people who made it possible for me. I would not have been on The Great Peking to Paris Expedition without an invitation from my father, John, who gave me the Contal, financial support and, best of all, an adventurous spirit. My mother, Jane, is responsible for my passion to write and went out of her way to keep things under control in Australia while I went gallivanting across Asia and Europe. The intelligent, cool, witty and insightful Chris 'Jowls' Boyle, whom I'd spend mere hours with before Peking to Paris, is the best travelling partner I could have chosen. The irrepressible Kim Traill's inspiring knowledge, enthusiasm and grasp of languages made the adventure twice what it would have been without her. Sophie Hamley at HarperCollins has been flatteringly generous and helpful as I have provided my share of this book, the first I have written. And everybody on the Expedition deserves more praise than I have space for now.

Mick Matheson, Paris, July 2005

LANG KIDBY

The concept of a 14 000 kilometre drive across the world in 100-year-old cars seemed a far-fetched idea in mid-2004 but, within a year, five vehicles of the same type which undertook the 1907 Raid had arrived safely in Paris.

The details of the beginnings and en route adventures are well documented in this book, along with a selection of Bob Barker's excellent photographs.

The Expedition was not a tour but a drive by five individual teams on a historical re-creation. We are extremely grateful to those companies which supported the event. All members of the organising team worked hard on sponsorship but a special thanks must go to Keith Brodie and Lana Hurst for their outstanding contribution.

Everyone involved spent a great deal of time and money preparing their cars and the fact all five completed the route is a credit to their work.

There are many people who helped and encouraged along the way and they are formally acknowledged in the book, but I must personally thank Warren for his constant good humour, even when he had the psychological stuffing knocked out of him. He adopted the role of class clown when required and lifted tired spirits with a joke or prank to put a smile on weary faces.

My final thanks go to my wife, Beverley, who put in hundreds of hours behind the scenes to get the show on the road and had the thankless task of trying to find somewhere to sleep each night. Her even temper and willingness to 'just do it' has allowed me to complete projects in the past far more difficult than this one.

As they say, 'There is no such thing as trying — only doing or not doing.' I am pleased we did what we said we would do: led a group of vehicles across the world. I am pleased five crews did what they said they would do: keep five 100-year-old cars going on an impossible journey to victory.

What more could you ask for?

Lang Kidby, Paris, July 2005

Introduction
by Mick Matheson

What should I feel right now? We've been going for 59 days and there's the end, 50 metres away. In a few seconds I'll steer the Contal under the banner, pull up and switch off the engine for the last time on The Great Peking to Paris Expedition. Is this really the end? I don't know what I feel. I hadn't given much thought to this moment, which always seemed impossibly far away.

Instead, I'd concentrated on discovering how much the world has changed since the Peking to Paris Raid in 1907, the motoring event we have now, successfully, re-created. What has motoring done for the world since then? How has motoring itself changed? How has humanity changed? It's been a fascinating century and our Expedition has dived into a significant chunk of its story.

We had many expectations before the start. The idea of driving four veteran cars and a replica of a failed century-old three-wheeler from Peking to Paris via the Gobi Desert and most of Russia filled us with dread, excitement, anxiety and enthusiasm from the very beginning. We'd tell our friends about it and they'd either plead to come along or smirk and shake their heads, wondering why anyone would be so silly.

Friends with veteran cars understood our passion but thought we had no chance. A big drive with a veteran car club is 200 kilometres, a journey done maybe once a year and planned six months or more ahead of time. We proposed to go more than 13 000 kilometres through some of the world's worst driving conditions.

And those conditions turned out to be far tougher than we could have imagined. There were times in the Gobi when we struggled to do 120 kilometres in a 16-hour day, but we remember those tracks with fondness after the nightmare of China's 'seven-day traffic jam', an entire highway crammed solid with thousands of trucks going nowhere. Siberia's roads were so bad that it's almost impossible to describe them to people. The highway from Moscow to Vladivostok was so appalling that trucks got bogged on it, potholes were like bomb craters and our cars suffered more damage than they did in the Gobi.

Sometimes we actually envied the 1907 Raiders, who only had to put up with mud, slush, collapsing bridges and encroaching forest.

It's still a struggle to drive through these remote regions but it's not just the conditions that make life hard. As in 1907, the Chinese authorities seemed to delight in putting bureaucratic barriers before us, frustrating us at every turn and even sending a military spy truck to shadow us. Russia's 'service' industry — its awful hotels in particular — revelled in making its customers furious, and when there was no translator nearby we often saw the people behind the counter just turn away and ignore us.

There was also a lingering suspicion of foreigners, a hangover from the paranoia instilled in the population during the Soviet era. This echoed the wariness of Russians about Japanese spies in 1907, when the Raiders were warned that they might be attacked as spies.

Yet the people of Russia were so warm and open towards us, again reflecting the experience of 1907. We fell in love with them — except the pests who'd arrive with a skinful of vodka — and whenever our cars broke down we knew we'd find the right people to help us get moving again as quickly as possible.

The cars exceeded our expectations. They became dependable machines and eventually we vanquished any doubts about reaching Paris. One of the De Dions broke down on the very first day, which seemed an ominous sign, but we got it mobile again and carried on. And on. We suffered broken driveshafts, broken differential housings, broken springs and a typical array of electrical and mechanical woes, but no car was ever off the road for more than three days, no one was left so far behind that they couldn't catch up and, despite the odds, all five cars drove into Paris. Funnily enough, the same De Dion broke down as we entered Paris. Again, we had it up and running within minutes and the convoy carried on to the end.

Throughout the Expedition we faced our own personal challenges, too. We were essentially a group of strangers thrown together with a common goal. There was no guarantee we'd like each other, no certainty about whether anyone would be loyal to the Expedition when things got difficult. The only thing we could be sure of was that we'd be tested to our limits on many occasions.

We were deprived of sleep when long days turned into all-nighters trying to service and repair cars. We were sorely tried when we faced breakdowns that would usually mean trucking the car home ... if only we were home. But we managed to rise above the trials, coaxing each other along when necessary and pitching in to fix things.

And, of course, we partied hard together on many nights, from China through to France. We joked, we laughed, we shook off each day's hardships with humour and mateship, forming new, strong friendships that will last beyond Paris.

As I swing right and idle the Contal under the banner beside the Eiffel Tower, the whole journey floods into my consciousness, overwhelming me and filling me with emotion. I switch off the engine and lean forward, resting my elbows on my knees and receding deeply into reverie. I don't how long it lasts — I'm off in my own little world, oblivious to the throng around me. Suddenly Andrew Snelling's outstretched hand and hearty shout of 'Congratulations, Mick!' snaps me out of it. I laugh as I shake his hand. I feel fantastic.

USSIA

asnayoyarsk

rkutsk ●
● Ulan-Ude
an Baatar ●

MONGOLIA

● Zhangilikan

PEKING ★
(Beijing)

NORTH KOREA

SOUTH KOREA

JAPAN

PACIFIC OCEAN

TAIWAN

NMAR

LAOS

THAILAND

VIETNAM

KAMPUCHEA

PHILIPPINES

BRUNEI

MALAYSIA

SINGAPORE

I N D O N E S I A

PAPUA
NEW GUINEA

FIJI

NEW CALEDONIA

AUSTRALIA

NEW ZEALAND

PEKING TO PARIS 1907

The Great Peking to Paris Raid of 1907

Will anyone agree to go this summer
from Peking to Paris by motorcar?

Le Matin

In the embryonic days of the automobile, it was France that really embraced the motorcar. True, it was two Germans, Gottlieb Daimler and Wilhelm Maybach, who in 1886 built the first self-propelled, four-wheeled vehicle that can be described as a motorcar. But it was the French who pounced on their idea, muscling in on the emerging automobile industry in a way that made other industrialised nations' heads spin.

Before Henry Ford dropped the equivalent of an automotive atomic bomb on the world in 1908 with his Model T, France held court, designing, building and exporting cars of all shapes and sizes around the world.

If you owned a motorcar in the early 1900s, the chances were it was a De Dion Bouton, a Peugeot, a Renault, a Delage, a Darracq or one of scores of cars designed and manufactured in France. Paris had fashioned itself as the centre of the automotive universe; not in the way we think of Detroit or Tokyo today, but a place where the motorcar was fêted almost as a work of art.

At the turn of the twentieth century, French car manufacturers became increasingly preoccupied with two things — speed and reliability. Being able to travel at speeds previously undreamt of, and driving without fear of being stranded miles from home, were the keys to persuading a cautious public of the benefits of owning a motorcar. Salesmen realised that there was no better way to entice potential buyers into the showroom than by dazzling them with displays of speed coupled with reliability: long-distance motor racing was the perfect way.

In the first few years of the twentieth century, Europe went speed crazy. Car-obsessed fans turned up in their thousands to watch dramatic inter-city races such as the 1902 Paris to Vienna Marathon, where cars reached speeds of up to 100 km/h. Demonstrating speed was never a problem. The philosophy was simple: build a bigger engine, burn more fuel, and your car goes faster. But the crowd's enthusiasm for racing on public roads was suddenly doused in 1903, when, during the race from Paris to Madrid, the mix of uncontrolled spectators and incredibly fast cars left ten drivers dead and hundreds injured. The race was cancelled midway, at Bordeaux, and the competitors were not even allowed to drive their cars back to Paris. The race left a bad taste in everyone's mouth.

Instead of highlighting performance, manufacturers switched their focus to promoting improvements in reliability. However, this was clearly a formidable task. Despite the ever-increasing numbers of motorcars on the road, owning one was not proving as wonderful as showroom salesmen promised. Cars were still contraptions; machines made up of a lot of fiddly parts that could be easily broken. On top of that, motorists had to be constantly mindful of the perils of everyday driving: fuel availability, tyre punctures, overheating, losing oil pressure … or something that was both spectacular and catastrophic suddenly happening under the bonnet. Those well-heeled enough to buy one of these new-fangled automobiles more often than not found themselves standing at the roadside by their smoking car, suffering jibes from farmers shuffling by in horse-drawn carts. As far as the public was concerned, motoring had become synonymous with danger and being stranded somewhere. What was needed was a serious test, something that would prove to the public that the automobile was the way of the future.

In January 1907 the Parisian newspaper *Le Matin* offered a challenge: 'Will anyone agree to go this summer from Peking to Paris by motorcar?' *Le Matin*'s proposal seemed far too preposterous to be taken seriously, but its sheer audacity captured Europe's imagination. Everyone knew you could drive, even race, from one neighbouring European country to another, but what if you were to take a car from one side of the world to another? To drive 14 000 kilometres where no one had ever heard of a car, let alone seen one; where there were no maps, no roads, no support?

ETTORE GUIZZARDI STEERS
THE ITALA WITH PRECISION
AS CHINESE COOLIES DRAG
AND PUSH THE CAR UP THE
KALGAN MOUNTAIN PASS.
BOULDERS OBSCURING THE
PATH WERE ROUTINELY
CHIPPED AWAY WITH PICKS
AND DRIVEN OVER, OFTEN
AT PERILOUS ANGLES.

BOGGED IN A RICE PADDY NEAR THE BANKS OF THE HUN HO RIVER, THE ITALA IS STUCK FAST
IN A MASS OF SUBMERGED TREE ROOTS. GUIZZARDI IS AT THE FRONT OF THE CAR,
HACKING AT THE ROOTS WITH A TOMAHAWK TO FREE THE WHEELS.

The Peking to Paris Raid, as it was called, became a hot topic across the Continent. In the words of one car manufacturer, the Marquis De Dion, 'This is a real Jules Verne undertaking … but nothing is impossible!' The Marquis understood the Raid's potential: here was an opportunity to prove the worth of the automobile and for France to cement its rightful position as the dominant presence in car manufacturing. Initially, *Le Matin* was flooded with entries from all over Europe, but as an understanding of the logistics and financial enormity of such an undertaking filtered through, one by one potential participants dropped out.

The challenge was ultimately taken up by the drivers of five automobiles — two French 10 hp De Dion Boutons, a 15 hp Spyker from Holland, a 35/40 hp Itala from Turin and a French three-wheeled 6 hp Contal cycle-car. The two factory-entered 2-cylinder De Dion Boutons were driven by the handlebar-moustached Georges Cormier and his subordinate, Victor Collignon (another devotee of impressive finger-twirling facial hair). With them travelled De Dion factory mechanic Jean Bizac and Italian journalist Edgardo Longoni, a reporter for Rome's *Il Secolo* newspaper and the *London Tribune*. Cormier, a Parisian car dealer, had had some success driving De Dion Boutons in endurance trials and was a staunch advocate of small, lightweight cars rather than heavier, more powerful types.

The unorthodox three-wheeled Contal Moto-Tri, piloted by the young Auguste Pons and his mechanic, Octave Foucault, seemed an unlikely starter: the contraption was configured much like an ice-cream delivery trike. The rider sat astride a conventional motorbike chassis fixed behind a passenger's chair, which in turn was positioned between two front wheels. Pons, like Cormier, had achieved some success with the Contal in local motor races, but whether or not the tricycle was capable of such an arduous journey as the Raid remained to be seen.

Perhaps the Raid's most remarkable character was Charles Godard, a gregarious French carnival worker and part-time con-artist who was paired for the journey with *Le Matin*'s correspondent, Jean du Taillis. Through some fast talking, Godard had convinced Dutch car manufacturer Jacobus Spijker to loan him a Spyker car for the 14 000-kilometre journey, no mean feat when you consider that Spykers were the Dutch Rolls-Royces: top-of-the-range automobiles with the price tag to match. Always the life of the party, Godard made virtually no preparations, and sold the Spyker's spare parts to buy a first-class ticket aboard the ship to Peking. When derided by du Taillis for his reckless planning, Godard leapt to his feet in typical theatrical fashion and responded,

'Either I shall never see Paris again or I shall come back to it in my Spyker, hot from Peking!'

Italian aristocrat and military man Prince Scipione Borghese announced to the world that he would enter the Raid driving a 7-litre, 4-cylinder Itala. With him would be his long-serving mechanic, Ettore Guizzardi, and Luigi Barzini, a journalist with the *Corriere della Sera* newspaper. While serving in the military, Borghese had acquired considerable experience of some of the remote regions the Raid was to pass through, giving him a superior understanding of just how difficult the journey would be. A meticulous planner renowned for his mountaineering feats and horse-breaking skills, the Prince immediately began plotting the Itala's route so that he would be the first across Asia and into Europe.

But of all the obstacles the motorists would face crossing two continents, the first was to be the diplomatic impasse between China and Europe. In 1907, China was still seething from humiliating terms forced upon it by European nations after the Boxer Rebellion seven years before. The secret Chinese society of 'Righteous and Harmonious Fists' — or 'Boxers', as they were called by foreigners — had sought to destroy any trace of Western influence, instigating a violent revolt.

After the European Legations in Peking had been under siege for two months, military forces from Britain, Germany, France, the United States and Russia arrived to quash the uprising. Once they had done that, they proceeded to exact revenge. The Empress Dowager, who fled the capital as Western forces reclaimed the Legations, was only allowed to return under the strictest conditions. The arrival of the Peking to Paris motorists and their five automobiles caused instant alarm among Chinese officials, who were convinced that the members of this strange entourage were actually spies. No one had ever seen a motorcar in Peking before — was it some sort of new military weapon? Were these foreigners searching for an invasion route from the north, so that an enemy could enter China in the same way Genghis Khan had done centuries before? Furthermore, that the expedition was actually called a Raid seemed absolute proof of the foreign devils' intentions. The Chinese set about obstructing the motorists' progress at every turn; they tried to impose an impractical route, delayed the administrative process and eventually issued unacceptable visas through Mongolia. Frustrated, all the motorists could do was wait as Chinese officials refused to co-operate.

Meanwhile, Prince Borghese went on a 300-kilometre horse ride north into the Kalgan Mountains near the Mongolian border, and spent days carrying a bamboo stick the width of his car, painstakingly measuring to see whether or not the Itala was capable of squeezing through the tight mountain passes. On his return to Peking, Borghese learnt that diplomatic negotiations between the Chinese and European Legations had completely broken down. The French Minister in Peking had received a letter from the Wai Wu Pu, the Grand Council of the Celestial Empire, stating that the Chinese government was completely opposed to the Raid's passage through Mongolia. Unable to secure a guarantee for the motorists' safety, the Peking to Paris Raid was cancelled. The drivers called a meeting, at which any suggestion of pulling out was dispensed with by Prince Borghese. 'Gentlemen,' he announced, 'whatever conclusion you come to, my own decision is made, and nothing can change it. I shall start on Monday.' The French teams had no choice: they could not allow an Italian to enter a French event unchallenged. The Raid was back on.

On Monday, 10 June, the five cars departed the International Legation in Peking for the 14 000-kilometre journey to Paris, fêted with a spectacular fireworks display and military bands pumping out the national anthems of Italy, Holland and France. But it was to be a debilitating start: teeming rain soaked the crews as they approached their first real difficulty — crossing the ruined ancient marble bridges over the Cha Ho River. Centuries of neglect had seen the approaches to the disintegrating bridges washed away; the height between road and bridge was sometimes as great as 5 metres. With block and tackle, crowbars and perseverance, the cars were hoisted and dragged on top of each bridge and driven carefully across the cracked and uneven surface, the drivers trying to keep the wheels from plunging into the wide ruts that separated the flagstones. Once across, the whole process with block and tackle was reversed, to lower the cars down the other side. The crews were soon approaching the Great Wall, and facing the daunting task of finding a path through the Kalgan Mountains, which separate China from the Mongolian Plateau.

The drivers had been told in Peking that the mountain range was impenetrable, and that any attempt to find a way through with a motorcar would prove impossible. This was no deterrent: the cars wound their way deep into cavernous, mist-filled gorges that grew so narrow the drivers could touch both walls by spreading out their arms. The path then grew worse, strewn with razor-sharp rocks and boulders that needed to be either broken with pickaxes or levered out of the way. Massive willow tree roots were chopped away to clear watercourses that were now being used as thoroughfares. The further the motorists went, the steeper the incline became; the cars were lashed to teams of mules and manhandled by Chinese porters.

Desperate for water and believing they'd been left to die by their companions, Pons and Foucault tried to walk back to civilisation.

Day after day the crews and their porters dragged the cars higher into the mountains, with mudguards and wheels scraping the sides of seemingly endless twisting passages. Drivers negotiated the cars along the crumbling edges of dramatic precipices, then lowered them with ropes down near-suicidal ravines, only to have to then haul them up the other side. Every inch forward brought them closer to the Mongolian Plateau.

It took five days to get to the summit, and there the Raiders faced their next hurdle: the burning sands of the Gobi Desert, littered with the bones of camels, horses and oxen. Luigi Barzini wrote that the Gobi had 'an indescribable spirit of death', and felt like 'a place of agonies'.

Although the two De Dions were committed to travelling together, the vast expanse of the desert allowed Prince Borghese to gain an impressive lead over the rest of the field. But not everyone was faring so well.

Somewhere in the Gobi, the Contal crew ran out of petrol. Desperate for water and believing they'd been left to die by their companions, Pons and Foucault decided to abandon their tiny vehicle and try to walk back to civilisation. After a fruitless 20-kilometre march in the shimmering desert haze, they returned to their machine, resigned to an agonising death in the Gobi's sands. Then, as if by some miracle, Pons and Foucault were rescued: they were discovered, lying unconscious, by Mongolian cameleers. The pair eventually made their way back to Peking, having left the Contal to perish in the desert.

The Spyker, meanwhile, had also run out of fuel. Godard knew full well that he did not have enough petrol to cross the desert, but had presumed he'd be able to score some from the De Dion crews when they caught up to him. Cormier and Collignon had already loaned Godard several litres of fuel, and on discovering the stranded Spyker, they sped past without stopping, promising to send fuel back once they reached the next town. For three days Godard and du Taillis waited by their car — suffering blistering heat during the day and freezing cold at night. In desperation, they had even begun to drink the oily water from the Spyker's radiator. When they had given up all hope of rescue, the pair suddenly saw two galloping horsemen on the

THE ITALA'S FRONT END PROTRUDING THROUGH THE REMAINS OF A ROTTING SIBERIAN BRIDGE WHICH COLLAPSED UNDER THE CAR'S WEIGHT. A TEAM OF RAILWAY WORKERS HAULED THE CAR OUT AND GUIZZARDI STARTED IT FIRST GO.

THE SIBERIAN ROADS WERE SO BAD THAT PRINCE BORGHESE DECIDED TO USE THE TRANS-SIBERIAN RAILWAY TRACKS — JOLTING ALONG THE SLEEPERS WAS PREFERABLE TO BEING BOGGED IN THE COUNTRYSIDE. HERE THE ITALA IS PICTURED ON THE BANKS OF LAKE BAIKAL.

horizon. As they rode closer, the horsemen give the thumbs up: they were carrying cans filled with much-prized petrol. Godard and du Taillis were saved. They were days behind the others now, but Godard was determined to catch them up, and drove 617 kilometres nonstop in 23 hours. Godard didn't know it at the time, but he had set an individual world record for long-distance driving.

Once inside Russia, Prince Borghese followed the recently completed Trans-Siberian Railway, the construction of which had had an unexpected side effect: the roads running parallel to the railway had virtually disappeared due to a lack of traffic and maintenance. On top of this, the summer rains had turned Siberia into a vast morass. All this resulted in the car being bogged frequently. Frustrated, the Prince sought permission to drive along the railway itself; he was allowed, and so his car jolted along the sleepers for hundreds of kilometres.

Despite the bone-jarring ride, driving along the railway seemed like a good idea — until the Itala's wheels suddenly became stuck on the tracks in the path of an oncoming freight train. The car was prised free and moved to safety only moments before the locomotive thundered past. Trains weren't the only near catastrophe for the Itala; it came even closer to disaster when, while crossing a derelict road bridge, the rotting planks under the rear wheels gave way. The car plunged backwards into a ravine, crashing on its rear end in a shower of debris. The Itala finished up held in an almost vertical position by the bridge's remaining beams. Miraculously, no one was seriously injured and the car itself seemed to have escaped too much damage: the spare tyres lashed to the rear had cushioned it against the worst of the impact. After local railway workers built a makeshift derrick, the car was hauled out. The crank handle was turned … and the Itala started first go.

Godard, meanwhile, had been experiencing problems with the Spyker's magneto, and an unwelcome chicken had come home to roost — he'd sold his spare magneto in Europe before departing for Peking. He was no mechanic, so he put the Spyker on a train and sent it 1300 kilometres west from Tcheremkhovo to a university in Tomsk, where the electrical engineering department would attempt to fix the problem. When the Spyker was finally repaired, Godard put the car back on a train, heading east this time, to return to the spot where the magneto had failed — Tcheremkhovo — and start the Raid again. Or so he said. Godard's heroic attempt to stay in the Raid was all very well, but he sent the bill for the cost of transporting the Spyker by rail to *Le Matin*; this move infuriated the newspaper's managing director, who set in train a course of action that would eventually backfire badly on Godard.

By the time Prince Borghese arrived in Moscow, on 31 July, he was 17 days ahead of the rest of the field. Borghese was so confident of his lead that he made a detour of 1000 kilometres to attend a grand ball in St Petersburg. The following day he drove back and rejoined his original route. He arrived in Paris, to a welcome from frenetic, cheering crowds, 21 days ahead of the De Dion Boutons and the Spyker. Wheeling the Itala around to a stop in front of the red velvet stage, the Prince gave a speech in impeccable French: 'Gentlemen, you have exaggerated. We were not heroes; we were simply patient.'

The three remaining cars were now travelling through Russia in convoy, intending to stay together at least until the German frontier. But unbeknownst to Godard, plain-clothes policemen were waiting at the German border to arrest him for extradition to France on the charge of false pretences. More to the point, the proprietor of *Le Matin* wanted Godard removed from the race. The Raid had, from the outset, two purposes: to promote the newspaper and to provide a huge boost for the French automobile industry. An Italian car had already arrived first in Paris, and the second was certainly not going to be anything but French. But Jacobus Spijker had been prepared for this: he had a factory driver standing by to take over the car when Godard was dragged away. Godard was duly released on appeal, but *Le Matin*'s plan to knock him out of the race had worked.

However, Godard had not given up. When the three cars had stopped for lunch, only 10 kilometres outside Paris, a crowd suddenly gathered around the Spyker. There was Godard, fixed firmly in the driver's seat, desperate to get one of the team mechanics to swing the crank handle. It was not to be. He was overpowered by security men and the police and dragged back through the crowd.

The victory parade began to roll towards Paris, the De Dions in the lead, and the Spyker driven — for the first time in 14 000 kilometres — by Godard's close friend du Taillis. Doused with champagne and presented with flowers, Cormier and Collignon were fêted as heroes. It was a proud day for France.

THE CARS, THE DRIVERS

Itala 1907

I hereby enter my name for the Peking to Paris race in an Itala motorcar.

Prince Scipione Borghese

There's little doubt that such a bold and concise acceptance of *Le Matin*'s motoring challenge would have shocked the French organisers and participants of the Peking to Paris Raid. Not only had Prince Scipione Borghese decided that this long-distance endurance trial was going to be a race — he was throwing down the gauntlet by entering a French motoring event in a car boasting the name of one of France's great rivals: Italy.

Although the Itala marque existed for 30 years, its moment in the sun came before World War I, particularly when the Peking to Paris victory rocketed the company's name to fame around the world. Founded in Turin in 1904, Itala was one of many exclusive marques created by the Ceirano family, whose philosophy was simple: build big, sporty cars with big, sporty engines that could travel exceedingly fast.

Just like today's quality car manufacturers, Itala decided early on that motor racing was a good way to both promote their vehicles and do research and development. The early racing Italas, which had engines up to a gigantic 14 litres, won undying fame in the first long-distance races and grands prix.

In the very first large, organised motor race in Italy, the 1905 Meeting in Brescia, Italas took out every prize and trophy — against some very tough opposition. They followed this up with numerous victories in the legendary Targa Floria, an event that runs to this very day; leading race drivers, past and present, and numerous enthusiasts from around the globe, still gather annually to race their classic racing and sports cars along this winding 600-kilometre course.

There were lots of Itala victories in Europe, South America and even Australia, but motor racing alone never made a successful car company. Itala built on its reputation for strength and reliability and entered the super-luxury market. It made large, comfortable vehicles with coachwork that was something to behold; the vast majority were designed to be chauffeur-driven.

The list of owners is impressive: Queen Marguerite of Italy had six Italas; Prince Borghese owned three, while six other European kings had Itala limousines. These limousines were the darlings of the nobility for many years and were seen regularly at the legendary Brooklands racing circuit in England. During World War I, the famed Vickers Aircraft Company started manufacturing at Brooklands by occupying Itala's English assembly buildings.

The fact that the rich and famous loved the marque was good for the company's luxury sales, but did not help a management looking at becoming a high-volume car manufacturer. Right from the early days, Itala experimented with smaller engines and chassis, all based on their top-shelf models. They achieved a modicum of success with this: a number of less wealthy buyers found what they were looking for in these cars — lively vehicles that performed well, had a reasonable price tag and still had the Itala badge on the radiator.

The decision by Prince Scipione Borghese in 1907 to use an Itala on the 14 000-kilometre race from Peking to Paris immortalised the name of the most famous pre–World War I brand. His car was built by the factory to his specifications. It had their large — by modern standards, mid-size — 7-litre engine as a power plant. Using a 7-litre engine was diametrically opposed to contemporary thinking about cross-country motor trials. Motorists in France generally agreed that lightweight cars would have superiority over heavier, more powerful types in off-road situations. In many cases this was true, but the Prince was banking on being able to use raw horsepower across the Gobi Desert and Siberia to arrive in Paris first. The chassis, axles and gearbox were off-the-shelf items selected from various models. The four other cars in the race were basically standard factory models in appearance, with everything stacked into or onto the normal car body.

This combining of elements was not unusual in the days before mass production. Most manufacturers offered owners numerous combinations of engine, chassis and other parts. Bodies were, of course, hand-built, often onto a chassis sent to the owner's local coach-builder. Almost every car was different, in some way, from all the others. This has led, 100 years later, to huge difficulties for restorers, who find the different construction specifications of the 'same' model cars almost impossible to identify exactly.

Apart from a heavier-than-normal gauge steel chassis, Borghese's battleship-grey Itala was more or less a standard 7-litre, 4-cylinder, 35/40 hp model. The engine's cylinders were cast in pairs and bolted to a cast-iron engine block. The electricals consisted of a low-tension magneto ignition and specially patented Itala spark plugs with carbide-powered head- and sidelights. A 4-speed gearbox driving the differential with a shaft was one of the Itala's most advanced features — most racing cars of the day were chain-driven.

Seating was for three: two seats in the front, with a third seat positioned between two 150-litre fuel tanks mounted at the rear. A tank for oil and a tank for water were also positioned at the back, along with a large locker-style tool chest. Initially, four iron planks to be used as sand channels were attached to the car in a V shape, like mudguards, but these proved heavy and useless and were dispensed with once the journey got under way. So distinctive were the huge fuel tanks and toolboxes, and the planks, that several model makers to this day produce a Pechino-Parigi Itala model car.

Despite the care and thought Prince Borghese had put into his special requirements for the car, the company was nervous about adverse publicity if it failed to complete such a gruelling course, and begged the Prince to withdraw his application. Unfazed, the Prince declared the car 'an excellent machine, but only the tool by which success is achieved, the chisel used by the artist to shape the statue which the inspiration of his own mind had created'. The sculptor was taking his chisel from Peking to Paris, and that was that.

During the 1907 race, the Itala performed beautifully. Although there is little detailed information in the various books on the event, reading between the lines suggests that Ettore Guizzardi was constantly tinkering with it. Oil and water were

PRINCE BORGHESE'S MECHANIC, ETTORE GUIZZARDI, AT THE WHEEL OF THE ITALA
IN THE COURTYARD OF THE ITALIAN LEGATION IN PEKING.

DUE TO THE CONSTRUCTION OF THE TRANS-SIBERIAN RAILWAY ONLY A FEW YEARS BEFORE THE RAID,
MANY ROADS AND BRIDGES WERE LEFT TO DETERIORATE. WHILE CROSSING ONE SUCH BRIDGE,
THE ROTTING PLANKS GAVE WAY UNDER THE ITALA'S REAR WHEELS. THE CAR LANDED ON ITS END
AND TIPPED SKYWARD. FORTUNATELY, NONE OF THE THREE OCCUPANTS WAS SERIOUSLY INJURED.

watched closely, and a new spoked artillery wheel was constructed in Siberia by a local blacksmith using only an axe. Numerous flat tyres were repaired; most of these were a result of the poor rubber compounds of those early days — they could not withstand treatment a modern tyre would take in its stride.

The condition of the roads for much of the journey was very poor, and speeds were generally slow: Luigi Barzini finds a full day driving at 60 km/h worthy of mention in his book, for instance. The road conditions plus overloading also led to broken springs in all the vehicles; the drivers either carried spares or had them sent via the Trans-Siberian Railway while the cars were en route.

The combination of the superior leadership, experience and determination of Borghese and the reliability and agility of his Itala saw the team cross the finish line in Paris 21 days before his rivals — they'd even managed to take a detour to St Petersburg!

The Italian national motor museum holds a post-race report by Itala on the state of the engine, gearbox and rear axle. The good condition of all items amazed the engineers — one comment states that the replacement of a few bearings and seals would see the car ready to undertake a second Peking to Paris. Prince Borghese's Itala is the only survivor of the great Raid, and is on display in the Museo Dell'automobile in Turin.

Prince Scipione Borghese

In reading contemporary accounts of the original Peking to Paris Raid, it's tempting to dismiss Prince Scipione Borghese almost as if he were some Boys' Own character: aristocrat, artillery officer, devoted husband and the dashing winner of the Raid. He was a perfect hero in an era when class-conscious Europeans expected nothing less than the Peking to Paris Raid to be won by a peer of the realm ... and the rest of the field to arrive in their correct social pecking order.

Newspaper illustrations at the time show Borghese to be an aloof, clean-shaven, ramrod-straight military man with chiselled features and piercing eyes; he was described to the world as an accomplished Italian explorer and diplomat, fluent in five languages, a man who did not drink, gamble or smoke. Whether he was conducting scientific expeditions in Mesopotamia or Turkestan or pitting himself against his own fears on the side of a mountain in the Alps, it was as if the Prince had spent his entire life preparing for the Peking to Paris Raid.

Born in Migliarino near Pisa in 1871, Prince Scipione Borghese was a descendant of Pope Paul V, 'Borghesius' (1550–1621), and grew up in one of the most respected aristocratic households in Europe. At the age of 18, Borghese joined the army. He was sent to artillery school, where he encountered other young officers from all social spheres — and became something of a socialist. In an age when many had begun to question the relevance of the upper classes, the young Prince rebelled against the traditional attitudes of old Europe: he was interested in technology, machinery and adventure in far-off places. He grew into a confident and complex man who seemed determined to cement his place in history through actions rather than birthright.

During his military service, the Prince acquired experience of some of the remote regions the Raid would later pass through. He conducted expeditions that took him through Siberia and the Pamir Mountains of Central Asia; these trips gave him a clear understanding of the problems the expedition was to face. The Prince was very good at interpreting and using maps, and had an unusually sharp memory: he could recall terrain he had traversed years before almost as if it were a photograph. He also had an extraordinary talent for planning, organisation and command. These skills would prove invaluable throughout the Raid.

When *Le Matin* issued the challenge to drive from Peking to Paris in 1907, 36-year-old Borghese immediately decided to enter, and devised a plan. It had three parts: tackling the route; organising a supply line; and preparing and maintaining his car. He was determined to win. In Peking the Prince discovered that the newspaper had cancelled the Raid, but he told the other drivers that, regardless of their intentions, he was going anyway; this forced them all to compete.

There must have been little doubt that Borghese would arrive in Paris first. He had the money, the fastest car, impeccable contacts, experience and training. He must have been the other drivers' worst nightmare. Further, Borghese's signature was notably absent from an agreement struck in Paris to travel in convoy. Unlike the other participants, who were either making pacts with each other for support or relying on sheer luck and bravado to get through, Borghese was totally self-reliant, and made no arrangements with anyone except his own suppliers.

In later years Borghese rejoined the army, and was sent on a diplomatic mission to Russia during the revolution of 1917, to urge Lenin to take up arms against Germany. He retired from public life, disillusioned, around the time of the emergence of Mussolini's Fascism. He died in 1927.

ITALA 1907

HAVING PUSHED AND PULLED THE ITALA ONTO THE GRASSY PLAINS OF THE
MONGOLIAN PLATEAU, CHINESE PORTERS RELAX AT THE MONGOLIAN BORDER
AS PRINCE BORGHESE AND GUIZZARDI PREPARE TO JETTISON AS MUCH
UNWANTED WEIGHT FROM THE CAR AS POSSIBLE.

BORGHESE AND BARZINI WAITING FOR THE RACE TO START —
THEY SIGNED THEIR NAMES ON THE ORIGINAL PHOTOGRAPH.

Ettore Guizzardi

Of all the teams that entered the Peking to Paris Raid of 1907, none could have hoped to match the unique combination of Prince Scipione Borghese and his mechanic, Ettore Guizzardi. It wasn't just the Prince's famous planning skills and the fact that he entered the event in the most powerful car that brought the Prince to victory — it was his unquestionable trust in his longtime servant and friend that brought the Itala first over the line in Paris.

Guizzardi had an amazing mechanical aptitude. Born a Romany (gypsy) of peasant background, the young Ettore displayed a fascination with all things mechanical. At the age of 15 he was working with his father as a fireman in the cab of a steam locomotive when it slid off the rails and crashed down an embankment. The accident injured Ettore, but it killed his father.

Guizzardi was taken to the nearby Borghese Villa, where he recuperated slowly under the care of Prince Borghese, who had recognised the boy's mechanical genius. The Prince provided an education for Guizzardi, including sending him to a polytech to study engineering.

When the Peking to Paris event was announced in January 1907, there was no question as to whom Prince Borghese would take with him as mechanical overseer.

While the drivers waited in Peking for the diplomatic tangle between governments to sort itself out, Guizzardi spent his time familiarising himself with the Itala; he regularly stripped and rebuilt the gearbox, tightening and retightening every nut and bolt in the car. Correspondent Luigi Barzini recorded his first meeting with Guizzardi. 'He was flat on his back under the Itala, lying quite still, with his arms folded. My first thought was that he was busy working. But he was relaxing. I discovered later that he was in his favourite place of off-duty pleasure. When there is nothing else to do he simply lies on his back under his motorcar and observes it, contemplates it item by item, every bolt and screw, in mystic communion with his machine.'

In the course of the 16 000-kilometre event (the Itala drove further than its rivals due to the St Petersburg detour), the Itala had many close shaves with disaster, but every time the car pulled through, thanks in no small part to Guizzardi's mechanical skills and maintenance.

The perilous ascent through the Kalgan Mountains early in the event seems to have been the greatest moment of concern for Guizzardi. In order to get the Itala on top of the Mongolian Plateau, the car had been stripped to the chassis in Peking; the bodywork and fuel tanks had been lashed to mules and sent on ahead for Guizzardi to reassemble after the great climb. With the toolbox locker placed across the chassis rails like a bench seat, Guizzardi leant over the steering wheel, carefully negotiating a path with utmost precision as the Itala was manhandled over jagged rocks which scraped the underneath of the car.

For five days his nerves were on edge — every crunching boulder underneath could crack the differential, gearbox or sump irreparably — but thanks to his careful nursing through the twisting passes, the car made it to safety.

After the Peking to Paris Raid, Guizzardi continued working for the Prince as a mechanic and chauffeur on the Borghese estate. In 1963, at the age of 83, Ettore Guizzardi — the last of the Itala's crew of three — died in Rome.

Luigi Barzini

Of the three journalists who travelled with the 1907 Peking to Paris Raid, the best remembered is Luigi Barzini, correspondent for the *Corriere della Sera* newspaper and author of *Da Pechino a Parigi* (*From Peking to Paris*), the most popular record of the event. In an age long before radio and television, Barzini was one of a new wave of twentieth-century newspaper journalists whose colourful writing, telegraphed from the field, enthralled and excited readers every day.

By the time of the Peking to Paris Raid, 33-year-old Barzini was already a household name in his native Italy. Interestingly, he began his career as a cartoonist for the Roman newspaper *Il Fanfulla*, but changed direction in 1899 when he secured an interview with the reclusive opera singer Adelina Patti. Impressed, the editor of the Milan newspaper *Corriere della Sera* approached Barzini to become the London correspondent — he accepted Barzini's claim that he could, of course, speak English.

Arriving in London with an Italian-English dictionary, Barzini commenced filing impressive stories about secret Chinese opium enclaves and an impending Boxer revolt in Peking. He was therefore a natural choice for *Corriere della Sera* to send as its correspondent with the International Expeditionary relief force to the besieged European Legations in Peking. His articles and drawings made him famous overnight, and he spent the next few years filing stories from around the world: in 1900 he was writing in Argentina on Italian migration; in 1903 he was in Russia covering political unrest; and in 1904 and 1905 he was in Japan reporting on the Russia–Japan conflict. Barzini was the only European journalist with the Japanese Army at the decisive battle of Mudken; the fighting lasted 30 days — in -30ºC temperatures.

He was also the perfect person to be *Corriere della Sera*'s correspondent for an adventure such as the Peking to Paris Raid. Eagerly filing stories by telegraph as Prince Borghese headed west, Barzini's adventures were also translated into English for London's *Daily Telegraph*. Bearing in mind the fact that he was reporting almost a century before satellite communication, email, digital photography and laptop computers, Barzini's reporting efforts were remarkable. While attempting to file a story from a remote telegraph post in Mongolia, Barzini noticed the telegraphist pencilling the message as 'Number 1' on the telegraph sheet. He asked the telegraphist if this was the first message transmitted that day; the man replied that it was the first transmitted since the telegraph office opened, six years before.

Even though his colourful writing style seems positively florid by today's standards (the noun *Barzinismo* was coined as a description), Barzini's account of the Peking to Paris Raid, published in 1908, is one of the biggest-selling motoring books of all time. Translated into 13 languages, *Da Pechino a Parigi* was constantly in print somewhere in the world until 1973.

Barzini clearly admired Prince Borghese, but he knew his place: this was an era when journalists had low social standing, particularly when compared with royalty, so he quietly accepted that when the Prince was invited to an official function somewhere along the route, Barzini himself was generally excluded. After the Raid, he and the Prince never met again.

Barzini had a fascination with machines and all forms of transport, particularly trains, motorcars and the newly emerging fad, aeroplanes. While in the United States covering the aftermath of the San Francisco earthquake of 1906, he achieved a personal goal: an interview with the Wright brothers. Barzini worked as a war correspondent during World War I and later moved to America, founding *Il Corriere d'America*, an Italian newspaper in New York. He moved back to Italy, and died there, in 1947.

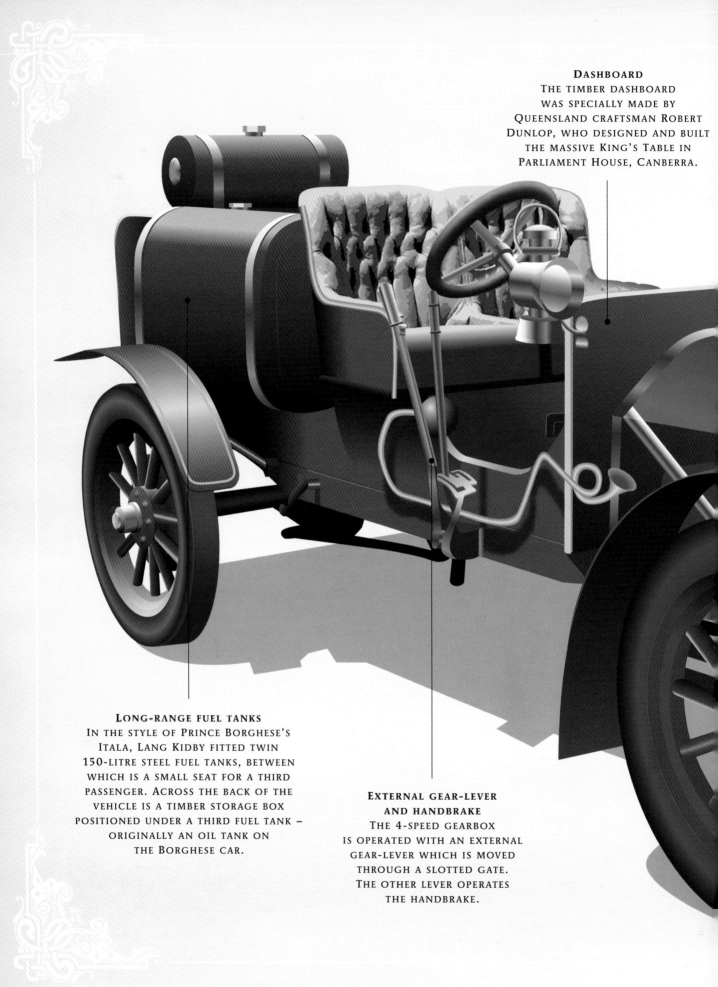

DASHBOARD
THE TIMBER DASHBOARD
WAS SPECIALLY MADE BY
QUEENSLAND CRAFTSMAN ROBERT
DUNLOP, WHO DESIGNED AND BUILT
THE MASSIVE KING'S TABLE IN
PARLIAMENT HOUSE, CANBERRA.

LONG-RANGE FUEL TANKS
IN THE STYLE OF PRINCE BORGHESE'S
ITALA, LANG KIDBY FITTED TWIN
150-LITRE STEEL FUEL TANKS, BETWEEN
WHICH IS A SMALL SEAT FOR A THIRD
PASSENGER. ACROSS THE BACK OF THE
VEHICLE IS A TIMBER STORAGE BOX
POSITIONED UNDER A THIRD FUEL TANK –
ORIGINALLY AN OIL TANK ON
THE BORGHESE CAR.

**EXTERNAL GEAR-LEVER
AND HANDBRAKE**
THE 4-SPEED GEARBOX
IS OPERATED WITH AN EXTERNAL
GEAR-LEVER WHICH IS MOVED
THROUGH A SLOTTED GATE.
THE OTHER LEVER OPERATES
THE HANDBRAKE.

Itala 2005

MODEL:	ITALA 18/24
ENGINE:	4 CYLINDER, BUILT IN TWO BANKS OF TWO
EXHAUST:	TWIN CAM CROSS-FLOW INDUCTION/EXHAUST SYSTEM
BORE:	90 MM
STROKE:	130 MM
DISPLACEMENT:	3.1 LITRES
MAXIMUM RPM:	1700
GEARBOX:	4-SPEED CARDIN TYPE
TOP SPEED:	90 KM/H
BODY:	3 SEAT WOOD CONSTRUCTION
FUEL TANKS:	2 X 150 LITRE PLUS 1 X 37 LITRE GRAVITY FEED
WHEELS:	WOODEN SPOKE 500X24 DETACHABLE RIMS
WEIGHT:	2100 KG
BRAKES:	CABLE-OPERATED FOOT BRAKE ON REAR WHEELS ONLY; LEVER-OPERATED HANDBRAKE ON TRANSMISSION

3-LITRE MOTOR

THE LOW-REVVING 3-LITRE MOTOR HAS 4 CYLINDERS CAST IN PAIRS BOLTED TO AN IRON BLOCK. THE MASSIVE FLYWHEEL IS CLEVERLY CAST WITH THE BLADES OF A FAN OFFERING SOME ENGINE COOLING. ALTHOUGH THE CAR STILL HAS MAGNETO IGNITION, FOR THE 14000 KM JOURNEY IT HAS BEEN FITTED WITH A GENERATOR AND SELF-STARTER.

ALTHOUGH LANG KIDBY AND WARREN BROWN'S ITALA IS ALMOST THE SAME SIZE AS PRINCE BORGHESE'S CAR, THE ENGINE HAS LESS THAN HALF THE CAPACITY OF THE 7-LITRE PEKING TO PARIS WINNER OF 1907. EVEN SO, THE CAR IS STILL CAPABLE OF REACHING SPEEDS OF OVER 100 KM/H.

Itala 2005

What other colour could it be but Italian racing red?

The Itala prepared for the 2005 event was a rare find indeed. Only a handful of these pre–World War I models are known to exist in Australia, and there is only a very tiny number in the rest of the world. Australia's greatest early motoring name, James Flood, was the original Itala dealer in Australia. Based in an inner-Melbourne workshop, James Flood and Company had considerable success in selling these quality cars, which was quite an achievement, as they were competing against dozens of different brands at that time.

The more egalitarian Australian society did not lend itself to the chauffeur-driven limousines of the European nobility, but several wealthy businessmen did operate such vehicles. Flood concentrated on the mid-size Italas — they were probably in the class of the modern Mercedes or the more sporting BMWs.

Numerous photos from this era show Italas with nicely built tourer bodies being driven by obviously well-dressed owners with equally well-dressed passengers. They were not tradesmen's vehicles, even in a classless Australia.

In the chase for victory on the racetrack, Australian drivers followed the results of the famous European events. There are many photographs of Italas, stripped to their bare essentials, charging along, wheel to wheel with a competitor, on a rough road outside Sydney or Melbourne.

The history of the 2005 car is almost a total mystery, though. There is evidence to suggest that it was imported and sold by James Flood and Company in 1907. Because it was discovered in ruins in the 1970s in country New South Wales, one might surmise that it was ordered by a Sydney businessman, or possibly a wealthy grazier.

The model is the mid-range size, Flood's specialty. The wheel base on all the models was very similar, at around

2.5 metres; the chassis on the larger cars was made of heavier material. While engines up to 7 litres were on offer, the 2005 car has what is probably the most popular size: it is 3.1 litres, and produces around 70 hp (in modern terminology), described as 18/24 hp at the time.

The differential is huge and would not look out of place on a modern 8-tonne truck. Italian enthusiasts report that there is no documented failure of an Itala differential.

The engine is of amazingly advanced design. It has magneto ignition to send the current to the spark plugs; this system has not been seen on cars since the 1920s (but is still standard on aircraft engines). It also has twin cams to operate the intake and exhaust valves; this was only seen on the most advanced racing or sporting vehicles until very recent times, but is now standard for road cars. The twin cams allow the valves to be placed on opposite sides of the cylinders to give 'cross-flow' heads, a design that modern car manufacturers are touting as advanced technology.

The engine bay is completely sealed, and there is a tightly fitting tray under the engine. At the rear of the engine is a huge 70-kilogram flywheel in the shape of a fan. Apart from providing excellent smoothness to the engine, the fan draws air through the radiator, past the hot engine, and blows it out the back. There are none of the pulleys or troublesome fan belts found on modern cars.

The clutch is a multi-disk design with about 10 steel plates that squeeze up against each other to smoothly transfer the power from the engine to the wheels. Once again, this basic design is found in automatic transmissions 100 years later.

The gearbox, like the rear axle, is extremely robust. It is a 4-speed, fairly conventional design (Cardin) with a big gear lever on the outside of the vehicle. Like most cars of the period, it takes considerable skill to change gears without crunching. The Raid took place 25 years before Ferdinand Porsche invented the synchromesh gearbox, so the driver must be adept at 'double declutching'. This requires the driver to match the engine speed to that of the gear he is about to select. He then pushes the clutch in and pulls the gear stick to neutral, then quickly lets the clutch out to match the spinning gearbox speed to that of the engine, then pushes the clutch back in and moves the gear stick to the next gear. If the driver knows what he is doing, he will have selected the perfect time, judging by the sound of the engine, and the newly selected gear will match perfectly with its mate in the gearbox. Poor coordination results in expensive crunching noises.

Going down a gear requires even more skill, as the driver must rev the engine during the short period the clutch is in neutral to match the gearbox to its higher speed in the lower gear. New drivers find this operation extremely difficult, and many people crunch through the gears of their veteran and vintage cars for years, slowly destroying their gearboxes. Some are so incompetent that if a down-shift is required, they have to stop the car then start up through the gears again.

Perhaps this is why so many people who could afford it had professional drivers or chauffeurs in the very early days of motoring.

Mal Garthon, the enthusiast who completed the Itala restoration — after many owners had fiddled with the project for many years — selected a nice period sports/racing body style. Mal drove the car in rallies for a number of years in the Sydney area, and it became a well-known participant in veteran car events.

When Warren Brown and Lang Kidby bought the car in late 2004, they planned a very extensive upgrade and modification program. Entering a local veteran rally required completely different performance, reliability and equipment from that needed for a 14000-kilometre drive across the world.

Right from the start, the Itala was planned as a tribute to Prince Scipione Borghese and Ettore Guizzardi for their heroic pioneering efforts a century earlier. There was no intention to claim that the vehicle was an exact replica, but it was hoped that people would see, as much as possible, what the 1907 car looked like.

The only way this could be accomplished was by a visit to Turin in Italy, where the original 1907 car is displayed in the national motor museum. Lang Kidby spent a whole day there with a sketch pad, tape measure and camera, noting every feature of the Borghese car. On return to Australia he stripped the Itala down to its bare chassis, storing the sports body for possible future use.

The original car was painted a somewhat depressing grey; it was an easy decision to brighten up the 2005 vehicle a little. As an Italian car with a fabulous racing heritage, what other colour could it be but Italian racing red? The chassis, mudguards and other parts were sent off to Kev Cranston for a 100 per cent colour change.

Meanwhile, the long task of going through every mechanical part began. A new magneto, water pump, tyres and brakes were only a small part of the list. The engine was balanced, and an electric starter motor and generator (unheard of in 1907) were designed and built. The lights, originally powered by acetylene gas created by dripping water on calcium carbide, were considered too unreliable for an expedition dealing with modern traffic, so a pair of the very first 1910 Cadillac electric lights was fitted.

The body was a major construction project. Finding tradesmen capable of doing the work was quite a task, but eventually the detailed plans, drawn during Lang's visit to Turin, were in the hands of cabinet-makers and sheet metal workers. Graham Chapman rolled the huge 150-litre fuel tanks, Terry Pampling set to work on the wooden body, and Bryan King and Bill Cardno modified, rebuilt or adjusted various mechanical parts.

Once everything was finally back in the shed, Lang set to work assembling the vehicle, running fuel lines and electrical cables, fitting shock absorbers, cutting, bending and securing the vast amount of brass trimming. Hundreds of hours were required before the Itala was finally in one piece.

Then the long process of getting the engine running perfectly commenced, with changes to magneto timing, carburettors, oil pressure adjustment, spark plug specifications and water flow modifications eventually being completed.

At last, the most beautiful of veteran cars appeared outside the workshop, ready for some short test runs. Although it only had a 3-litre engine, and with the original Itala specifications nominating a maximum speed of 90 km/h, the car reached almost 100 km/h unloaded down the runway at Caboolture airport near Brisbane.

Happy with these results, Lang Kidby and his wife, Bev, set off on a proving run — a 1500-kilometre rally from Brisbane to Sydney through some fairly high mountain country. Despite suffering numerous flat tyres (the result of a poor batch of inner tubes), the car ran well. Sufficient information was gained from the run to justify another couple of hundred hours of work on further modifications, adjustments and improvements.

There comes a time when preparation must be converted into action, though, so the book was closed and the car readied for packing into a container for shipment to Beijing — and the great adventure.

Warren Brown

Warren Brown has been a car enthusiast for as long as he can remember. His first memory is as a three year old standing on the running board of a derelict 1920s Dennis fire engine parked behind a service station somewhere on the New South Wales Central Coast. The fire engine was for sale, but despite Warren's older brother pleading with their father to buy it, the rust-riddled Dennis didn't come home those Christmas holidays. Nevertheless, the episode sparked in Warren a fascination with old cars that continues today.

Born in suburban Sydney, Warren first read of the Peking to Paris Raid of 1907 as a kid, when it was described in exciting detail in a holiday annual. There were dramatic illustrations of cars whizzing by the Great Wall of China, with the goggle-wearing drivers hunched forward, their wild handlebar moustaches trailing into the wind. Little did he realise that 30 years later he'd be hammering across the Gobi Desert doing the same thing.

One of Australia's best-known newspaper cartoonists, Warren has been the editorial cartoonist for the Sydney *Daily Telegraph* for 10 years, and during that time he has received many awards.

Warren's keen interest in history and motoring are now combined in a classic motoring column, 'Warren's Wheels', which appears in every Friday's *Daily Telegraph*.

In 1995 Warren was appointed to the national committee of Australia Remembers, a federal government initiative commemorating the 50th anniversary of World War II. Warren organised the largest historical re-enactment ever seen in Australia — a pilgrimage for veterans who served in the Northern Territory.

Warren is an Australia Day Ambassador and a regular guest on Channel Nine's *Today* show and ABC-TV's *Insiders* program. He has recently completed a 15-part historical series, 'National Treasures', for Film Australia.

It was while attending the 60th anniversary of the D-Day landings in Normandy that Warren met Lang Kidby, a kindred spirit when it comes to a fascination with things motorised and audacious expeditions. It didn't take long for the pair to concoct the brazen scheme to recreate the 1907 event with the five original types of cars.

Warren's love of cars has never died: he has restored and still owns several vintage and classic cars, including the first he ever saw — a vehicle he tracked down only a few years ago ... a 1920s Dennis fire engine.

Lang Kidby

One of Australia's great adventurers, Lang Kidby concedes that he was probably born in the wrong era. Rather than living the mundane routine of everyday 21st century life, Lang would much prefer to be tracing the source of the Nile, or hacking his way through the jungles of the Dark Continent, or struggling to reach the North or South Pole.

Lang's remarkable achievements have earnt him a reputation for adventure second to none. His impressive military career and tremendous historical knowledge will stand him in good stead for the 2005 Peking to Paris Expedition.

An Australian Regular Army pilot with the Aviation Corps for 14 years, Lang served in numerous locations, including Southeast Asia and the United Kingdom, and spent six years flying Pilatus Porter aircraft in Papua New Guinea.

Since leaving the army, Lang has owned and run a marine construction company, organised expeditions in Papua New Guinea and Indonesia to recover crashed World War II aircraft, contract-captained a deep-sea fishing mother ship for a television crew off the coast of Papua New Guinea, been awarded a Churchill Fellowship, and commanded relief truck convoys in Iraq.

But he is best known for his spectacular aviation achievements, which include conceiving of and operating the largest long-distance vintage aircraft rally ever held, from England to Australia, featuring 25 aircraft built before 1950. The rally required setting up workshops in the US and Australia to construct a 1919 Vickers Vimy twin-engined aircraft (the largest replica aircraft ever built). Lang flew the Vimy with fellow pilot Peter Macmillan, and was awarded the Order of Australia Medal for the project.

To mark the 70th anniversary of Bert Hinkler's first solo flight from England to Australia, Lang restored an Avro Avian biplane and flew it 40 000 kilometres through 18 countries from England to Australia, fêted wherever he went.

But Lang's the first to admit that his success is due in no small part to his wife, Bev. She is his greatest supporter, and the backbone of a brilliant partnership that has seen them succeed in some of the world's great adventures.

And when Lang and Warren Brown met in France and hatched the idea for recreating the Peking to Paris Raid, Lang was able to realise a boyhood ambition — to follow in the steps of Prince Scipione Borghese, in an Itala, on yet another of the great adventures of all time.

1907 ITALA

De Dion Bouton 1907

It is my belief that if a motorcar can get through, the De Dion Bouton will get through.

Marquis Albert de Dion

When *Le Matin* published the challenge to drive from Peking to Paris in January 1907, the first to reply was the founder of the Automobile Club of France, car manufacturer Marquis Albert de Dion. His response was delivered to the newspaper's offices by special courier: '... it is my belief that if a motorcar can get through, the De Dion Bouton will get through'.

The reason for the Marquis's unbridled optimism was largely the success of these little cars in cross-country events in the hands of works drivers such as Georges Cormier and Victor Collignon. Tiny cars with excellent ground clearance would always win out against heavy, truck-like vehicles such as Prince Borghese's Itala or Charles Godard's Spyker — or so the Marquis thought.

The Marquis de Dion and two brother-in-law mechanics, M. Trepardoux and Georges Bouton, were amazing innovators and pioneers in the production of cars in quantity. Unlike many other French car manufacturers such as Peugeot and Delage, which arrived at car manufacturing via bicycle building, the De Dion Bouton boys fell into the automotive business from the world of steam; De Dion steam-powered carriages were being built from as early as 1883.

Trepardoux was an engineering genius who devised an ingenious rear-axle arrangement which transferred power to the wheels through a differential on a fixed mounting connected to short half-shafts which, in turn, turned the rear wheels. The wheels were supported by a curved beam axle which carried the car's weight on the springs. This meant the car could follow wheel ruts of different depths with the wheels remaining vertical. The De Dion rear axle would remain famous in motor racing for a century.

Suspecting that steam may not be the path of the future, the Marquis de Dion built a successful single-cylinder petrol engine in 1895. An outraged Trepardoux considered dabbling with petrol engines heresy; he hit the roof and resigned from the company. What followed probably made him wish he'd reconsidered. De Dion's little single-cylinder motor was a hit across Europe, powering tricycle cars and quadricycles, including the 402 cc, 3 hp voiturette, a natty contraption frequently piloted by none other than Britain's King George V.

De Dion engines were produced in large numbers for other car manufacturers — by 1904, De Dion's Puteaux factory had built some 40 000 units. De Dion Bouton cars offered all sorts of nifty innovations, including a gearbox which employed the same basic principles as a modern automatic transmission, including epicyclic gears and automatic clutches. In Australia, for an extra £10, you could get reverse gear as well. And as well as having contracting-band drum brakes on the rear wheels, De Dions sported 'decelerator' pedals, which were fundamentally a transmission brake.

Officially, the cars supplied by the De Dion factory for the Peking to Paris Raid were two identical field-grey, 10 hp 2-cylinder AV models fitted with timber box bodies specially constructed for the event. But when comparing the cars in photographs of the Raid, is it clear that the two De Dions were not identical; De Dion enthusiasts suggest that the cars were probably of different horsepower. Both cars, however, sported oversized wheels and tyres — useful for overcoming obstacles such as sand and rocks.

Certainly the little De Dions would have been easier to manhandle up the Kalgan Pass than the heavier Itala and Spyker, but once on the Mongolian Plateau, Cormier and Collignon would have had to concede to the raw horsepower of the Itala's whopping 7-litre engine.

That Prince Borghese arrived in Paris 21 days ahead of the De Dions made the Marquis rethink — in some circumstances, it seemed, spindly light cars with tiny engines were just not able to compete with the big, no-nonsense, agricultural-style petrol-guzzling motors. Immediately after the Peking to Paris Raid, De Dion Bouton built a massive 6.1-litre engine; it was the first successful V8 engine in the world.

DE DION BOUTON 1907

THE PEKING TO PARIS RAID WAS ONE OF THE FIRST CORPORATE-SPONSORED MOTORING EVENTS IN THE WORLD. HERE THE SPECTACULARLY MOUSTACHED GEORGES CORMIER IS DESCRIBED ON THIS SOUVENIR POSTCARD AS THE WINNER OF THE RAID. FRENCHMAN CORMIER ARRIVED IN PARIS 21 DAYS AFTER THE ITALIAN PRINCE BORGHESE.

VICTOR COLLIGNON AT THE WHEEL OF THE DE DION, WITH GEORGES CORMIER AT THE FRONT AND JEAN BIZAC UNDER THE REAR, ON THE GROUND.

Georges Cormier

Georges Cormier was one of the world's most experienced long-distance drivers when he fronted for the Peking to Paris Raid. A De Dion dealer, he'd already been signed by the factory to participate in several adventurous drives in eastern and southern Europe, as well as Africa, so he was a natural to lead the company's charge across two continents. He was also a good leader of men — second only to Prince Borghese on the Raid — and known to be dependable in difficult situations. He must have been trustworthy too, for those who travelled with him left him in charge of all their money. His methodical planning and good organisation were a given, and his angry moods were either ignored or forgiven by his companions; twice they enjoyed roadside celebrations and toasts while he sat broodingly behind the wheel of his De Dion.

Not everyone got along with him, though. He sacked a mechanic, Lelouvier, in Peking. Lelouvier had been sent to assess road conditions across Asia and, according to one report, came to Peking with flawed intelligence. Perhaps that's why Cormier sent him home, but it's also recorded that they didn't like each other.

Cormier was not so strong in a war of diplomacy, and was the first to throw in the towel when the Chinese authorities, through political manoeuvring, created so many difficulties that it seemed the Raid would never begin. He was already in Peking by then, and proposed selling the cars and going home. Yet he could play the game well on a personal level, and left the ever-devious Spyker driver, Charles Godard, admitting defeat in the Gobi Desert during a mental tussle over fuel supplies. This encounter almost left Godard and his co-driver, Jean du Taillis, dead, but Cormier couldn't have predicted this, and he later showed plenty of loyalty towards his fellow competitors and crew. He publicised Godard's stoic performance in the raid when the French press (du Taillis excepted) refused to acknowledge the driver of the Dutch car.

The huge, drooping handlebar moustache Cormier sported in Peking became a full and massive beard during the journey, as he didn't shave till he reached Paris. An enthusiastic hunter, he carried two rifles and two revolvers in his car and often went stalking across the countryside in search of sport or food.

Cormier was deservedly heralded as France's hero of the Peking to Paris Raid. It was his greatest, but not only, achievement for French motoring, and his memorial is the highly respected Georges Cormier College of automotive trades in Coulomiers.

DE DION BOUTON 1907

Jean Bizac

'God, this god is ugly,' commented Jean Bizac when he met the Grand Lama in Urga. Bizac was a matter-of-fact Frenchman who wasn't easily impressed and had little tolerance for ostentation. Bizac was amazingly stoic, too: he had spent seven years in the engine rooms of France's Navy despite suffering badly from seasickness. Ironically, he was the only De Dion Bouton team member who went to Peking by sea. His response to his seasickness, in this case, was to install himself in a deckchair, wrap himself in heavy clothes and broil all the way through the tropics, getting up only for meals.

Bizac was a De Dion Bouton employee who was a brilliant mechanic and loved engines. He lavished care on the 1907 De Dions. In one photo taken in a European city, with drivers and spectators crowded around in proud poses, Bizac is hunched under the car looking after some important piece of maintenance.

Bizac was very disciplined, very organised and able to function with little rest — mechanics had extra-long days, as they were required to work on the cars for hours after each day's drive was over. He was always the one up before dawn to make sure the others were awake for an early start.

He was happy to accept his junior ranking on the Peking to Paris Raid, even to the point of piggybacking Godard across a Chinese river so that the driver would stay dry. However, Bizac wasn't silly, and when he began to lose his balance he dropped Godard in the cold water rather than fall himself.

Amazingly, Bizac had never ridden in a car before he got to Peking. His first drive would be the greatest automotive adventure the world had ever seen, but when this was pointed out to him he shrugged it off without a word. He didn't talk much, but as with his comment about the Lama, when he did speak it was pointed. His only words on crossing into France, when everyone around him could barely contain their joy, were, 'None too soon.'

Victor Collignon

If Cormier was a leader, Victor Collignon was a natural follower, and thus the ideal man to drive the second De Dion Bouton. He was an imperturbable and reliable man who carried on with little change in mood regardless of miserable weather, beautiful scenery or anything else — unless he ran out of cigarettes, in which case the chain-smoker would finally complain. He always backed Cormier's decisions and followed instructions. Perhaps he didn't like confrontation, because he looked away as the De Dion team left Godard in the Gobi and again when *Le Matin*'s heavies wrestled Godard out of the Spyker before the final drive to Paris. But he was not a weak or incapable man, and when the New York–Paris race was proposed in 1908, De Dion appointed him to drive it (the factory later pulled out).

Collignon was almost as experienced a driver as Cormier, and had been on some of Cormier's previous journeys. He'd also learnt a lot about mechanics, and often helped Bizac maintain and repair the vehicles.

Somehow Collignon managed to put on weight between Peking and Paris, while everyone around him grew leaner from months of tough living. His taste for beer may have contributed — he was nicknamed 'Pivo' after a Russian brew he developed a thirst for. The poor Frenchman seemed to attract misfortune: someone threw a stone that hit him squarely in the face just before he reached Europe (Cormier and Bizac avenged him by beating the thrower), and he was attacked by a drunken Russian in an inn room a few days later (fortunately, he was not hurt).

He took all this with little more than a shrug of the shoulders. He was the kind of man who, when everyone else was heatedly debating how long the trip would take after they'd suffered the first 150 miles (240 kilometres), simply said, 'We shall get there when we get there.'

De Dion Bouton 2005

ENGINE:	TWIN-CYLINDER 4-STROKE
CRANKSHAFT PHASE:	180 DEGREES
CAPACITY:	1250 CC
POWER:	10 HP
IGNITION:	ELECTRONIC
GEARBOX:	IN-UNIT 3-SPEED TRANSAXLE
REAR SUSPENSION:	DE DION TYPE
WHEELS:	CAST ALUMINIUM
WEIGHT:	APPROX. 600 KG

ACETYLENE HEADLIGHTS
IT WAS SOME TIME BEFORE EARLY MOTORCARS CAME FITTED WITH GENERATORS AND BATTERIES, SO ELECTRIC HEADLIGHTS WERE CONSIDERED ALMOST SCIENCE FICTION. IN THE SAME WAY EARLY MINERS' HELMET-LAMPS WERE ILLUMINATED, BLOCKS OF CARBIDE PLACED WITHIN THE LAMP WOULD REACT WHEN IN CONTACT WITH DRIPPING WATER, CREATING A BRILLIANT LIGHT. ON THE TOP OF THE LAMP, A SMALL VENTILATED BOX ACTED AS A CHIMNEY.

ALLOY ARTILLERY WHEELS
TIMBER ARTILLERY WHEELS CAN PRODUCE SERIOUS PROBLEMS OVER LONG DISTANCES IN ROUGH TERRAIN. PRINCE BORGHESE'S ITALA HAD A SPOKED WHEEL COLLAPSE IN SIBERIA – ONLY THE INGENIOUS WORK OF A LOCAL BLACKSMITH WITH HIS AXE SAVED THE DAY. ALTHOUGH THEY LOOK LIKE THE REAL THING, THE WHEELS ON THIS DE DION BOUTON ARE MADE OF CAST ALLOY – STRONGER, LIGHTER AND MUCH LESS PROBLEMATIC.

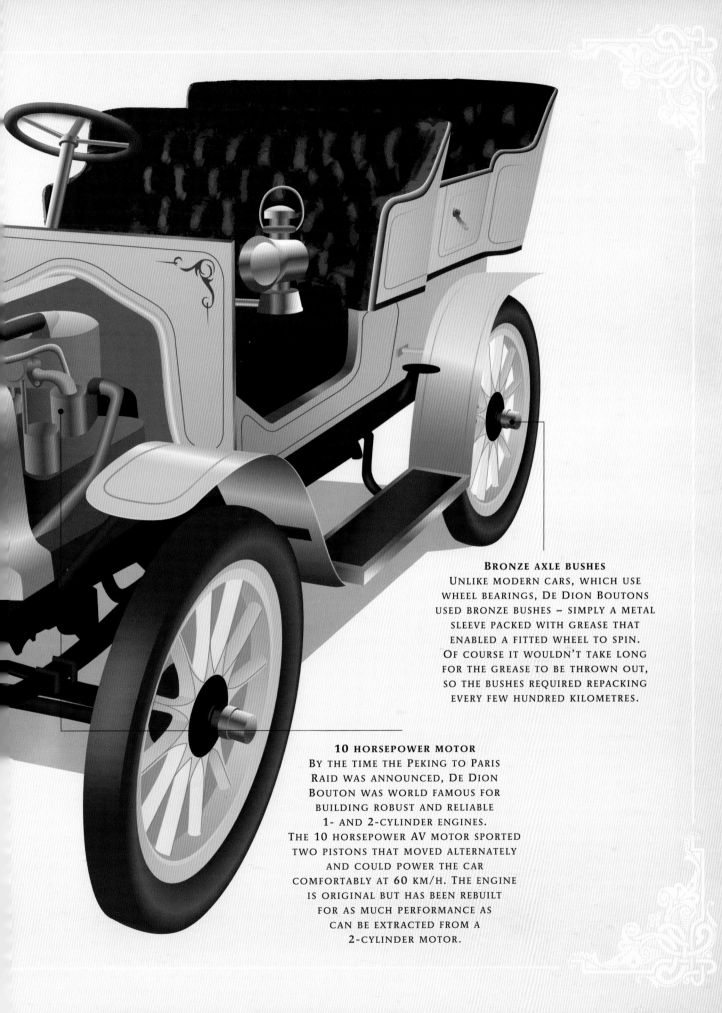

BRONZE AXLE BUSHES
UNLIKE MODERN CARS, WHICH USE
WHEEL BEARINGS, DE DION BOUTONS
USED BRONZE BUSHES – SIMPLY A METAL
SLEEVE PACKED WITH GREASE THAT
ENABLED A FITTED WHEEL TO SPIN.
OF COURSE IT WOULDN'T TAKE LONG
FOR THE GREASE TO BE THROWN OUT,
SO THE BUSHES REQUIRED REPACKING
EVERY FEW HUNDRED KILOMETRES.

10 HORSEPOWER MOTOR
BY THE TIME THE PEKING TO PARIS
RAID WAS ANNOUNCED, DE DION
BOUTON WAS WORLD FAMOUS FOR
BUILDING ROBUST AND RELIABLE
1- AND 2-CYLINDER ENGINES.
THE 10 HORSEPOWER AV MOTOR SPORTED
TWO PISTONS THAT MOVED ALTERNATELY
AND COULD POWER THE CAR
COMFORTABLY AT 60 KM/H. THE ENGINE
IS ORIGINAL BUT HAS BEEN REBUILT
FOR AS MUCH PERFORMANCE AS
CAN BE EXTRACTED FROM A
2-CYLINDER MOTOR.

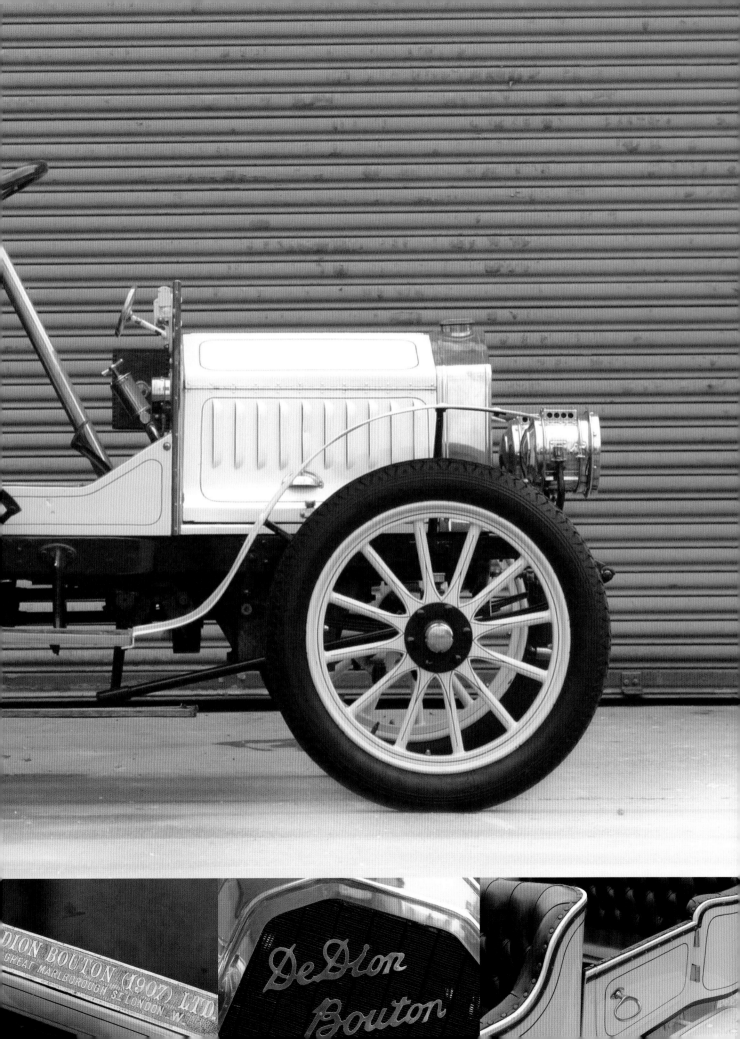

Yellow De Dion Bouton 2005

*It's always been a good car.
It's almost like a modern car to drive.*

Geoff Simmons

The yellow De Dion Bouton is one of the sweetest and fastest cars of its kind you're likely to come across. From a restoration that began 20 years ago, it's now a beautiful example of how practical and useable a veteran car can be.

The 1907 AV model has the same 10 hp, 1250 cc engine used in the De Dion Boutons that completed the 1907 Peking to Paris Raid. It's a twin-cylinder with a 180-degree crankshaft throw, meaning the pistons travel in opposite directions to each other — when one is rising, the other is falling. In a twin this is a better solution than a 360-degree crank, which produces more vibration and big changes in crankcase pressure.

Geoff Simmons, restorer and former owner of the De Dion, believes it's the quickest twin-cylinder veteran car in Australia. 'It's a fast car,' he says. 'It'll

probably do 90 km/h, and I've done 80 in it. With a higher diff ratio it'd do more.'

Geoff and his brother John bought the car as a basket-case project in 1985. The whole car came stripped to bare bones, but it was mostly complete — the previous owner, who'd given up his hope of restoring it, had at least tracked down many parts. Unfortunately, most of what Geoff and John inherited was completely worn out. There was a lot of work to do, and the job took two and a half years.

The Simmons brothers already had three similar vehicles; they decided to put this one together as a spare car to lend to people who wanted to enter veteran car events. Geoff also says they had a mischievous plan to race the solar-powered cars that were regularly running north–south across Australia at the time, just to prove that a 1907 car could do it. However, they didn't follow through on this.

'It was restored to be easy to drive and bulletproof,' says Geoff. 'It's always been a good car. It doesn't break things or do stupid things. It vibrates like hell, but all twins do. If anything's going to cause it to break ... the vibration will, but I think that's all been sorted out now.'

Geoff made two crucial changes that have improved the De Dion's practicality: he fitted a more modern carburettor and electronic ignition. The engine originally used twin ignition systems, with spark from magnetos.

The engine is basically standard, but of course many original parts were no longer available and had to be manufactured or replaced with modern items. The pistons, for example, are cross-flow Ford Cortina parts.

The De Dion's in-unit, transaxle, 2-speed gearbox was missing when Geoff got the car. Finding one was not easy, but a friend remembered seeing an ad for one some time ago — an Australian farmer was trying to sell one. In a situation that was typical for antique car parts, there were no buyers when the farmer was advertising it, and now there were no ads when Geoff wanted to buy. However, Geoff tracked the farmer down, negotiated a price and sent a cheque. The farmer put the gearbox on a train to Geoff.

It never turned up. The railways people shrugged their shoulders and told John to file the insurance claim and wait for the payout instead. Completely unimpressed over the loss of such a rare thing, not to mention the poor attitude of the railways people, John filled out the forms and casually valued the gearbox at $80 000! Miraculously, it was found.

This car has the famous De Dion rear end. This suspension design was well ahead of its time in the 1900s, was adopted by Formula One race cars in the 1950s, and is still sometimes used almost 100 years later.

Contrary to common belief, it is not an independent suspension system, although developments later in the century added independent wheel control. The De Dion Bouton uses a solid axle between the rear wheels but the differential is mounted to the chassis rather than incorporated into the axle, as it is on most cars.

This reduces unsprung mass, improving ride quality and handling. The solid axle means the wheels remain parallel and vertical during cornering, which also helps handling. The design is one of the major contributors to the De Dion Bouton's easy-to-drive characteristics.

'It's so light to drive,' says Geoff. 'It's almost like a modern car to drive. It's light on the steering, all two-finger stuff, not like the normal veterans. It has delicate controls. It's soft on the suspension.'

One of the odd things De Dion Bouton did was install brass bushes on the rear wheels and bearings on the front ones. Doing it the other way around would have made much more sense; this is one of the car's few drawbacks. Provided the bushes are well lubricated, though, they give a decent service life.

The wheels look like wooden originals but are actually cast aluminium. Like the modern carburettor and ignition, the cast wheels lend modern practicality and solidity without detracting from the De Dion's style. Wooden wheels don't last long and may collapse while driving, so metal replacements are a safe alternative — especially for a 14 000-kilometre trip from Peking to Paris.

Driving the De Dion Bouton isn't hard if the driver has sampled the odd vintage or veteran machine before. The only thing the driver needs to adjust to is the centre-mounted accelerator, which looks like a plunger mounted between the clutch and brake pedals. This is no big deal, and no one has hit the wrong pedal by mistake.

Geoff eventually sold the car to Lynne Brown. Lynne had planned to come on the 2005 Peking to Paris Expedition; when he had to pull out, he sold the De Dion to Keith Brodie. It was hard to part with such a sweet vehicle, and Geoff has been having pangs of conscience ever since. But selling it has at least ensured that the De Dion has a chance to prove itself in the tyre tracks of its nearly 100-year-old sisters.

Keith Brodie

Driving a vintage De Dion Bouton is a bit of a culture shock for Keith Brodie, 56 — his motoring history is much, much faster. He's competed seven times in the Targa Tasmania: five in an MGB, one in an Austin-Healey MkII 3000 and the other in an Elfin Streamliner. He also raced the Healey in the New Zealand Targa. He almost killed himself in the Streamliner during his final Targa, in 1998. Then he took up Formula Ford racing. He fielded a 1976 Bowin P6F in historic and NSW State championships until a couple of years ago.

Born in Brazil and educated in Scotland, Keith is fluent in Portuguese and can speak a fair amount of Spanish and French. He married an Australian, Louise, in 1973 and the couple settled in Australia five years later. They have three children.

Meanwhile, Keith had gained a law degree and qualified as a chartered accountant. He worked with companies such as Price Waterhouse, rising through the ranks. He is now Group Human Resources Director of News Limited, after serving 14 years as company secretary for News Corporation.

Keith has a passion for sport — for instance, while he was living in Brazil in the 1970s he played some standout cricket matches against touring teams such as Argentina, the MCC and Combined Oxford & Cambridge — and a knack for business, and the two have often merged. He earnt the Australian Sports Medal in 2000 for services to Australian hockey, and he has held many senior roles in hockey's administration, including a post as director of the 1994 Hockey World Cup.

He was also director and later chief executive of Pacific Sports Entertainment Limited, which owns the Brisbane Broncos rugby league team, and has held directorships at several local and national rugby league clubs. True to form, he has continued to rise, and is now the chairman of Australia's National Rugby League.

Keith also serves on the executive committee of the CARE Australia Corporate Council, helping to raise much-needed funds from corporate Australia.

Warren Brown convinced Keith to buy a De Dion Bouton for the Peking to Paris expedition. For Keith, it's something completely different, and a serious challenge — and it beats working.

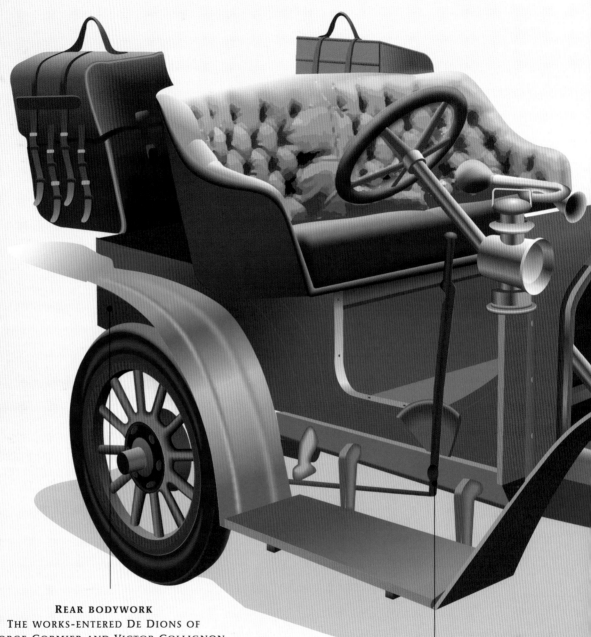

REAR BODYWORK
THE WORKS-ENTERED DE DIONS OF
GEORGE CORMIER AND VICTOR COLLIGNON
HAD SPECIALLY CONSTRUCTED,
BOX-LIKE BODYWORK FOR THE PEKING TO
PARIS RAID OF 1907. TO CAPTURE THE LOOK
OF THOSE CARS, JOHN MATHESON'S
DE DION BOUTON HAS BODYWORK FITTED
THAT CLOSELY RESEMBLES THE ORIGINAL
PEKING TO PARIS CARS, COMPLETE WITH
SPECIALLY MADE LEATHER PANNIERS FITTED
TO EACH SIDE. WITHIN THE BODY IS
A STAINLESS-STEEL FUEL TANK AND
A STORAGE COMPARTMENT.

HANDBRAKE LEVER
STOPPING MANY VETERAN CARS WAS
A SKILL REQUIRING CAREFUL MANIPULATION
OF BOTH THE FOOT BRAKE AND THE
HANDBRAKE. THE EXTERNAL LEVER OPERATES
THE MECHANICAL BRAKES ON THE REAR
WHEELS ONLY, THE FOOTBRAKE OPERATING
AS A TRANSMISSION BRAKE. ORIGINALLY
THE GEAR-CHANGE LEVER FOR THE STRAIGHT-
PULL 3-SPEED GEARBOX WAS FITTED
EXTERNALLY ALONGSIDE THE HANDBRAKE
BUT WAS MOVED 'INSIDE' THE CAR BETWEEN
THE DRIVER AND PASSENGER.

De Dion Bouton 2005

ENGINE:	TWIN-CYLINDER 4-STROKE
CRANKSHAFT PHASE:	360 DEGREES
POWER:	6 HP
IGNITION:	MAGNETO
GEARBOX:	3-SPEED TRANSAXLE BEHIND ENGINE
REAR SUSPENSION:	LIVE AXLE
WHEELS:	CAST ALUMINIUM
WEIGHT:	APPROX. 600 KG

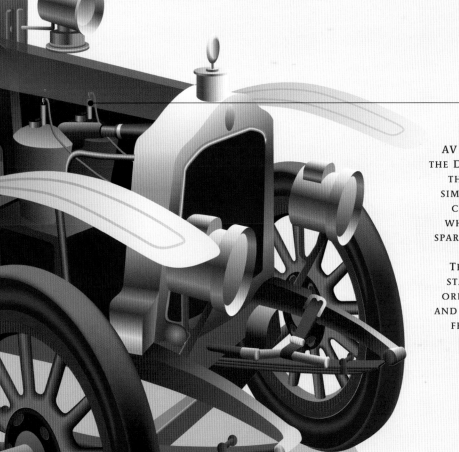

6 HORSEPOWER MOTOR
UNLIKE THE 2-CYLINDER AV MODEL DE DION BOUTON, THE DE2 MODEL HAS TWO PISTONS THAT TRAVEL UP AND DOWN SIMULTANEOUSLY, MAKING THE CAR SHAKE SPECTACULARLY WHEN IDLING. THE IGNITION SPARK, HOWEVER, FIRES ON EACH CYLINDER ALTERNATELY. THE ENGINE IS COMPLETELY STANDARD, FITTED WITH THE ORIGINAL MAGNETO IGNITION AND A GRAVITY-FED FUEL-SYSTEM FROM A TANK IN THE REAR.

STEEL WHEELS
ORIGINALLY THE DE DION BOUTON DE2 WAS FITTED WITH TIMBER ARTILLERY WHEELS BUT FOR RELIABILITY OVER THE 14000 KM JOURNEY, JOHN MATHESON OPTED FOR METAL WHEELS. WITH TIME RUNNING OUT TO HAVE THE CAR PREPARED FOR PACKING FOR CHINA, JOHN FOUND A COMPLETE SET OF WHEELS FROM A MORRIS COWLEY WHICH WERE THEN MACHINED TO FIT THE AXLES.

Blue De Dion Bouton 2005

The car was ready for its first road test a mere two weeks before it went to China.

There were five cars entered in the 2005 Peking to Paris Expedition — John Matheson's blue De Dion Bouton struggled every inch of the way to get to the starting line in Beijing. Only four months before the event was to start in China, the De Dion DE2 was nothing more than a chassis stacked with cardboard boxes full of parts.

The youngster of the group of veteran cars, the 1912 6 hp 2-cylinder De Dion DE2 is mechanically quite different from the 1907 AV 2-cylinder car. The bigger-engined 1907 De Dion AV has two pistons which travel up and down alternately, whereas the little 1912 DE2 model's pistons move simultaneously. The engine in fact operates like that of a single-cylinder car, where the two pistons throw themselves up and down as one; this results in the car shaking like a wet poodle on the Champs Elysées when idling.

The DE2 of 1912 was the last hurrah for the Marquis de Dion's renowned mass production of tiny, small-engine cars. The Marquis had become famous for his single- and twin-cylinder engines, but the company's defeat in the Peking to Paris Raid of 1907 by the bigger, heavier and more powerful Itala led directly to the De Dion Bouton moving away from little engines and into developing the world's first successful V8 engine.

The DE2 was the absolute bargain-basement model offered by De Dion Bouton, and was promoted as a utilitarian light commercial vehicle. An advertisement in *The Motor* magazine of 13 August 1912 contains a testament from biscuit company Peek Freans, which used a fleet of DE2s around London, claiming that one of their cars covered a distance of 941 miles (1506 km) in four weeks, with a total running cost of '.9 of a penny per mile'.

Bought as a partially finished project from South Australian veteran car collector Julian McNeil, the little French racing blue De Dion was initially to be completed for Keith Brodie to drive but it was then sold to John Matheson, who was already in the process of building the Contal replica. John bought the car sight unseen and was faced with a restoration project far greater than anticipated, as there was no way the car was ready to undertake the long drive. So the engine was stripped and rebuilt by Sydney De Dion expert Geoff Simmons, who had the two tiny pistons fitted with oil rings, a feature not available when the car was new. The timber artillery wheels were replaced with stronger steel ones from a Morris Cowley picked up at a vintage car swap meet in Queensland. At the rear, the car was fitted with a large timber box, much in the style of the one on Georges Cormier's 1907 De Dion, inside which was fitted a new stainless steel fuel tank.

John and co-driver/mechanic Andrew Snelling spent every spare second working on the car, but it seemed that for each problem solved, another two would appear. Unable to start the car, Andrew discovered that the refurbished magneto was not producing a spark to ignite the fuel — but every time the magneto was removed and tested on the work-bench, it operated perfectly. The mystery was solved after days of frustration when Andrew accidentally scratched paint off the home-made brackets which held the magneto in place: they were made of steel and were stealing the electrical charge from the spark plugs and sending it through the car's chassis instead.

Finally the moment arrived to start the car. Andrew clenched his teeth as he threw his weight behind the starting handle. The car erupted into life. As the two tiny pistons threw themselves up and down inside the cylinders, the car shuddered so violently that the brass side lamps fell off. Nuts and bolts shook themselves from their holes, and the crank handle ripped a 20 cm gouge along Andrew's forearm.

Doubting that the car would be ready in time, John and Andrew nevertheless continued to resolve each problem as it arose: they altered gear linkages, changed clutch pressure-plate springs, replaced incorrect brake springs, renewed stretched axle half-shafts and repaired the leaking radiator.

A mere two weeks before the cars were to be shipped to China, the little blue De Dion went for its first road test. With John at the wheel, it shuddered and sputtered but seemed to go okay. Still ironing out each new problem as it appeared, John and Andrew were confident that the little car was making progress, and eventually Andrew was able to take it for a two-hour, trouble-free drive. 'I'm happy,' sighed a grinning Andrew, and the car was loaded in the box for China.

John Matheson

John Matheson drove a vice-regal Rolls-Royce Phantom V in the 1997 Peking–Paris Motor Challenge with his wife, Jeanne. He has a collection of Rolls-Royces and Bentleys, and has driven many of them in rallies all over the globe. He has always had passion for cars and for travel. The 2007 Peking–Paris Challenge was on his mind, but when the chance came to drive in the 2005 event, with original vehicles, he grabbed it.

Born in Palestine in 1938, John lived in a different country every year during his early life, thanks to World War II and his father's career as a BOAC pilot. The family settled in Australia in 1952. While studying medicine at university, he was a member of the anti-establishment Sydney Push. He volunteered as a civilian doctor for service in Vietnam in 1974, operating on civilian casualties, and went on to become one of Australia's most prominent neurosurgeons, renowned in particular for his work in vascular brain surgery and operations for epilepsy. He has now retired from surgery.

Through the 1970s and 1980s John co-owned cattle properties in New South Wales, where visitors were often horrified to see the hands of a surgeon thumping a crowbar into the ground as he dug post holes into rock. He had four-wheel drive vehicles and explored parts of outback Australia in them, often with Michael and James, his sons from his first marriage. After selling the land, he indulged in boats for a few years before he began buying Rolls-Royces and Bentleys.

John gave his eldest daughter, Marion, her first driving lesson one Christmas day in his 1926 Rolls-Royce 20 hp. Meanwhile his younger daughter, Eloise, not yet old enough for a driver's licence, gained her pilot's licence.

John restored the historic sandstone keeper's cottage at Sydney's Macquarie Lighthouse and the family lived there for a decade before moving to the inner city. When Sydney's Motor Museum closed down, leaving dozens of classic car owners with nowhere to store their cars, he opened Motorworks in a large, disused factory near Botany Bay as a place where others could store their cars and he could keep and maintain his own vehicles.

DE DION BOUTON 2005

Andrew Snelling

Andrew Snelling is a larrikin with a dry sense of humour and a reputation for practical jokes. The 35-year-old electrical engineer is also an excellent troubleshooter who can fix just about anything. He grew up watching and learning as his father repaired everything that broke around the house, including the family's Wolseley, and by the time he was three years old Andrew was mad about cars, and showing mechanical aptitude.

Andrew and his late father, Graeme, shared a love of Wolseleys, and began competing in the charity-raising Redex Variety Club Bashes throughout rural and outback Australia — these are events for pre-1972 cars. They gave Andrew an opportunity to hone his 'bush mechanic' skills, fixing vehicles using a limited supply of parts, and he became used to working on cars late into the night and then driving the next day.

He has now completed 11 Bashes, and the adventure-driving bug bit deeply along the way. Andrew joined a three-person team in a Wolseley 24/80 on the 1997 Peking–Paris Challenge, earning a gold medal by finishing 17th overall and second in class. He also drove in the Amsterdam to Arctic Circle Rally and the Around Australia Overlander.

Such wanderlust — which also includes trips to the United States, Canada and New Zealand — is almost at odds with the fact that the Snelling family has lived in the same Sydney suburb for three generations. Andrew has three sisters and is the favourite uncle to his nieces and nephews. The Snellings are involved in community activities, and Andrew has been a Scout leader for six years. His parents, Graeme and Elaine, believed strongly in giving practical help whenever possible to others on life's journey, and Andrew has adopted the same philosophy.

As well as his work as an electrical contractor, Andrew deals in Wolseley and MG parts. He is an active member of the Wolseley club and also enjoys abseiling, canyoning, scuba diving, skiing, water skiing and four-wheel driving.

Contal 1907

We came here with the object of showing that the motorcar is the machine of the future, and that nothing can stop its progress.

Auguste Pons

No one had agreed on any rules or conventions for engineering motorcars and cycles in 1907. Anything and everything was worth a try, and dozens of weird, wacky and woeful designs rattled onto the roads. Many failed — and deservedly. The Contal Moto-Tri must have seemed like a good idea at the time. It wasn't. The design might have worked on Parisian streets when traffic was slow and sparse, but it was hopelessly inadequate for trailblazing in remote deserts, boggy plains and rugged mountains.

The Tri-Contal (its name is recorded in several informal ways, with the 'tri' added to differentiate it from Contal's lightweight four-wheeled *voiturette*) was more motorcycle than car. Like all bikes of the day, it had no rear suspension, just a sprung saddle to cushion the rider's *derrière* and kidneys from the shocks of cobbles, potholes and bumps.

The front end had a large frame section that carried a solid axle on leaf springs, just like a car. Its two front wheels were hub-steered; the rider held long handlebars that moved like a tiller.

The 6 hp, 2-stroke engine was water-cooled. Its single cylinder had a bore and stroke of 80 x 86 millimetres, making it 433 cc. A large tank in front of the steering head held water, and two small coolers protruded from its sides, but these weren't adequate for the heat and hard work of the Gobi Desert — the engine often overheated.

A drive chain ran directly from the engine to the rear hub, which contained two gears and the clutch mechanism. The Contal had a small drum brake at the rear and none up front. Effective front brakes would probably have been terrifying, as they'd have tipped the front-heavy tri-car on its nose.

Contals were intended to be delivery vehicles, and were usually fitted with purpose-built ramps that would form a solid base under its wheels in mud and sand.

Pons's laden Moto-Tri weighed 700 kilograms, which seems good compared with the 1400-kilogram De Dions and Spyker, and the 2000-kilogram Itala — until you remember that the bare Contal weighed only about 200 kilograms. It was seriously overloaded. Consequently, its handling was dreadful. Most of the weight was over the front axle, but the Contal needed plenty of weight on the back to keep its driving wheel in solid touch with the road. With no rear suspension, the wheel frequently bounced off the ground, and the unbalanced load encouraged the wheel to reach higher and stay up longer. The rear wheel often wouldn't ride out of ruts in the road. If the front wheels sank into sand or deep ruts, sometimes the Contal's momentum would carry it over its front axle until it planted its nose into the ground.

The Contal didn't even complete the first day of the Raid successfully. Pons turned back to Peking and put it on a train to Nankow.

It's tempting to ask, 'What if?' What if the Contal hadn't run out of fuel in the Gobi? What if someone had come back to give it more petrol? What if it had been given a sporting chance to prove itself, rather than failing completely for want of a few litres of petrol? But its demise was inevitable. Pons and Foucault had exhausted themselves getting as far as they did. They'd had to rely on the generosity of Godard and others to carry their luggage. They were always much slower than the rest. If the Gobi hadn't claimed the Contal, it would have bogged endlessly in the mud further west. At best, had the Spyker and De Dions stayed in convoy, the Contal would have delayed their arrival in Paris by weeks.

Pons set out to show that lightweight vehicles were superior, but all he managed to prove was that you can push a lightweight tri-car further than a car when you're dying in the desert.

Auguste Pons

Auguste Pons was absolutely certain that the Contal tri-car would succeed, but he was hopelessly optimistic about many things. His optimism was as much to blame as anything for his failure in the Peking to Paris Raid, for it encouraged him to make several bad — almost fatal — decisions. It underlined his conscientiousness and

CONTAL 1907

reinforced his often dogged determination in the face of certain defeat. His optimism probably led him to trust his fellow competitors with his life, which is ultimately what he did when he unloaded even his water and fuel into the Spyker in an effort to lighten the Contal for its Gobi crossing.

Even when Pons was stopped in the Gobi with less than a litre of fuel left in his tank, he replied with a cheery '*Ça va!*' ('All okay!') as Borghese came past asking if he needed help; Pons knew there was no one else coming after the Prince.

Pons was a tough man, though, physically and mentally. He drove himself and Foucault beyond exhaustion on several occasions when the Contal had to be pushed for miles. He didn't flinch at the Wai Wu Pu's machinations before the start of the race, immediately affirming his intention to get home across country — or at least make a valiant effort to start. He knew the gravity of what they were attempting: 'We came here with the object of showing that the motorcar is the machine of the future, and that nothing can stop its progress.' He probably didn't appreciate the irony of the statement in relation to his own vehicle.

Feeling bitter and betrayed after recovering from his Gobi ordeal, Pons returned to his family in France, including Lily, his three-year-old daughter, who would later become a world-renowned opera singer. Pons wasn't quite ready to settle down, though. He entered a tiny Sizaire-Naudin four-wheeler in the 1908 New York–Paris race. The little car was a step up from the ill-fated Contal, but Pons hadn't learnt much: he overloaded the car with luggage and three people and broke it before he'd driven 100 miles (160 kilometres).

Octave Foucault

Octave Foucault is the most shadowy figure in all the histories of the Peking to Paris Raid. Little was recorded about him by any of the journalists and diarists. Pons seemed to do the talking for the Contal pair, and Foucault obediently followed orders — even when it may have cost him his life in the desert.

One personal detail noted was his nickname, Apache; it was given to him by his companions on the way to Peking because he had 'sinister' features.

THE CONTAL OUTSIDE THE EUROPEAN LEGATIONS BUILDINGS IN PEKING; AUGUSTE
PONS IS IN THE BACK SEAT, DRIVING, WHILE OCTAVE FOUCAULT SITS UP FRONT.

THE CONTAL BEING ASSISTED BY A CHINESE LABOURER.

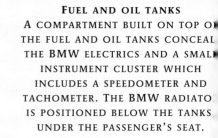

FUEL AND OIL TANKS
A COMPARTMENT BUILT ON TOP OF
THE FUEL AND OIL TANKS CONCEAL
THE BMW ELECTRICS AND A SMALL
INSTRUMENT CLUSTER WHICH
INCLUDES A SPEEDOMETER AND
TACHOMETER. THE BMW RADIATOR
IS POSITIONED BELOW THE TANKS
UNDER THE PASSENGER'S SEAT.

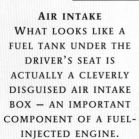

AIR INTAKE
WHAT LOOKS LIKE A
FUEL TANK UNDER THE
DRIVER'S SEAT IS
ACTUALLY A CLEVERLY
DISGUISED AIR INTAKE
BOX — AN IMPORTANT
COMPONENT OF A FUEL-
INJECTED ENGINE.

TUBULAR STEEL CHASSIS
THE CHASSIS FOR THE CONTAL WAS
CUSTOM-MADE BY MOTORCYCLE BUILDER
MICK COSTIN FROM PLANS BASED ON
PHOTOGRAPHS OF THE ORIGINAL THREE-
WHEELER. THE BEST SEAMLESS TUBULAR
STEEL WAS USED IN A LADDER-STYLE
FRAME THAT FLARED FROM THE REAR TO
THE FRONT. THE WHOLE CHASSIS WAS
THEN POWDER-COATED BLACK.

BMW F650 ENGINE
WITH NO CONTAL MOTORS THOUGHT
TO SURVIVE, MICK MATHESON DECIDED
TO USE A NEW BMW F650 MOTORCYCLE
ENGINE, GIVING THE REPLICA ALMOST
TEN TIMES THE POWER OF THE 1907
433 CC ORIGINAL. THE FUEL-INJECTED,
WATER-COOLED F650 MOTOR WOULD BE
IDEAL FOR SLOW SPEEDS DUE TO ITS LOW-
REV TORQUE, MAKING DIFFICULT TERRAIN
JUST THAT MUCH EASIER TO NEGOTIATE.

Contal 2005

ENGINE:	BMW F650GS
CAPACITY:	652 CC (100 X 83 MM)
POWER:	50 BHP AT 6500 RPM
FRAME:	TUBULAR STEEL
FRONT END:	AUSTIN 7, MODIFIED
WHEELS:	CUSTOM 21 INCH
BRAKES:	DISC (REAR)
WHEEL BASE:	1560 MM
KERB WEIGHT:	200 KG (APPROX)

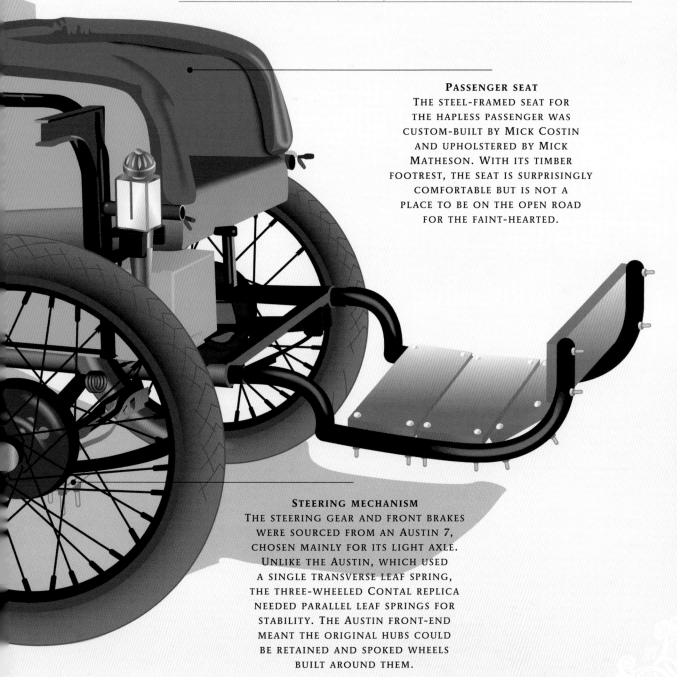

PASSENGER SEAT

THE STEEL-FRAMED SEAT FOR THE HAPLESS PASSENGER WAS CUSTOM-BUILT BY MICK COSTIN AND UPHOLSTERED BY MICK MATHESON. WITH ITS TIMBER FOOTREST, THE SEAT IS SURPRISINGLY COMFORTABLE BUT IS NOT A PLACE TO BE ON THE OPEN ROAD FOR THE FAINT-HEARTED.

STEERING MECHANISM

THE STEERING GEAR AND FRONT BRAKES WERE SOURCED FROM AN AUSTIN 7, CHOSEN MAINLY FOR ITS LIGHT AXLE. UNLIKE THE AUSTIN, WHICH USED A SINGLE TRANSVERSE LEAF SPRING, THE THREE-WHEELED CONTAL REPLICA NEEDED PARALLEL LEAF SPRINGS FOR STABILITY. THE AUSTIN FRONT-END MEANT THE ORIGINAL HUBS COULD BE RETAINED AND SPOKED WHEELS BUILT AROUND THEM.

Contal 2005

*It promises to be the most dependable
vehicle on the Expedition.*

There appeared to be no Contals left in the world when, with four months to go until cars had to be shipped to Beijing, the 2005 Peking to Paris crew decided that the only way to have a Contal was to build a replica. They had no blueprints, no instructions — not even the basic dimensions of the 1907 Contal. They'd have to cobble together a design from the handful of photographs available. The photos showed the Contal from several angles but not all, and the details were indistinct or obscured. Perspectives changed from shot to shot, some making the tri-car appear larger or smaller than it was. Artistic touch-ups altered the Contal's appearance in misleading ways.

To complicate things, the only clear sketch they found of a Contal turned out, on closer examination, to be a different, smaller model. Its engine sat lower in a frame with two top rails and the wheel base was shorter. Perhaps Pons's Contal was built specially for the challenges it faced? The photos hinted that maybe the frame was a heavier construction and perhaps the wheels were larger than normal.

Then in late February 2005 word came through of an unrestored Contal in Europe — but it was far too late for anyone to contemplate getting it up and running in time for the expedition. This one wouldn't even be any use for reference because the replica was almost complete by then.

John and Mick Matheson had taken on the project in late November 2004, less than four months before the cars had to be loaded into containers for Beijing. They found a builder in England who'd create a Contal replica, but the quoted price was far too high. Mick had written a story about Mick Costin, a motorcycle enthusiast who builds replicas of 500 cc Grand Prix motorcycles using his own handmade aluminium frames. Costin had also made a custom Harley-style frame, just for fun. His skills and knowledge were perfect for the job. He was perturbed by the lack of proper plans, but enthusiastically took on the challenge.

The Mathesons decided that they could make up the rules for their replica. As long as it looked the part and was as close to the spirit of Pons's machine as possible, it didn't matter how modern the technology was. And with no Contal engines in existence, John wanted a brand new, modern motorcycle engine that would guarantee no breakdowns. Mick had researched the reliability of many bikes in his work for *Two Wheels* and knew that the Rotax-based BMW F650 engine was as strong and long-lasting as they came. It would also provide the low-rev torque required for the slow speeds the replica would meander along at. So John bought a new F650GS.

Costin chose the strongest seamless tubular steel available for the chassis, and crafted it into a ladder-style frame that was narrowest at the rear and flared out as it went forward. John sourced an Austin 7 front end, mainly because of its lightweight axle. The Austin used a transverse leaf-spring suspension, which was fine on a car with two rear wheels, but the Contal replica needed parallel springs. Costin made adapters so that box-trailer springs could be fitted. Using a complete Austin front end meant Austin wheel hubs would be used too, simplifying the job.

George Kay, an experienced wheel builder, laced the Austin hubs to aluminium 21-inch motorcycle rims using heavy-duty spokes. The rear wheel is the same but with a Yamaha XTZ660 hub.

The Austin's front brakes were fitted but not connected, as front brakes had the potential to tip the Contal onto its nose. Fortunately, the Yamaha hub's disc brake worked very well — this became the Contal's only brake.

The tank behind the front seat served several purposes in the replica: the fuel oil tanks were built into it, and the BMW's electrics and dash were hidden in its top. The BMW's radiator was mounted under the front seat. The tank behind the engine, which carried fuel in 1907, became an airbox, which is essential for a modern fuel-injected engine.

The engine was about ten times as powerful as the 433 cc unit from 1907, and would be lethally fast on full throttle. But the basic flaws in the Contal's design and its woeful suspension ensured that the replica would never handle well. The only question was whether it'd handle well enough to keep up with the other cars.

The tight deadline left the team little time to test the replica before it was shipped to China, but with an over-engineered chassis and a brand new engine, it promised to be the most dependable vehicle on the Expedition.

Mick Matheson

Mick Matheson was 16 when he decided he wanted to work on a motorcycle magazine. His mother and stepfather ran the Australian edition of *Rolling Stone* while Mick was growing up, so journalism was an easy progression for him. Despite failing English in his final school exams, Mick became a copyboy at News Limited. He landed a cadetship on Australia's *Two Wheels* when he was 21, and couldn't imagine how life could get any better. However after becoming the magazine's youngest editor, he realised that freelance journalism was even better — and has pursued it ever since, with a few brief and unsuccessful detours into real jobs along the way. He also edited *Streetbike*. Now 37, Mick contributes regularly to *Two Wheels*, *Street Machine*, *4x4 Australia*, *Ralph* and a number of other magazines.

Mick's father's influence has been as strong as the journalistic upbringing of his mother. Before Mick was 10, John had taught him to drive and to shoot. He took Mick down the Birdsville Track in 1976, when it was still a difficult outback trek, and now Mick ventures into Australia's arid heart as often as he can. In 1997 Mick completed a solo coast-to-coast crossing through the centre of the continent by motorcycle. In 2004 he 'accidentally' crossed the Simpson Desert: 'We didn't mean to go all the way, but we got there and thought, "Why not?"' he says.

After many years riding motorcycles, Mick spent two seasons racing them in his early 30s, and finished third in the Streetfighter class. He never won a race, but he once crashed out of the lead. Recently Mick has taught himself to weld, sew and paint — he is restoring and customising a 1962 Pontiac. His daily drive is a 1965 Dodge, and his current bike is a well-used old BMW R80G/S.

Mick's work has taken him to various parts of the United States, Europe and Asia. His future plans centre around building a four-wheel drive vehicle he can live and work in, then hitting the road until he runs out of stories to write.

Christopher Boyle

Christopher Boyle is a very capable man who conquers physical and mental challenges the way the rest of us sit down to meals. Underlined by intelligence and level-headedness, his pragmatic and logical approach to everything he does ensures that he's successful. And because he's able to harness his restless energy, he gets things done.

He rose into senior management roles in his early 20s, working in New Zealand's electricity industry, and now, at 38, is a company director, a partner in a consulting business, part-owner of two companies, sits on eight company boards and, just for fun, is acting part-time CEO of NZ's Manfeild Park raceway. For Chris, this last role is like being the boss of the playground.

Chris has spent most of his life trying to make motorcycles go as fast as possible. He jokes that he's a fast crasher but a slow learner. He began racing motorcycles in 1987, navigated for NZ rally champion Joe McAndrew in a Subaru and spent a season racing Formula Ford. He took up multisport and adventure racing in the late 1990s, competing in New Zealand, Australia and China. Recently he's taken to racing mountain bikes downhill.

Perhaps his biggest adventure to date has been climbing to within 300 metres of the summit of the 6957 metre Mount Aconcagua in the Argentine Andes in 2004, but it's not his only one. He's dived the Maldives and ridden many times into the Australian outback on motorcycles. Chris has a soft spot for Ducati motorcycles — at last count, he has owned 34.

Meanwhile, Chris has gained a Bachelor of Electrical and Electronic Engineering and Master of Business Administration. His work has taken him to Bhutan, Nepal, India, Australia, the United Kingdom and the Maldives, and somehow he still finds time to spend with his partner of twelve years, Donna, and their blue heeler, Jess.

Chris loves adventurous travelling. Like many of us, this passion began when he was a child — he was inspired by the crazy stunts of Alby Mangels and John Field, who drove a little DAF car across the Sahara. He has always wanted to ride a motorcycle around the world. The Contal will take him halfway, but perhaps a lot more slowly than he's used to when he's behind handlebars.

Tomsk
Sibérie
le 20 Juillet 1907

Pékin — Paris

Go and Paris

Voici l'état de ma dpijk
murailles de chim, roire

Spyker 1907

The Rolls-Royce of the Continent.

When the irascible Frenchman Charles Godard discovered Belgian car manufacturer Metallurgique had withdrawn its entry in the Peking to Paris Raid and his driving services were no longer required, his desire to participate in the 14 000-kilometre event suddenly intensified. Godard needed a manufacturer to supply him with a car. But not just any car: there was no way he would be motoring to victory along the Champs Elysées in anything but the best automobile money could buy. In England he might have approached Rolls-Royce, but on the Continent there was only one manufacturer Godard was interested in: the Dutch firm of Spyker.

In an age when the automobile was still considered a novelty, Spyker cars had earned an enviable reputation for quality, robustness and reliability in just a few years. In 1898 Jacobus and Hendrik Spijker, two coach-building brothers in Amsterdam, built their first

motorcar: a Benz-engined automobile that won them enormous praise for its excellent build quality and workmanship. Jacobus and Hendrik decided to move into the car-making business full time, and changed the name of their company to Spyker for easier recognition in non-Dutch-speaking markets.

Just as a Rolls-Royce is instantly identified by its distinctive grille, Spykers were recognised by their circular radiator; in later years the car earnt a reputation as 'the Rolls-Royce of the Continent'.

Spyker cars pioneered the first of many amazing innovations that would pave the way for motoring for the next century. In 1902, they designed a 6-cylinder, four-wheel-drive racing car — it was both the first 6-cylinder car ever made and the first four-wheel-drive car ever made. Not a bad start. But their innovations didn't stop there. In an age when most roads were still nothing more than horse tracks, motorists would arrive at their destination coated from head to foot in dust. Spyker cars patented a 'dust shield chassis' which was more or less a giant, streamlined shield fitted under the car to prevent it from making dust on unpaved roads. It was a tremendous selling point.

Despite relatively small sales on the Continent, Spykers proved popular in England. The *Automotor* journal of Great Britain described the Spyker of 1905: 'high-class workmanship and materials in the construction of the chassis, silence in the running of the engine and transmission, and the dustlessness in the motion of the car have been the three characteristics of Spyker cars ...'

But the company's moment in the sun began in 1907 when Charles Godard walked into Jacobus Spijker's office, determined to convince him of the merits of entering a Spyker car in the Raid. He succeeded. The car supplied was a standard 15 hp 4-cylinder model, with the engine configured as two double blocks with T-formed heads.

Lubrication involved an external oil pump and wet sump. In anticipation of difficult terrain, the 3-speed transmission had special low gearing and the car was fitted with oversized artillery-style wheels. Like Borghese's Itala, the Spyker's drive-train was shaft-driven rather than chain-driven; this was typical for racing cars of the day.

But the most striking feature of Godard's car was its lurid paint scheme. Upon arriving at the Spyker factory in Trompenburg, Godard instructed the painter to paint the sides of the car, the bonnet and even the radiator in the vertical red, white and blue of the French flag. Such a colour scheme would no doubt have got up the nose of Dutchman Jacobus Spijker, who had just supplied this Frenchman with Holland's finest car. The words PEKIN and PARIS were then painted over the top, along with the route: 'la Siberie, la Russie, l'Allemagne'.

Even though Godard didn't win the Raid, Spyker's reputation for reliability and ruggedness rocketed around the world, earning the marque a name it deserved. But, sadly, the company lost momentum in 1907, when Hendrik Spijker drowned in a shipping accident — Jacobus spent days viewing hundreds of corpses as they were brought ashore, hoping to identify him.

SPYKER 1907

Jacobus's grief seriously affected the company's performance and he was removed from the board of directors before the company went bankrupt in 1908.

Spyker was resurrected, with new directors, and continued operations, building aircraft during World War I and still making beautiful cars, but the company ceased trading in 1925.

Incredibly, in 1999 the marque was revived yet again, and Spyker continues to build luxurious sports cars in Holland today.

Charles Godard

Every great story needs a colourful rogue, and Frenchman Charles Godard filled the role as if it had been written specifically for him. Unlike the methodical and meticulous Prince Borghese, Godard relied on pure rat cunning to get from Peking to Paris. He was not motivated by ill will; he just did whatever he could get away with.

Small, and with a beard in the style of King George V, Charles Godard was a *bon vivant*, raconteur and small-time con artist from Burgundy whose background was … well, nobody was really quite sure, but it had all the aroma of something mildly on the nose. More than likely he'd served a little time in prison for obtaining money through some nefarious method. Money was always a problem for Godard.

People were naturally drawn to him, and Godard held court wherever he went, making jibes, pulling faces, cracking jokes: always the life of the party. He earnt a living working for a Parisian carnival riding a motorcycle in 'The Wall of Death', and despite his relentless bravado and practical jokes, as a driver he was second to none.

When *Le Matin* issued the challenge to drive from Peking to Paris, Godard was approached to drive in the event by Belgian car manufacturer Metallurgique, which intended to enter three works cars. However, as the realisation of what this undertaking would actually cost filtered through, one by one car companies pulled their entries from the event, and Godard found himself unemployed when Metallurgique bowed out.

Desperate to enter the Raid, Godard headed straight to the office of Spyker cars in Amsterdam, and proceeded to dazzle and impress the proprietor, Jacobus Spijker, with the merits of giving him a car to drive in the event.

He succeeded: Spijker gave him a car and a heap of spare parts, paid his entry fee, and promised him a 10 000-franc bonus if he won. In typical Godard fashion, he promptly flogged his spares and tyres; he was going to travel on the steamer to Peking with a first-class ticket, with or without spare parts. During the race, Godard would leave a trail of bouncing cheques, broken promises and IOUs from Peking to Paris which would eventually bring him undone, but for now he was at least on his way.

On board the ship to China, Jean du Taillis, the correspondent *Le Matin* had appointed to travel with Godard, chided him about his reckless lack of planning: 'You can't run these risks over such a long trip with the resources you've got. You can't do it!'

'Why not?' replied Godard. 'Either I shall never see Paris again or I shall come back to it in my Spyker, hot from Peking!'

Already pressuring poor Jacobus Spijker for an advance on his winnings, Godard arrived in Peking penniless but confident that he'd be able to work out some way to finance his journey. And there was still the small matter of the 3000-franc shipping fee to be paid before his Spyker could be unloaded at the dock. Who better to impress with the arrival in China of such a magnificent Dutch car than the Dutch Consul — more to the point, wouldn't it be a shame if Holland's finest automobile was not able to participate in the Raid because of a mere 3000 francs? Godard had done it again.

His optimism was both his greatest asset and his undoing, and on more than one occasion it nearly cost him his life. Crossing the Gobi Desert, for example, required careful preparation. Even though Godard knew he didn't have enough fuel for this leg of the journey, he decided to attempt the drive anyway; he assumed he'd be able to snare petrol from the De Dion crews when the Spyker's tank finally ran dry. But instead the De Dions left Godard and du Taillis in the desert; Georges Cormier promised to send fuel back once he reached the next town. The pair waited by their car in the blistering desert for three days and nights. Fearing a slow death from thirst, they had even begun to drink the oily water from the Spyker's radiator. When two horsemen finally arrived bearing cans of petrol, a reinvigorated Godard became determined to catch up to the rest of the field, so he drove a distance of 617 kilometres nonstop in 23 hours. He didn't know it at the time, but he had set an individual world record for long-distance driving.

The further the Raid travelled, the more Godard's stamina and determination shone. This was never more evident than in Russia, when he loaded the

Spyker on a train to be sent for repairs 1300 kilometres away, then freighted the car back by train to the place where it had broken down, turned it around to face the correct direction, then rejoined the Raid in an astonishing marathon drive.

But Godard's trail of chicanery finally caught up with him once *Le Matin* received the bill for his Russian train travel adventure. The editor had him arrested at the German border, and he was charged with 'false pretences'. Though he was not jailed, Godard was out of the race — and was ordered to repay some of the money he'd jagged from the Dutch diplomats.

The following year he entered a contest inspired by the Peking to Paris Raid: it was to travel from New York to Paris via Japan. However Godard, in a Motobloc car, retired from the race with mechanical trouble before reaching San Francisco.

Jean du Taillis

The headache for Jean du Taillis, *Le Matin*'s correspondent on the Peking to Paris Raid of 1907, was being both the newspaper's official representative and the passenger accompanying serial rogue Charles Godard on the 14 000-kilometre journey.

Du Taillis, a man in his early thirties, cut a plump figure. He had a ruddy round face with rosy red cheeks, a mop of blond hair and a trimmed beard. He sported gold pince-nez on the bridge of his nose, behind which his eyes were constantly dancing around the room. He was notorious for spontaneously erupting into bursts of laughter so loud that they would shock those who had not met him before. At times he was forgetful and disorganised, but he was a courageous newspaperman who had served in many parts of the world; he was familiar with the responsibilities and dangers of being a foreign correspondent. 'All I am and all I want to be is a modest globetrotting reporter,' he said.

In Peking du Taillis attempted to take on the role of the event's leader, and called the drivers to a meeting. He was keen to remind the participants that the Raid was not a race but would be executed in convoy, as agreed in a document signed some months earlier in *Le Matin*'s office in Paris. 'We shall go in convoy, heavy and light.' Slapping fellow journalist Edgardo Longoni on the back, he nervously called for unity: 'The little Italian and me, the colossal Itala and the tiny Contal — stick to that understanding and we shall all get through.'

But du Taillis was aware that Prince Borghese was not a signatory to the agreement; further, it was becoming clear that the Prince had no intention of following any agreement and would run his own race. When negotiations between the Chinese and the French governments concerning permission to travel through China and Mongolia broke down, *Le Matin* cancelled the expedition. Du Taillis called another meeting to discuss developments, and was politely informed by Prince Borghese that as far as he was concerned, the Itala was driving from Peking to Paris whatever the French decided. Du Taillis was powerless: the Raid was going ahead whatever he said. Any aspirations he'd had to control the event had vapourised.

Once Prince Borghese had turned the proposed convoy into a race, du Taillis struggled to elicit co-operation from anyone. His difficulties with this were never more evident than when he desperately tried to organise a search party for Pons and Foucault, who had gone missing in the Gobi Desert. Prince Borghese blithely announced that the Contal crew would be fine and that he intended to continue. The others did not want to give the Prince the opportunity to race ahead while they turned back. But as for Pons and Foucault — they were, in fact, dying.

However, it was his time as Godard's companion in the Spyker that would prove that du Taillis was a man of strong character. Du Taillis watched with disbelief as Godard sold off the Spyker's spare parts before the event. This was a worrying move that could — and ultimately did — put both their lives in peril.

Godard put du Taillis's life at risk on more than one occasion; perhaps the most serious occurred when the Spyker ran out of fuel in the Gobi Desert. Godard's plan was to flag down the De Dions and use some of their petrol. But the plan went wrong: the De Dions did not stop. For three days and nights du Taillis and Godard waited by the motionless Spyker in the Gobi's blistering heat, ultimately drinking water from the radiator to stop themselves dying from thirst.

SPYKER 1907

CHARLES GODARD AT THE WHEEL OF THE SPYKER, WITH THE PRESIDENT OF THE MOSCOW
AUTOMOBILE CLUB BESIDE HIM. A YOUNG SPYKER MECHANIC NAMED BRUNO STEPHAN
LOOKS AT THE CAMERA; HE WAS SENT TO RUSSIA WITH SPARE PARTS.

GODARD AND THE SPYKER IN PARIS, BEFORE LEAVING FOR PEKING.

Petrol did arrive at last, and the Spyker crew battled on; their near-death experience in the desert had somehow cemented their comradeship. Ill with dysentery for most of the journey from there on, du Taillis agreed to use *Le Matin*'s money to pay for Godard to send the Spyker 1300 kilometres by train to be repaired and freighted back to the point where it broke down — and then rejoin the Raid.

An outraged *Le Matin* had Godard arrested at the German border; the Spyker car company replaced him with a works driver. Just outside Paris, Godard returned (he had been released from jail) and attempted to climb aboard the Spyker, but was seized by police. Du Taillis fought to have the police let him go, but he failed, and Godard was dragged back through the crowd. Determined that one of the original Spyker crew should have the honour of driving the car into Paris, du Taillis, for the first time in 14 000 kilometres, put the car into gear and motored on to the finish line in honour of his friend.

45 HORSEPOWER MOTOR

THE BIG 4.6-LITRE 4-CYLINDER 45 HORSEPOWER MOTOR IN STIJNUS SCHOTTE'S CAR IS MUCH MORE POWERFUL THAN THE 15 HORSEPOWER ENGINE FITTED TO CHARLES GODARD'S 1907 CAR. WHEN THE ENGINE WAS DISMANTLED TO BE REBUILT FOR THE 2005 EXPEDITION, THE CENTURY-OLD PISTONS WERE CONSIDERED TO BE IN SUCH GOOD CONDITION THAT THEY WERE SIMPLY REINSTALLED. AT GREAT EXPENSE, THE CAR'S MAGNETO WAS SENT FROM HOLLAND TO THE UK SEVERAL TIMES TO BE OVERHAULED BUT IT CONSTANTLY FAILED TO OPERATE. TWO WEEKS BEFORE THE START OF THE EXPEDITION IN BEIJING, THE SPYKER WAS FITTED WITH A MORE RELIABLE ELECTRONIC IGNITION.

RADIATOR

IN ITS DAY, THE SPYKER'S CIRCULAR RADIATOR WAS AS INSTANTLY RECOGNISABLE AS THAT OF ITS ENGLISH RIVAL, ROLLS-ROYCE. FOR THE RE-CREATION OF THE PEKING TO PARIS RAID, STIJNUS SCHOTTE'S SPYKER'S RADIATOR WAS FULLY REBUILT — THE WORKMANSHIP OF SUCH A HIGH STANDARD THAT THE RADIATOR WAS PLACED ON DISPLAY IN THE 2005 RETROMOBILE MOTORSHOW IN FRANCE.

Spyker 2005

ENGINE:	4 CYLINDER
POWER:	45 HP
IGNITION:	ELECTRONIC
FRAME:	AUSTRALIAN MADE
GEARBOX:	3 SPEED
TOP SPEED:	55 M/H
BORE:	110/120 MM
WHEEL BASE:	3000 MM

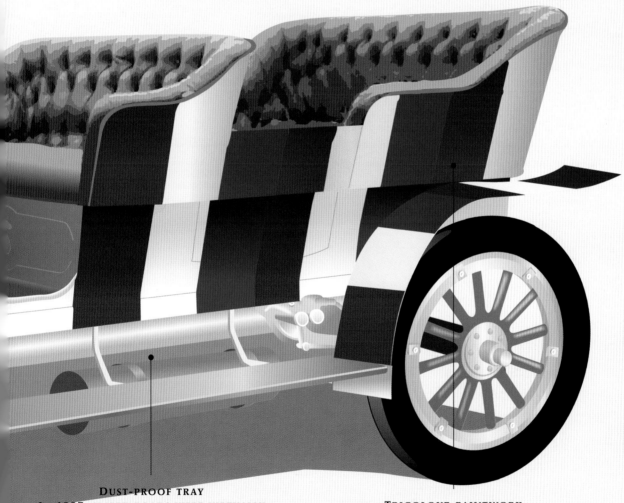

DUST-PROOF TRAY

IN 1907, SEALED ROADS WERE VIRTUALLY UNHEARD OF ONCE VENTURING OUTSIDE CITY LIMITS — DUSTY ROADS BECAME A MAJOR PROBLEM FOR MOTORISTS AND THEIR PASSENGERS. THE SPYKER CAR COMPANY PATENTED AN INGENIOUS DUST-PROOF DEVICE THAT WAS FUNDAMENTALLY A GIANT CAR-LENGTH TRAY FITTED UNDERNEATH WHICH PREVENTED DIRT AND DUST BILLOWING UP THROUGH THE CAR.

TRICOLOUR PAINTWORK

WHEN FRENCHMAN CHARLES GODARD CONVINCED JACOBUS SPYKER TO GIVE HIM A CAR FOR THE 1907 RAID, HE CHEEKILY HAD THE CAR PAINTED IN THE COLOURS OF THE FRENCH FLAG, MUCH TO THE ANNOYANCE OF THE DUTCH MANUFACTURER. ALMOST 100 YEARS LATER, STIJNUS SCHOTTE HAD HIS SPYKER PAINTED IN THE SAME STRIKING LIVERY.

Spyker 2005

This Spyker would have given the Borghese Itala a run for its money.

Of the five cars entering the re-creation of the great Peking to Paris Raid, the most exclusive and expensive is the 1907 Spyker belonging to Stijnus Schotte of Holland. When the idea for locating the five original marques and using them in the 2005 Expedition came about, the most difficult to find (aside from the nonexistent Contal) was always going to be the Spyker. Surviving pre–World War I Spyker cars are extremely rare — there are thought to be only around 16 worldwide.

Why are there so few survivors? The answer can be found in the European climate: cars were likely to be driven through snow dissipated with copious amounts of salt. Salt and steel are not happy partners, of course, and corrosion saw the premature demise of too many marvellous cars.

It's no coincidence that all the cars in the Peking to Paris re-creation have an Australian connection: the dry climate has proven ideal for their survival.

In the early part of the twentieth century Australia's economy was booming, and wealthy farmers and graziers were only too keen to buy some of the world's most expensive cars. Stijnus Schotte's Spyker was delivered from Holland, new, to a Mr Smith of Elizabeth Street, Brisbane, in 1907. This Spyker is much more powerful than Charles Godard's standard 15 hp model, sporting an impressive 6.5-litre 45 hp 4-cylinder engine that would certainly have given Prince Borghese's Itala a run for its money. Mr Smith's Spyker had a 4-speed transmission rather than the standard 3-speed in Godard's car, and was capable of giving exceptional top-end performance.

In the early 1960s the car was restored by Brisbane resident Alan

Dunshea; it was a familiar sight at veteran and vintage car rallies all over Australia. In 1971 a photograph of the car at one such rally was spotted in a magazine by wealthy Dutch industrialist and car collector Max Lips, who had been scouring the world in an attempt to amass a collection of the last surviving Spykers for his museum in Holland. Lips sent representatives from England to Australia to buy the car, and it returned to Holland for the first time in 66 years. (Interestingly, many of the Spykers in the Lips collection were sourced in Australia — one car in the museum still wears a New South Wales registration sticker.)

The Spyker was painted like the French flag to replicate Godard's car, and was on display for many years commemorating the Peking to Paris Raid, complete with Chinese coolie hauling the car by rope, as occurred on the Kalgan Pass.

In the early 1990s the car was purchased from the museum by Stijnus Schotte's father, a car museum owner himself, and regularly used in car club rallies. Since Stijnus's father passed away in 1999, Stijnus has continued to rally the car. He decided to completely strip and rebuild the vehicle for the 2005 Peking to Paris Expedition.

Restoration has been a costly exercise. Refurbishing the circular radiator alone cost several thousand dollars — but it was considered such a fine example of restoration work that the radiator was put on display at the 2005 Retromobile motor show in France.

Stijnus has had the gearbox and engine completely overhauled, and despite the cylinders being machined to the finest tolerances, the car is still using the original pistons and bearings — this is a sign of its unquestionable strength and quality.

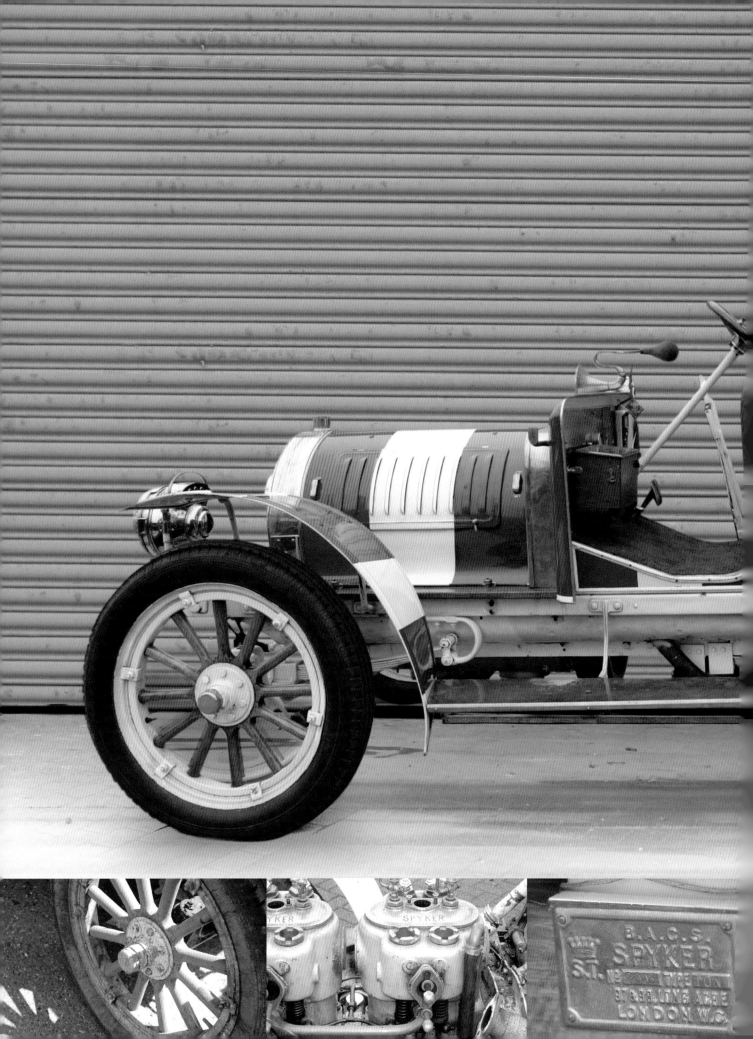

Stijnus Schotte

When the idea of tracking down the five types of original cars and re-creating the Peking to Paris Raid took hold, one of the key problems was finding a Spyker car. Warren Brown and Lang Kidby made contact with a renowned European veteran car dealer and were told that nearly all the world's remaining pre–World War I Spykers belong to wealthy Dutch industrialist Max Lips. And Mr Lips's Spykers are museum pieces. It was thought that a Spyker car existed somewhere in Scotland, and that one belonged to a descendant of the Spyker brothers in New Zealand. The only known Spyker for sale anywhere in the world was the bare bones of one in Venezuela, for which the owner wanted 200000 Euros.

Undeterred, Warren contacted the Veteran Car Club of New Zealand and was put in touch with Rob Spyker, a descendant of the famous car manufacturing family. Rob owned the chassis and engine of a 1907 Spyker. Rob's Spyker was clearly in no state to undertake the Expedition, but he suggested contacting Stijnus Schotte, a Spyker owner in Holland. Warren emailed Stijnus, outlining the plan for the Expedition and asking him if he was prepared to join. Warren was absolutely amazed when he read Stijnus's emailed reply — 'Yes'.

Stijnus Schotte is a born and bred car enthusiast: his family owns a vintage and veteran car museum in Holland which is housed in a converted farmhouse. Packed with automotive memorabilia, the museum contains about 25 cars, including such delights as a 1908 Mitchell and a 1920 Packard. When he's not turning the spanners on old cars, Stijnus earns his living dismantling factories in some of the world's most remote locations.

In 1992, Stijnus's father had an opportunity to buy a 1907 Spyker from Max Lips's collection — the car had been on display in the tricolour livery of Charles Godard's Peking to Paris car. Stijnus's dad regularly rallied the car until he passed away in 1999. Though Stynus is primarily a 1960s cars man, he fell in love with the Spyker and began to track the car's history. He discovered that it had been restored in Brisbane by Alan Dunshea in the 1960s. Stijnus contacted Mr Dunshea's widow, and they have been in contact ever since.

The Spyker is now Stijnus's favourite car in the museum's collection: 'In Holland, when people see the round radiator and realise the car's a Spyker, they stand up and cheer. It makes me feel very proud.'

Rob Spyker

In re-creating the Peking to Paris Raid, it seems only appropriate to have a descendant of one of the original players involved in the arduous 14 000-kilometre journey as the co-driver of the car that bears his family name. Veterinary surgeon Rob Spyker is a descendant of brothers Jacobus and Hendrik Spijker, founders and proprietors of the Spyker car company from 1899 to 1908.

Handlebar-moustachioed Jacobus Spijker found himself involved in the original Peking to Paris Raid when small-time con man Charles Godard presented himself on the doorstep at Spyker Cars' head office requesting the loan of a car to drive the journey. Jacobus Spijker was an extraordinarily enthusiastic individual, and he quickly became entranced with the promotional opportunities a Spyker victory would provide. He gave Godard a car, and a heap of spare parts, and agreed to a 10 000-franc bonus if he won.

Godard, of course, promptly sold the spares and set a series of problems rolling for Jacobus. He was constantly cabling for more money, requesting deliveries of spares for the car and writing IOUs on behalf of the Spyker car company across two continents.

Rob Spyker's father emigrated from Holland to New Zealand in the 1950s, still with the Spijker name, but as Jacobus and Hendrik did with their cars, he altered the spelling to make pronunciation easier in English. Rob remembers his father often talking about the two brothers and the luxurious cars they built, and collecting any reference or memorabilia he could find that related to the car company. In his lifetime Rob's dad had never heard of a Spyker car in New Zealand, but Rob, who gradually fell into car restoration, began a crusade to track down any trace of the marque, no matter how small, on either island.

Amazingly, not far from where he lives in Christchurch, a local turned up a 1907 Spyker engine. Four years later Rob was offered a Spyker chassis, possibly from the same car: enough bare bones to begin a restoration. Rob intends to fully restore his Spyker, which is one of only about 16 left in the world.

SPYKER 2005

Prepped and Packed for Peking

Which department have you been dealing with to gain approval for this?

Mr Du Wei, Chinese Deputy Consul General in Australia

Sometimes years of fastidious planning and preparation can't hope to match the spark of an ingenious idea that fires up the imagination and then takes on a life of its own, gathering momentum like a locomotive down Everest.

This was certainly the case in January 1907, when the French newspaper *Le Matin* offered the world a challenge to drive from Peking to Paris. Within a few months, Prince Scipione Borghese was hurtling down the Champs Elysées, cheered on by enormous, frenzied crowds, having achieved what many thought was impossible.

In the same way, The Great Peking to Paris Expedition rocketed ahead from a chance meeting on the Normandy coast in 2004, to turning the crank-handles on a line-up of vintage cars in Beijing eleven months later.

How a group of Australians, a few Kiwis and a Dutchman came together to re-create a century-old French motor race won by an Italian is a story in itself.

So that they could participate in the 60th anniversary of the D-Day landings in France, former Australian Army pilot Lang Kidby and his wife, Bev, decided to make an adventure of it. Not content with merely buying a couple of tickets to fly to Europe, Lang restored a World War II ex-Australian army Dodge staff car and shipped it to Aqaba in Jordan. For the next six weeks, Lang and Bev drove the old 3-speed, desert-yellow Dodge across Jordan, Syria, Turkey and into Europe. For Lang and Bev, this Middle Eastern sojourn was a breeze: after all, they'd organised and completed some of the world's truly great adventures. Lang has organised many expeditions around the world; his most famous followed the 1919 path of aviators

Ross and Keith Smith from London to Sydney in a purpose-built replica Vickers Vimy bomber.

Among the exhaust and congestion of several thousand WWII trucks, Jeeps and tanks marshalling on the French coast for the D-Day anniversary, Lang and Bev met another Australian, Warren Brown. Warren, a fellow military vehicle enthusiast and Editorial Cartoonist for Sydney's *Daily Telegraph* newspaper, was also in Normandy for the anniversary, invited by the Military Vehicle Trust of Great Britain to jump aboard a WWII truck and cross the English Channel by ferry. Warren, Lang and Bev hit it off immediately. One warm evening in the tiny village of Etreham, they found themselves in the local pub in a fug of cigarette smoke with a crowd of serious drinking French Air Force personnel.

As Lang remembers, 'We regaled each other with our ever more exciting tales of past adventures. In the true Aussie tradition of "never let the truth get in the way of a good story", even the Frenchmen who could not speak English hung on our every word. Warren's atrocious Peter Sellers Inspector Clouseau French accent got stronger as the evenings wore on, endearing him to the locals. They could not understand a word he said, but he *sounded* like a Frenchman.'

In the ensuing days, Lang and Warren's conversation turned to the great motoring adventures of the early twentieth century and inevitably arrived at the showstopper of them all — the Peking to Paris Raid of 1907. To retrace the steps of Prince Borghese, Charles Godard, Georges Cormier and the others was something Lang had always wanted to do but he had been repeatedly stumped whenever the opportunity arose. Warren explained to Lang that he had intended to enter an event scheduled for 2007 which would see all sorts of cars heading from Peking to Paris. In fact, for the centenary, no less than twelve separate groups were endeavouring to make the journey: vintage car groups, four-wheel drive clubs, motorcycle packs, anti-pollution/anti-car groups on bicycles — even a flock of ultralights.

This started Lang thinking. 'Going in somebody else's event with a great crowd of tourists is not my style,' he says. 'I thought that Warren's great enthusiasm was too good to waste on a tour and he could be a fine ally for my own Peking to Paris aspirations. He obviously had a great interest in the event and had done quite a bit of research on the race of 1907.'

Lang recalls the conversation that followed.

'You don't want to be on a tourist drive with 100 other people, you should do it yourself.'

'Oh, yes, what do you have in mind?'

'I think we should build a replica Itala and do it alone.'

'What do you mean, "we"?'

'You and me.'

Lang was insistent that the two of them build a replica of Prince Borghese's Itala vehicle and hightail it 16 000 kilometres across two continents, following the Prince's original route.

'I thought Lang was mad suggesting we build a replica,' says Warren. 'It sounded impossible. But then it dawned on me: if this bloke could build a replica Vickers Vimy bomber and fly the thing from London to Sydney, then I was sure we could build an Itala.'

Within minutes Lang was on the phone to his car-building contacts. Warren remembers his plan: 'I was watching him and I could hear the cogs ticking over in his brain. Lang had it all worked out — "The car should have some great old, enormous motor, something with a really long stroke that could just power along effortlessly".'

Lang made the replica car bit sound easy, but the reality of actually driving across China, Mongolia and Russia might be something else.

Only seven years after the Peking to Paris Raid of 1907, the outbreak of World War I set in train a series of events that closed the original route across China, Mongolia and Russia to the Western world for almost 90 years. In the wake of the Great War, political change snowballed from West to East: the Russian Revolution of 1917, the Soviet annexing of Mongolia in 1921, and the establishment of Communist China in 1949. No doubt it was the thought of Borghese, Godard, Cormier and the others travelling across far-flung and mysterious countries long since locked away from the West that had tantalised the imaginations of motoring enthusiasts for so many years.

 Not that people didn't attempt to follow their path. In 1958, Luigi Barzini Jr tried to organise an expedition retracing his father's footsteps, but he was thwarted by Communist governments unappreciative of his enthusiasm. Barzini Jr gave up on the idea as being impossible. After the fall of the Soviet Union in 1990 and the thawing of relations between China and the West, retracing the original route gradually became feasible. In 1997, a Peking to Paris rally ran on a course that dipped southwards from Beijing, through Nepal and India, up through Iran, Greece, Italy and on to France. About 90 classic cars of all vintages entered; a 1942 Willys Jeep won the event.

But driving the route across China, Mongolia and Russia in a car like Borghese's — that's something different altogether. The plan at this stage was simple, but then, as they say, life turned on a dime.

Warren knew of someone in Sydney who had restored a real veteran Itala and rang him, hoping to come and photograph and measure the car in preparation for building the replica. Much to Warren's surprise, Malcolm Garthon's Itala turned out to be the correct year model, 1907 — and even more surprising was that Malcolm was considering selling it. Now, when you compare a real Itala with a replica, there's no contest. Warren contacted Lang immediately.

'I couldn't stand the thought of a replica when there was a real car still alive in the world,' Lang recalls, 'so within a couple of days\ Warren had bargained the owner down from his original price to something we could marginally afford. The car had been fully restored and sported the classic race-about-style body of the grand-prix-racing Italas of a century ago. I passed through Sydney on my way to a job in the US and within a half-hour of seeing it we stood beside our new Itala.'

Lang had a clear vision for this car: that even though it had half the engine capacity of Prince Borghese's Itala, it should still reflect the Peking to Paris car. On his return from America, Lang detoured to see the original Peking to Paris Itala in the Fiat Museum in Turin. Borghese's battleship-grey car is the only survivor of the five from the original Raid, and here it was in front of him. After explaining to the young security guard what he and Warren were doing, and asking if the guard would mind if he climbed over the barrier to photograph the car in detail, the guard graciously left the room for a few minutes while Lang measured and photographed every part of the car he could.

Once Lang returned to Australia, Warren took the Itala from Sydney to Brisbane on a car trailer. He had a nerve-wracking trip. While heading up the north coast of New South Wales, he noticed strange greenish-grey clouds hanging above a mountain range ahead. Realising that a hailstorm was imminent, he pulled over to put the small canvas tonneau cover over the Itala's leather seats. Continuing his journey, Warren rounded a bend and his Land Rover was suddenly pounded with large hailstones; as the storm worsened, he could no longer see the Itala on the trailer behind him. Parking the trailer under the little protection a eucalyptus tree can offer, he waited for the storm to pass, but after twenty minutes of relentless hail hammering the Itala's paintwork he decided to drive through it rather than watch the car being pounded to pieces.

Once the Itala arrived in Brisbane, Lang wasted no time in stripping it completely. The attractive race-about-style body was removed and stored. Lang's plan was to design and build the framework for a body in the style of the Borghese car: a three-seater with large fuel tanks on either side at the rear. He'd made detailed diagrams of the Borghese Itala, showing measurements of the wheel base, the dashboard, height, width: everything he could run a tape measure over.

To his amazement, despite their Itala having an engine half the capacity of Borghese's 7-litre vehicle, the car was of similar dimensions, give or take a few inches. Lang set about having the fuel tanks pressed and decided to paint the car bright red — the colour of the original racing Italas.

Soon afterwards, Lang received an email from Warren saying he'd approached the owner of a 1907 De Dion Bouton AV, two of which were in the 1907 race, to join the Expedition. Lang thought this was a great idea, but the request suddenly caused Warren to have a vision: what if they could get all five original cars? They could then really feel what it had been like in 1907.

Things had looked so simple a few days before. But now Lang and Warren had to find not only some of the rarest cars in the world but drivers willing to flog them on some of the roughest roads in Asia and pay the considerable costs of such an adventure. Lang had no doubt he could organise and run the event, and Warren's keenness buoyed his hopes of finding the necessary but elusive sponsorship, but they had made for themselves a pile of work.

For a start, even though Russia and Mongolia were now democratic countries and China today is particularly receptive to the West, Lang and Warren had no idea whether the various governments would actually co-operate. Warren's friend Dr Meredith Burgmann, who is the President of the New South Wales Legislative Assembly, offered to host an evening in the President's dining room in NSW Parliament House to which she would invite the consuls general for China, Mongolia, Russia and France, so that Lang and Warren could present their audacious plan and the consuls in turn could help troubleshoot foreseeable problems.

The President's dining room was the perfect venue to pitch such a crazy Jules Vernian adventure: cedar panelling, magnificent gilt-framed paintings, the finest crystal and silver cutlery. One by one the bewildered consular officials arrived, unsure as to why they had been invited to attend this unusual dinner. When Chinese Deputy Consul General Mr Du Wei arrived, Warren shook his hand, but the consul appeared suspicious and unimpressed, firing a question immediately.

LEFT: LANG KIDBY AND WARREN BROWN WITH THEIR UNREFURBISHED ITALA.

ABOVE: THE ITALA CAUGHT IN A HAILSTORM ON THE NORTH COAST OF NEW SOUTH WALES WHILE ON ITS WAY TO BRISBANE FROM SYDNEY.

ABOVE: THE ITALA STRIPPED TO ITS BARE BONES, ENGINE EXPOSED.

RIGHT: LANG SITS ATOP THE HALF-REBUILT, HALF-PAINTED CAR.

'Which department have you been dealing with to gain approval for this?' he glowered, holding out the dinner invitation, which depicted a presumptious map of the route. Mr Du Wei had obviously done his homework: official responses from China had declared that they knew nothing about the Expedition. It seemed to Mr Du Wei that Lang and Warren had organised an event through China which somehow left the Chinese government out of the loop.

So Mr Du Wei wasn't exactly sharing Warren's enthusiasm for the drive from Beijing: this was causing him a serious loss of face. 'Ah …' said Warren nervously, not sure how to respond, 'we haven't actually made any plans — that's why we've asked you here, you know, to see if you think our proposal can work.'

The consul's expression softened and he smiled. 'Okay, okay.'

During dinner, Warren and Lang gave their captive audience an enthusiastic presentation in which the guests learnt of the original race of 1907 and how the two of them were crazy enough to try to do it all over again. They were told of the pair's intention to drive the original route dressed in clothing of the Edwardian period and how they were going to find the line-up of the five original types of cars. Just how and where they would find the cars was incidental; they just would — somehow.

Lang had made sure he was seated next to the Russian Consul General, Georgy Toloroya, and chatted to him about the proposed journey across Siberia.

'Siberia,' sighed Georgy, reclining in his chair and swishing red wine around the bottom of his glass. 'We have bad wolves in Siberia, bad bears … and some very bad people.'

Warren sat next to Mr Yin Yali, the Chinese Consul for Culture (one of those euphemisms for 'spy' if you're a John Le Carré fan) who thoroughly embraced their idea as the night went on. He was at first reserved at their use of the pre-Communist name Peking rather than Beijing, but realised its historical context for the Expedition. 'I understand now, this is about tradition,' he smiled.

Also invited to the dinner was leading Sydney neurosurgeon John Matheson, who in 1997 drove a 1968 Rolls-Royce Phantom V that once belonged to Queen Elizabeth II in the Peking to Paris event that ran way south from Beijing through Nepal, India, Iran and up though Greece. Warren had once interviewed John about the Rolls-Royce for his motoring column in the *Telegraph* and thought it would be a good idea to have John attend, because he had some experience of driving from Peking to Paris — even if he'd gone nowhere near the original route.

John certainly seemed surprised at the audacity of Lang and Warren's proposal, but it obviously intrigued him; his parting words were particularly encouraging: 'If you can find me a Spyker, I'll buy it.'

From this point the hunt for cars and participants began in earnest. After the first few inquiries, Warren and Lang's hopes of finding the original five cars began to take a battering. Several very expensive De Dion Boutons turned up in Europe, but the duo's enthusiasm was dampened even further on learning that the chance of finding a Spyker for sale was almost zero. Lang and Warren discovered that virtually all of the surviving 16 Spykers in the world were housed in one collection in a museum in Holland and the only known Spyker for sale anywhere was the bare bones of a car in Venezuela with an asking price of 200 000 Euros. A road-ready Spyker would be worth around $A1 000 000.

Keith Brodie, the Company Secretary for News Corporation, had been approached by Warren to join the Expedition. Keith had a long association with motor racing and had become increasingly interested in the proposal. Lang had been steadily buying every copy of Barzini's classic book *From Peking to Paris* that he could find on the Internet, and sent a copy for Keith to read. Completely enthused, Keith decided to join and asked if Lang and Warren could find him a car.

Lang started the first of several hundred inquiries but eventually tracked down a 2-cylinder De Dion DE2 in Adelaide, South Australia. Keith was delighted and bought the car immediately, even though it required total restoration. Now they had three.

This left only two cars to find — the two most difficult. They were still no nearer to locating a Spyker of any description, and as for the other car, the little French three-wheel Contal cycle car, it would be totally impossible to find one, since the word around the world pointed to none surviving.

However, John Matheson is a quietly determined fellow, and, having thought of his options, he said, 'What if I build a replica Contal?' It was a prospect Lang found daunting. He had suggested a replica Itala initially but there was the original car in the Turin motor museum in Italy to copy and a vast number of photos, plans and specifications available. Hardly any historical material was available for the Contal.

Regardless, Warren and Lang thought building a replica would be an incredible undertaking and encouraged John to investigate the prospect further. Within a few weeks John and his son Mick, a motoring journalist and motorcycle enthusiast, were hard at work devising plans for the Contal from diagrams and photographs procured from around the world.

Finally, a great event was building: four of the five original types — an Itala, two De Dion Boutons and a Contal.

Then one night Lang received an excited phone call from Warren.

'We've got it!'

'Got what?'

'The Spyker!'

Stijnus Schotte, a Dutchman owning the last regularly operating 1907 Spyker in the world, wanted to come. Warren had found him through a most circuitous route. He and Lang had heard of the remains of a Spyker car somewhere in New Zealand and were astonished to learn the owner's name was also Spyker, a descendant of the original manufacturers. After several false leads, the Veteran Car Club of New Zealand put Warren in touch with Rob Spyker, a veterinarian in Christchurch who owned a Spyker chassis and engine.

Although Rob's car was years off completion, he asked if they had spoken to Stijnus Schotte, a Spyker owner in Holland; his car was rallied regularly.

Having the only road-going Spyker around, Stijnus had been approached to enter his car in a large veteran car rally intended for the drive from Peking to Paris in a few years' time. But when he learnt that only the original types of cars could enter the Aussie event, he was in.

Warren and Lang had now achieved what neither of them had believed was much more than wishful thinking. They would have been more than satisfied with three original cars, but now they had all five. Dozens of veteran car experts around the world had told them it was a ridiculous dream to think they could assemble the full 1907 field. But they had done it.

Suddenly, a potential disaster struck. The owner of the first De Dion called to say he was pulling out. It was now almost too late to start looking for another 1907 De Dion owner to come. What a blow to the team's enthusiasm.

Unrealised by Lang and Warren, the spirit of what they were trying to do was shared by others. When he heard the sad news, Keith Brodie refused to accept the situation. He demanded to know what the owner wanted for his De Dion and, for no other reason than to keep the purity of the event, purchased the vehicle - at huge cost. Keith now had two De Dions.

Where, at this late hour, were they to find someone willing to buy and drive Keith's second De Dion? Thankfully they didn't have to look far — he was already on the team. Within a few days John Matheson had completely handed the Contal project over to Mick and entered in his own right. John enthusiastically took up the challenge to buy Keith's first partly restored De Dion while Keith stepped into the original entrant's car he now owned.

Everyone felt excited about the situation. Denied the chance to compete in an original car, John Matheson had taken up the challenge to build the Contal replica to complete the field in what, to everybody involved, was as faithful a tribute to the original pioneers as could be mustered. Mick Matheson would continue the Contal construction and drive it himself; John now had his original dream fulfilled of driving from Peking to Paris in a genuine turn-of-the-century vehicle.

Meanwhile, Warren had convinced the Australian Broadcasting Corporation (ABC) to look seriously at the Expedition as the subject of a documentary. Denise Eriksen, the head of the documentary division, seemed intrigued by the sheer audacity of the event and, after careful consideration, gave a cautious okay.

Now the real work began. It was a huge undertaking by any standard to organise a journey for 100-year-old cars with their support crews and an eight-person film crew to cover at least 14 000 kilometres of what is still some of the most isolated country on earth.

One of the perennial problems for an event like this is to find sponsorship. Being a taxpayer-funded broadcaster, the ABC wasn't permitted to fund any of the expedition, despite having allocated considerable funds for a documentary. Warren and ABC publicist Lynne Shaw approached many of the original sponsors from the 1907 Raid, but either their time frame was too short or they couldn't get their head around what the hell the Expedition wanted to do. There was a Catch-22: why would Australian companies want to fund something that's happening across the other side of the world? Why would Europeans want to fund a bunch of crazy Australians?

Keith Brodie's incredible connections solved an enormous amount of trouble by sponsoring things in kind. Marsh Insurance underwrote the expedition; Cellhire donated satellite communications; R.M. Williams bushmen's outfitters sponsored clothing. But through Lana Hurst, a colleague of Keith's at News Corporation, the team snared sponsorship for shipping the cars with P&O Nedlloyd.

Lana had impeccable credentials: she had co-ordinated all the importing and exporting of equipment for the 2000 Sydney Olympics. She had worked for all sorts of transport companies and knew her way around shipping and customs better than anyone.

PREPPED and PACKED

LEFT: ORIGINALLY INTENDED FOR KEITH BRODIE, THIS STRIPPED-DOWN DE DION BOUTON WAS BOUGHT BY JOHN MATHESON (BELOW).

ABOVE: THE RESULT OF LOVING RESTORATION: THE BLUE DE DION, TO BE DRIVEN BY JOHN MATHESON AND ANDREW SNELLING.

RIGHT: KEITH BRODIE AND HIS WIFE, LOUISE (BOTH IN THE BACK SEAT), SHAKE HANDS ON THE DEAL TO TAKE OWNERSHIP OF THE YELLOW DE DION BOUTON.

RIGHT: THE 2005 CONTAL IN
ITS EMBRYONIC STAGES.

BELOW: JOHN MATHESON
WAS THE ORIGINAL DRIVER OF THE
CONTAL, AND CAN BE SEEN HERE TEST
DRIVING IT. WHEN JOHN BOUGHT THE
BLUE DE DION HIS SON MICK TOOK
OVER IN THE CONTAL, WHICH DROVE
WITH CHRIS BOYLE.

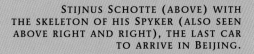

STIJNUS SCHOTTE (ABOVE) WITH
THE SKELETON OF HIS SPYKER (ALSO SEEN
ABOVE RIGHT AND RIGHT), THE LAST CAR
TO ARRIVE IN BEIJING.

The Expedition team had chosen three of the most difficult countries in the world to import and drive vehicles into. China recognises no international agreement regarding motor vehicles. Old cars are prohibited imports, temporary entry for even a few days requires a deposit (in cash) of 110 per cent of the value of the car, and no foreigner may drive in the country on an international or national driver's licence. Of course, foreign number plates are not recognised and temporary Chinese plates must be obtained in the most roundabout fashion imaginable.

The initial approach recommended by the Chinese Consulate in Sydney was to the Federation of Automobile Sports. All the Expedition wanted was to drive directly from Beijing to Erinhot on the Mongolian border, a distance of 600 kilometres — say, three days in all. Lang nearly fell off his chair at the first meeting with FASC in Beijing when the Deputy Secretary-General laid down a proposed bill of $US60 000 for those three days' driving. His list of permits from every possible department, local government, police and of course his own organisation went on and on. Amazingly almost every item on the list was exactly $US6000. When Lang explained that they did not want to rent the whole of China for three days, just travel along one road, with the stroke of a pen the Deputy Secretary-General generously reduced the FASC amount from $24 000 to $10 000.

Discussions went on for some time before the Deputy Secretary-General awoke to the fact the Expedition didn't have a bottomless pit of money (he had just finished dealing with the Formula One Grand Prix in Shanghai) and there was no milk, let alone cream, to be had out of the deal.

The whole show nearly stopped there, as the Expedition had no major sponsor at that stage and the entrants were certainly not prepared to put in an extra $10 000 each just to drive 600 kilometres of a 14 000-kilometre journey. The Deputy then informed the Expedition that, as they were not a large competitive motoring event requiring police escorts, road closures and huge public gatherings, they could do what they originally wanted as private tourists.

'This could be done through a travel agent,' advised the Deputy Secretary-General, 'and I just happen to know the very one who can help you ...'

This initial 10-day trip to China was a constant stream of meetings focused partly upon sponsorship opportunities but mainly upon the vexed question of obtaining drivers' licences and car numberplates. Patrick Chou, a board director of Audi cars, came to the rescue and undertook to provide the team with the required numberplates.

Licence discussions continued.

Lang's task was also to reach the Mongolian border on a survey trip to discover areas of interest for the film crews, as well as establishing the condition of the roads along the way. Not having a Chinese driver's licence, he was generously offered a four-wheel drive vehicle with a driver, by Jason Li of the Chinese Automobile Association (CAA), who eventually extended the organisation's support to a larger sponsorship.

The driver, Gao, was a delightful young fellow supplementing his income as a car club breakdown mechanic by 'guiding' Lang. His English was only slightly better than Lang's Chinese but a great few days was had by the two of them.

Gao was not the worst driver Lang had ever seen, but he was certainly well through the qualifying rounds. Lang doubted Gao had ever been out of Beijing, and he certainly had not driven on a dirt road before.

After two hours on the dirt Lang noticed twice, within a single 10-minute period, that Gao had stayed on the wheel tracks for distances approaching 50 metres at a time. He did even better on the freeway on the way home, when he regularly stayed entirely within their lane for distance as much as 200 metres at a stretch.

The country was barren and featureless, and they lost the track completely a few of times. Lang had Gao drive in a big circle to find it again. It was -23°C outside and the white knuckles and heavy breathing told Lang that death had a firm grip on Gao's shoulder. This bloody Australian had him stumbling through the shrubbery on a frozen wasteland and he would never see his family again.

When Lang finally found the track again, the release of tension was audible.

Back in Australia, the sponsorship hunt continued. Lynne and Warren had been trying for airline sponsorship, but it was the same old story: 'You want to do *what?*' Through Mike Smith, the travel writer at the *Daily Telegraph*, Warren was introduced to the graceful Helen Wong, who owns the most prestigious travel company for touring anywhere in China. Mike forewarned Warren: "Helen *is* China. If she can't get you all there, then no one can. All the airlines sit up and listen when she speaks.' Helen embraced the Expedition immediately. 'Leave it with me,' she said. A week later she had return air tickets for all the Expeditioners.

Time was running out and the deadline for loading the cars to be freighted to Beijing was fast approaching. Lang would be somewhere in Mongolia on a reconnaissance for the Expedition when the cars were loaded but he had devised a loading diagram for placing the cars in the two 40-foot containers. Loading and securing is straightforward but needs to be done correctly, otherwise you end up with a pile of smashed-up parts when you open the container at the other end. The idea is that even if the containers are banged around or tipped, the cars will stay in position. This is achieved by using heavy-duty truckies' ratchet-straps tied to the floor at 45-degree angles at each corner of the car. Pieces of 4 x 2-inch timber are then nailed to the timber flooring, pressing the blocks hard up against the tyres to create a sort of corral around the car so that it's 'fenced in'.

It was a dull, miserable day the morning the cars were being packed in their containers, the light rain making everything seem that much more ominous. Mick Matheson was still putting the finishing touches to the little Contal as the two four-wheel drives manoeuvred their way onto the trailer couplings . Keith's De Dion was lashed on top of the 'emergency' car trailer; the Nissan support vehicle was ready with the blue De Dion in a covered box trailer; the Contal and the Itala would be driven to the dock under their own power.

As the convoy of cars arrived at the container terminal, driving slowly through the drizzle, Lana Hurst was waiting at the P&O gates, flanked by an army of P&O employees. Given the okay at the boom gate, the convoy followed the flashing orange safety light of a well-used forklift truck which wound its way through dark canyons of stacked containers. The container terminal was a bizarre world of sheet steel in every possible direction — a claustrophobe's nightmare. Warren flinched as the Itala ducked under gigantic, multi-wheeled mobile cranes that lumbered unexpectedly from almost every corner. Mick piloted the tiny insectivorous Contal, looking particularly vulnerable in a location where everything else was beyond gigantic. The convoy snaked its way through the terminal, arriving at two open-mouthed containers where Lana Hurst and the packing crew waited.

The first in would be the Nissan with the car trailer. Andrew Snelling reversed the whole road train into the container in one go, the P&O workers descending on the boxed vehicles immediately. Armed with new ratchet-straps, lengths of timber and nail guns, they had the Nissan and trailer secured fast in no time. The next would be the Itala in the second box. Warren drove the red machine into the darkness of the container where was swallowed whole while the straps were anchored to the floor and the nail guns fired through the timber. Then it was the Contal's turn, and finally Andrew, the master of reversing, delivered Keith Brodie's yellow De Dion onto the trailer with only millimetres either side to spare.

The P&O official slammed the doors and tagged them shut. The Expeditioners looked at each other almost in shock. A wave of relief washed over everyone there. The cars were gone.

ON THE ROAD TO PARIS

In Beijing

Mick: It's the Wai Wu Pu all over again. Almost. China hasn't actively discouraged us in 2005 but as the week counts down to Sunday, 15 May, and Expeditioners begin arriving in Beijing, we're not feeling at all encouraged by the way things are turning out. Chinese officials expect bribery, and they block all your moves when you're not forthcoming. Even Lana Hurst, the event's shipping genius who thrives on the wheeling and dealing of international freight movement, struggles sometimes and briefly loses her ever-smiling composure.

Mr Lau (not his real name) from our sponsor organisation is our liaison, but he quickly proves to be a serious liability who seems more intent on extracting money from us than facilitating our logistics. We watch $US1000 disappear into a policeman's pocket while we're struggling to get cars off the docks. We're stalled, made to sweat on whether we'll ever succeed, while time runs out for other important meetings we must not miss. More money, more papers, and just when we think we've cleared the final obstacle, the Chinese reveal another expensive barrier.

It's infuriating and costs us an exorbitant amount of money. In the end we throw away tens of thousands of dollars just to spend a few days driving in China.

Stijnus cops the worst. His Spyker is airfreighted to Beijing from Europe, and because it arrives separately from the rest, the Chinese suddenly find a beautiful excuse to make it a completely separate transaction, despite the fact that the Spyker was factored into the cost of earlier bribes. But there's some justice in the end. Lau, after upping the price another few

grand, tells us we won't get the Dutch car until next week —
after our start date! But China has a Spyker importer who's keen
for any publicity in his efforts to sell the all-new sports cars,
and he manages to find new contacts for us. On Saturday
afternoon we finally pay around $5000 and pry the car from
Customs without Lau. At the eleventh hour all five cars are
registered and sitting together at Beijing's Kempinski Hotel.
We're relieved, rapt and ready to go now.

Sudden Lau shows up and demands his $US2000 'fee'.
With enormous satisfaction, we tell him to get lost.

These experiences, our lightened wallets and other
unnecessary impositions leave us with a bad taste. It's a
shame, because China may have a lot to offer. The shopping
is certainly cheap and the history is amazing, but none of
us is interested in coming back — ever. The Kempinski
employees form the only group we have an easy time with
but that's because it's a German organisation.

And now, on the eve of the adventure, we double-check
the cars in the hotel's car park. We have got luggage and supplies spread
everywhere as we get the cars packed and prepare for departure at six-thirty
tomorrow morning. Our spirits suddenly lift after having been repeatedly crushed
through the week and now, at last, The Great Peking to Paris Expedition is
tangible.

It's time to go.

LEFT: WARREN BROWN AND KEITH BRODIE WITH ALBERT ROUWENDAL, MANAGER OF THE KEMPINSKI HOTEL IN BEIJING, AT THE COCKTAIL PARTY HELD AT THE HOTEL TO FAREWELL THE EXPEDITIONERS.

RIGHT: WARREN ADDRESSES THE GATHERING, WITH LANG KIDBY TO HIS RIGHT.

ABOVE: WARREN WITH GUESTS FROM AIR CHINA, ONE OF THE EXPEDITION'S SPONSORS.

RIGHT: A GUEST TRIES ON SOME EXPEDITION HEAD GEAR WHILE LANG (RIGHT) LOOKS ON.

LEFT: Stijnus Schotte with Albert Rouwendal. All the Expeditioners are sporting 'uniforms' from R.M. Williams, although Stijnus is the only one in a maroon shirt.

ABOVE: Rob Spyker signs some Expedition memorabilia. Chris Boyle can be seen over his right shoulder.

ABOVE: John Matheson with Lynne Shaw from the ABC, who accompanied the Expedition as part of the ABC TV crew filming a documentary on the five cars and their drivers.

RIGHT: Stijnus Schotte and John Matheson sign memorabilia.

Peking to Xuanhua

Mick: We make an early start to beat the traffic that's heavy even on a Sunday morning in Beijing, hitting the road by 7 a.m. and meandering to what was once the Italian Legation in Peking, the very spot that Prince Borghese had made his home for a few days in 1907. Beauty queens in Qing Dynasty costumes ride in each vehicle as the cars motor onto centre stage for a function that includes hundreds of media people, as well as the French and Australian ambassadors. And then, at last, The Great Peking to Paris Expedition sets off.

Beijing is an amazing city dominated by the Forbidden City and Tiamanmen Square. We drive through the massive square, past the huge Forbidden City and into the old *hutongs*, a maze of ancient bungalows that resembles exactly the kind of streets that the 1907 Raiders experienced. They are narrow, crowded and lined by the most basic brick buildings you've ever seen, punctured by narrow alleys disappearing into what must have been a tangle of passages to who knows how many people's homes.

But the crowded and congested streets are tough on veteran cars. Keith Brodie's yellow De Dion boils and then its battery goes flat trying to run an electronic ignition with what has proven to be a limited charging system. As is often the case, it's the car's more modern modifications that bring it undone. But within minutes it's fixed and we're moving again.

All the way, locals line the roads and gawk. No one has seen cars like these in almost half a century, and most have no idea what they are. To contemporary Chinese people the car is a phenomenon of the past decade or two, and veteran cars are completely alien.

Then suddenly we are on the tollway heading out of the city. Cars and trucks stream past the slower veterans, and almost universally the Chinese peer and grin and wave. The Great Wall appears, snaking over rugged mountains on both sides. Tourists are climbing it like a multicoloured caterpillar as we drive past.

John Matheson's blue De Dion develops gearbox problems but Andrew Snelling keeps it going. Their little De Dion — the most modestly powered as well as being the least proven car after its hasty build-up for the trip — is the slowest of the five cars, but it's going well. On steep grades Andrew sometimes has to jump out on the push before the blue car stalls, but they keep at it.

The final leg comes at the end of what has become a very long day, and some of the cars arrive in Xuanhua after dark — never a good bit of timing on a veteran vehicle with their poor or nonexistent headlights. Few of us get to bed before 11 p.m. Each car has had a few little problems but no one has resorted to the back-up trailers to carry the cars, and no cars had major dramas. It's been a very successful first day.

Warren: There's no sun in Beijing — none that I can find, anyway. There's a layer of smog and smoke and dust that makes the sun sort of glow like a 20-watt light bulb in a snooker room. This city with a population of nearly 20 million is what's described to me by a mate living here as 'hard-core' China. Peking was already the Orient's busiest city when Godard, Cormier, Borghese and the others brought the very first cars here 100 years ago, but it's pure motoring chaos today: everything and anything with wheels is gridlocked on Beijing's roads.

Today we roll out of Beijing. At 6:30 a.m. the five cars are assembled in the forecourt of the Kempinski Hotel and their pith-helmeted drivers are hovering around them in a last-minute attempt to make sure every conceivable detail for preparation has been attended to. It's that kind of feeling where you're sure you've forgotten to do something and you're not quite sure what it is, but you know you'll discover it 5000 kilometres down the road.

Lang and I just made an agreement: I'll drive the Itala when we depart Beijing; he'll drive the car into Paris. It seems a fair enough deal to me — there's every chance the Itala could put a piston through the side of the engine block 500 metres from the Kempinski and I'll be on my way home to Australia that afternoon. And, besides, the thought of punting our century-old machine through the streets of Paris after having lived in it for two months and 14 000 kilometres isn't on my list of priorities this morning. Nevertheless, today is to be my day at the wheel.

H-Hour: saddle up. The crank handles are turned, the goggles are on and the cars wait to enter the madness that is Beijing's traffic. The road outside the hotel is a white-water river of buses, cars, tricycles and trucks meandering from lane to lane in every direction. Nothing happens quickly; the traffic flows roughly in the same direction; it's almost dream-like, the way cars gracefully cut each other off and brush past disinterested pedestrians who amble diagonally across intersections.

There is only one way to deal with this: put the car into gear, release the handbrake, close my eyes and nose out into the traffic. And we're out — for the first time in a century a Spyker, a Contal, two De Dion Boutons and an Itala are on the streets of Peking.

We are heading for an official farewell at the old Italian Legation building, the site where Prince Borghese and Ettore Guizzardi stripped their Itala before heading off for the Great Wall. The old Legation building is one of those grand colonial structures set in a courtyard behind an impressive set of gates. We swing our small convoy inside and line up the cars side by side.

The CAA, which sponsored the ceremony, has arranged an astonishingly grand farewell. Five models in exquisite traditional Chinese dress sit in each car as a phalanx of TV crews and photographers swarm over the vehicles in a kind of Chinese media feeding frenzy. The reality strikes me: there are no vintage cars in China. None. In a country with a population of over a billion people, these five machines are the only antique cars on Chinese soil.

As had been done a century before, the French ambassador's wife was invited to farewell the motorists — Madame Guelly doing the honours for us today. Lang and I shake the bottle of champagne, blasting the Itala's bonnet for luck — we'll need every bit.

Now there's no turning back — it's Paris or bust.

The cars file back out into Beijing's traffic, heading for Tienanmen Square. Overloaded buses sound their horns in approval as they pull alongside, their passengers' faces squashed against the windows as they wave and laugh at these lunatics in their wacky contraptions. Pedestrians cheer and we cheer back — a bit of colour and movement for everyone, it seems.

The five cars putter through the traffic along the edge of the square, where a giant portrait of Chairman Mao hangs over the front gate to the Forbidden City — a lot of things have come and gone since 1907.

Our goal today is to head for Nankow (Nankou), the first night's stop for the original Peking to Paris Raid; the Great Wall; the town of Bedaling, and on to the old military town of Xuanhua.

It's a very strange feeling to pilot the Itala on the path to Nankow. I've only read of the place, where the 1907 motorists arrived for their first night in teeming rain at the Nankow Inn. Nankow was the place they were warned by French Concessionaires they would never reach; the place Auguste Pons shipped his Contal to by train.

Nankow today is merely a grimy industrial outer suburb of Beijing: just a turn-off from an expressway chock-a-block with cars. The drive out here has proven that the De Dions are absolutely no match speed-wise compared to the big 4-cylindered Spyker and the Itala — it's a struggle for the little 2-cylinder numbers to keep up. Mick Matheson's Contal proves to be a real surprise to everyone, and Chris Boyle reports that being the passenger stuck out reclining amongst the traffic is a breeze, but, of course, that's travelling on modern sealed roads. I wonder how they'll go once we hit the dirt.

We can see through the relentless fug of smog and smoke the faint silhouette of a spectacular and forbidding mountain range ... somewhere up there is the Great Wall.

After passing through a particularly grim and grotty truck-strewn roundabout in Nankow, we receive a message from a CAA escort vehicle that John Matheson's blue De Dion has broken down with a gearbox problem and Anthony Eden, our mechanic, is with him. The four remaining cars press on, working their way higher towards the mountains.

The Itala requires serious concentration to operate when heading uphill, so much so that it comes as a shock to look up and suddenly see the overpowering vision of the Great Wall snaking its way along the dragon-toothed skyline above me. It doesn't matter how many photographs or postcards or commemorative ashtrays you've seen of the Great Wall: nothing prepares you for its breathtaking presence.

The climb from Nankow to the Wall is as you would expect — steep. Ultimately the point arrives where we pass through an archway in the battlements signifying that we've crossed the Great Wall. We pull up by the side of the road with the Contal and the yellow De Dion.

We've lost John Matheson in the blue De Dion and we've lost Stijnus Schotte in the Spyker. This is only Day 1 and we've suddenly realised that we have a serious communication problem. As it turns out, Stijnus is not far behind — he had a series of fuel blockages causing his car to conk out — but John has been trying to find us since his car broke down back outside Nankow. John eventually appears, having backtracked to the roundabout outside the town where he eventually worked out where he was and continued on the right road.

Now we were ready to head up toward Bedaling to cross the Wall again. Bedaling is Tourist Central when it comes to the Great Wall — the mighty barricade trivialised with souvenir shops, cafés, restaurants selling everything from Great Wall tea towels to snow domes. If the wall couldn't keep Genghis Khan and his hordes of Mongols out of China, how on earth can it keep out 100 coachloads of tourists per day?

Now it's a long run for the cars on the open road to Xuanhua, described as a military city when Prince Borghese passed though. It may still be a military city, but the exquisitely named Steelworkers Hotel suggests otherwise.

KEITH AND LOUISE BRODIE GLIDE THROUGH EARLY-MORNING BEIJING
ON THEIR WAY TO THE OFFICIAL LAUNCH.

KEITH IN THE YELLOW DE DION AND WARREN IN THE ITALA TAKE PART IN
A PARADE TO MARK THE START OF THE EXPEDITION.

MAY

S	M	T	W	T	F	S
	1	2	3	4	5	6	7
8	9	10	11	12	13	14
~~15~~	(16)	17	18	19	20	21
22	23	24	25	26	27	28
29	30	31				

DAY 2

Xuanhua to Zhangjiakou

Warren: No one here wants to take an easy option on this expedition. We all know the drive to Paris in these Edwardian contraptions will be hard, but we haven't brought our cars halfway around the world to do the journey like some Sunday lunch run to my old nana's.

We want to know what it is like to throw these old cars at some of the most diabolical mountain ranges China has to offer. We all now have a bit of an understanding as to how primitive and temperamental our cars are — dodgy brakes, poor performance, suffering from exposure to the weather — and how these mischievous little machines demand complete attention and maintenance every afternoon before you go to the pub, whether you like it or not.

So what must it really have been like to be Godard or Borghese or Cormier, having to deal with these rolling nightmares and then face the impossible in shifting these vehicles over the Kalgan mountains to reach the Mongolian Plateau? How did they hack away at rocks and massive tree roots to encourage the cars' progress, employing scores of Chinese porters to help haul and manhandle the cars up hills and through ravines? Not in my wildest dreams could I imagine that hardship.

Today we'll have a go at finding out how difficult it truly was. On a back road to Zhangjiakou, fifty locals are waiting at the base of a rocky hillside to help us with an experiment.

The locals, of both sexes and all ages, line up alongside two ropes attached to the Itala's front springs. Lang explains to them through an interpreter what we intend to do. He is now Prince Borghese, clear-headed and with one vision: to convince this group of people who have no idea what he's on about to get this car to the top of the hill. Like the dramatic photographs of the time, I am to be Ettore Guizzardi, perched high behind the steering wheel, ready to negotiate the car through the rocks and ruts.

Accepting the idea, the locals jovially raise the ropes across their shoulders, and with Lang bellowing the command to move, the Itala lurches forward. Up onto the hillside the Itala rolls, the porters suddenly straining against the dead weight. It's no fun now. I've often wondered about that photograph of Guizzardi, as to why he was standing on the floorboards, almost bent double looking at the ground in front of him. I can tell you why: with so many people jammed in each wheel rut in front of the car, it's nearly impossible to see where the wheels should be going. I find myself bent double, looking at the ruts ahead of me.

Lang, under one of the ropes, urges them to heave, and they do, everyone's feet slipping on the scree, the weight of the car proving more of a problem than anyone imagined. The Itala slowly moves uphill — 'Go! Go! Go!' Lang yells, the porters and Expeditioners straining on the ropes. Up over a steep rise, they continue to drag the car, a line of people pushing their physical limits for some stupid contraption still nowhere near the top. Finally the Itala reaches the summit, the locals dropping the ropes, relieved at their accomplishment. But it isn't over. John Matheson's De Dion Bouton, as tiny as it is, seems somehow heavier, and even with mules attached to Keith Brodie's car, the hauling becomes more exhausting.

It must suddenly seem infuriating to the locals that they agreed to such a painful exercise — and for what? Once the Itala and the De Dions are at the top, forget it. Just as a century ago, the locals have had enough.

Mick: We awake to broken clouds today but at least we can see the sky, a first in our experience of hazy northern China at this time of year. The forecast rain holds off all day, which is a huge relief. There's nothing worse than driving open cars in the rain, especially when you have special events planned. And we have a

LEFT: WARREN MAKING FRIENDS IN A CHINESE VILLAGE AS HE OFFERS TO DRAW A VILLAGER'S PORTRAIT.

RIGHT: IN THE ORIGINAL RAID, VILLAGERS OFTEN HELPED BY PULLING THE CARS UPHILL WITH ROPES AND DONKEYS. THE 2005 CARS DROVE UPHILL UNDER THEIR OWN POWER, THEN HIRED VILLAGERS RE-CREATED THE PAST AND HAULED THE CARS UP THE HILL. HERE, THE YELLOW DE DION GETS A PUSH.

ABOVE: THE SPYKER AND YELLOW DE DION ATOP THE RIDGE.

RIGHT: THE HAULING EFFORT IN FULL SWING.

beauty today: re-creating the time the 1907 Raiders were pulled up horrendous mountain passes by gangs of Chinese coolies.

First, though, we head to what we call the Breakfast Town, a tiny village where everyone pours into the main street to see the first Westerners who have ever stopped there. They're fascinated by Bev Kidby's sandy-blonde hair as much as by the weird cars. Toothless old men, slick youths, giggling girls — even a woman holding high the drip for a sick child — press around us.

Leaving town, we encounter our first section of rough road. The Contal replica, which was expected to be the worst-handling vehicle, sails along happily. Neither Chris nor I, who swap seats regularly, have any qualms about riding up front. Indeed we thrive on it, playing it up by feigning sleep or just lounging while the three-wheeler putters through the countryside.

A few dozen 'coolies' — in reality, rural workers — are waiting for us up the road, beside a track that struggles up a steep and rutted hillside. Each car tries the climb alone. None fails the test, even though the Contal stalls a few times as it bounces and tilts across the tough terrain. The Itala passes it when it's trying to back down to get another run at the steepest section. The Spyker follows the red car all the way to the top without a drama. The humble De Dions lack the torque to surmount the short, sharp rise halfway up and find a gentler detour — cross-country running is no problem as long as it's not too steep.

We all drive back down, Warren and Lang taking a difficult secondary route to the bottom without any hassles. These old cars will go almost anywhere a modern four-wheel drive can go as long as power is not crucial to success. Then the Itala and De Dions are pulled to the top again by the 'coolies'. They drag the cars to the top eagerly and easily. But the novelty wears off and, besides, our Chinese organisers haven't arranged any drinks or food for them, so they refuse to do any more. Never mind, we've seen enough and are happy to move on to our camp for the night.

But there's another problem — and there is always another problem in China, as we're discovering. The village up the road, which was expecting us for the night, hasn't arranged a single thing. No food, no nothing. So we opt instead to go on to Zhangjiakou, which was once called Kalgan, a major stop on the 1907 trip. We arrive before the rain finally falls, and gather to tell tales of our hill-climbing prowess over dinner.

MAY

S	M	T	W	T	F	S
1	2	3	4	5	6	7
8	9	10	11	12	13	14
~~15~~	~~16~~	(17)	18	19	20	21
22	23	24	25	26	27	28
29	30	31				

DAY 3

Zhangjiakou to Jining

Mick: The Chinese authorities — who stick by international visitors like mother hens and force their own agenda onto them — won't tell us until after 8 a.m. whether we will be allowed to use the route to Shangdu that we want or whether we'll have to follow a longer path on main highways. Of course their decision puts us on the main roads, which doesn't please us at all as we set off in light rain from Zhangjiakou. We were warned that the highway to Jining is 'a seven-day traffic jam'. We took that to be an exaggeration ... until we find the truck parking lot that masquerades as one of the nation's major roads. There are stationary trucks to the horizon — and they've been there since the day before.

Eventually we make some progress ... but not for long. No one is happy and we curse the authorities, who lied blatantly to us and even insisted that they'd chosen this god-awful route for our own safety and comfort. We are appalled.

But we laugh, too, because it's what we've come to expect, and then we each go at our own pace through the chaos of trucks. Somehow, in the end, the day finishes on a high note for all of us.

Keith needs more water for his De Dion's radiator and is invited into someone's house to get it, an experience he didn't expect. John and Andrew's De Dion plods along beautifully and John grins when he recounts the fun of dealing with the day's challenging traffic. This, he says, is what he wanted from this most bizarre of journeys: challenges that are thrown up at us, that challenge the cars, and that force us to deal with them on terms we understand.

Chris and I don't enjoy the highway on the Contal but are delighted by a dirt-road detour that takes us through fields and into a village where chickens scatter before us and locals stare with blank, uncomprehending expressions at the odd sight of the three-wheeler. We also spend an hour laughing and gesturing with locals on the side of the road towards the end of the day, making friends who help us buy local beer at a discount and then guide us to the hotel where everyone else has already arrived.

There was no chance any of us would make Shangdu on the imposed route, so we pull into a hotel in Jining. Still, no car has required major work today — not even the 1300-metre altitude hampered them significantly — but again we all experienced minor niggles that were quickly dealt with.

Warren: China proved the greatest problem for the original Peking to Paris Raiders of 1907 — and not because of the Great Wall or the Kalgan mountain pass. The Chinese government was convinced that the motorists were actually spies and attempted to obstruct their every move by refusing them access across the country to Mongolia.

Outside our hotel in Zhangjiakou sits a camouflage army radio surveillance truck, complete with blacked-out windows and a large rooftop antenna, looking somewhat like an oversize roof rack. It was there last night and its presence here this morning seems more than a little coincidental. Zhangjiakou is a military town, as it was when Cormier and the others passed through in 1907. It was explained to me that only twenty years ago no Westerners were allowed on the back roads through the district, and even today all levels of government are nervous about our intentions, particularly with a film crew in tow.

Last night a group of local officials was invited to dinner to discuss our planned route following the original 1907 path, taking in Shangdu. The local officials explained that it would be much better to take the highway — much safer. They would feel better if we took the highway directly west to Jining. West to Jining — why would we want to go there? We have to go north, we explained. The officials looked nervously at each other. Yes, yes — but it would be much safer for them to

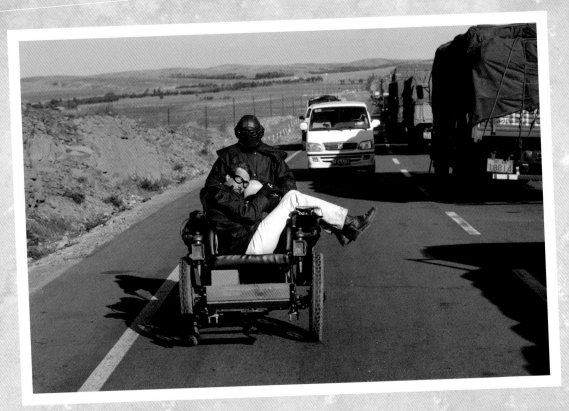

MICK MATHESON TAKES A NAP ON THE MOVE IN THE CONTAL,
PILOTED BY CHRIS BOYLE ON THE HIGHWAY TO JINING.

ACCORDING TO PHOTOGRAPHER BOB BARKER, 'THIS DAY WAS MARKED BY A TRULY SURREAL SCENARIO
OF THE MOST INCREDIBLE NUMBER OF TRUCKS, JAMMED AND MOVING, ANY OF US HAD EVER SEEN
– KNOWN AS THE SEVEN-DAY TRUCK JAM. BELCHING, FILTHY, DUSTY. SCIENCE FICTION!'
THE BLUE DE DION IS BARELY DISCERNIBLE AT THE FRONT OF THE PACK.

escort us to the edge of their province and farewell us on the road to Jining. It was obvious: they wanted us out of their district on the fastest road.

This morning we move off on the road from the city behind an official government vehicle; the army radio truck shadows us.

While fuelling up at a service station, the government official bounds over with the happy news we are allowed to drive the original route and that this is much better, because there's a seven-day truck jam to Jining on the highway. The radio truck glides by. Relieved, we drive on; then, twenty minutes later, the official vehicle pulls over — there is a problem: the original route is unsafe, apparently — there are major roadworks and the road is closed, so we must use the highway for the 150-kilometre drive to Jining. But isn't there are seven-day truck jam? The flustered official gives me an idiotic, hapless grin — he's been overruled. We press on and soon arrive at a gridlock of tens of thousands of trucks idling in a black fug of diesel exhaust. The queue of motionless vehicles stretches beyond the horizon.

The official is embarrassed — moments ago he warned us about this truck jam and now he's led us straight into it. He has to do something. An hour later a police car arrives, lights flashing, siren blaring, to lead us through the traffic jam — but how? The police car follows the centre line of the highway, blasting its horn until the trucks fire up and diverge, giving the cars just enough room to get through. We follow the police, our cars squeezing through this corridor of metal with only millimetres to spare.

Suddenly the police car is gone and we have to fend for ourselves. Stijnus in the Spyker is ahead of us and charges his car down the centre line of the highway. The wall of trucks part as if the road is the Red Sea. We're hot on the heels of the Spyker. Soon we're in the lead — a 100-year-old car taking, head-on, an endless river of coal trucks that decide at the very last second to lumber across onto the shoulder of the road, giving us the narrowest margin to scrape ahead.

The best way to drive in this situation is to select a gear and pull out into the oncoming traffic, then floor the accelerator relying on the good nature of the oncoming truck driver to not annihilate us. Any hesitation could prove disastrous. This incredible truck jam lasts 120 kilometres and on more than one occasion we nearly lose each car and crew. In the late evening the air becomes thick with exhaust, the road a miserable, muddy mess.

We arrive at the Jining Hotel as the sun descends into a bleak haze, glad to survive an adventure we never expected.

MAY

S	M	T	W	T	F	S
				1	2	3	4	5	6	7

1 2 3 4 5 6 7
8 9 10 11 12 13 14
~~15~~ ~~16~~ ~~17~~ (18) 19 20 21
22 23 24 25 26 27 28
29 30 31

DAY 4

Jining to Suniteyouzi

Warren: The Jining Hotel is a fairly appropriate monument to old-time communism in China. Big, marbley and empty, its cavernous foyer is fully staffed with countless attendants and porters — even on the mezzanine level there's a small army waiting to hold elevators and open doors despite a noticeable lack of any customers. I'm sure the place was intended as an example of a communist Michelin Guide four-star hotel, but it's everything you would imagine a 1980s, Cold War-style hotel to be: all ready to go if only someone wanted to go there.

Our wild-haired mechanic, Anthony Eden, is up early working on the old cars. Anthony's a young bloke who joined us a few weeks ago in Sydney, having driven the scenic route of 8000 kilomentres from Margaret River in Western Australia. He had quite an adventure himself, his Land Rover blowing the gearbox on the road between Kalgoorlie and Alice Springs. After being stranded for three days without seeing another car, he was eventually flat-towed by a Telstra Land Cruiser to an Aboriginal mission, where the car was loaded onto a four-trailer road train and sent to the Alice. This side trip took nine days for Anthony to travel 1000 kilometres.

We roll out from the hotel at 8 a.m., hoping to salvage whatever we can from the original route in this part of China. We are now well and truly inside Inner Mongolia, heading towards the town of Suniteyouzi, about 220 kilometres north of Jining. As the road climbs higher toward the Mongolian Plateau, the landscape becomes increasingly more arid — the rolling hills becoming vast, flat sandy plains and the sight of a wolf trotting across the road signals that we're approaching the wilds of the Gobi.

Suniteyouzi is the last Chinese town before reaching the showpiece border city of Erinhot (Erlian) — but a showpiece Suniteyouzi is not. Turning off the highway, the road into town travels through a squalid landscape of abandoned machinery, decaying brickworks and gargantuan quarries strewn with tens of thousands of plastic bags blowing around in the desert wind. This is a town the Chinese government is not keen for Westerners to see. Keith and Louise Brodie in the yellow De Dion Bouton are stopped by police, who instruct them that the region is 'off-limits to foreigners'. It's too late — most of the Expedition is already in town.

The streets are blasted by grit from the desert; footpaths are stretches of compacted sand littered with Chinese trucks in various stages of repair or ruination. Grimy barefoot locals peer out from sand-blasted buildings at the curious convoy that's just pulled up in the main street. The whole place has a Sergio Leone feel about it, tumbleweeds and all. Forget the West — this is the Wild, Wild East.

We find our hotel, a bland box-building distinguished by two giant green and blue plastic palm trees out front. Entry to our rooms is made via the fire escape at the rear, and, contrary to what we're expecting, the rooms are terrific. Furthermore, the restaurant cooks up a tremendous Beijing duck — I don't dare ask for the pre-communist Peking variety. Tomorrow we cross the border into Mongolia.

Mick: The Expedition motors into a bitterly cold headwind this morning on the 220 kilometre highway drive to Suniteyouzi. This is where the countryside changes from the distinctly Asian landscape you expect of China to the outback-like openness that defines Mongolia. Indeed, Suniteyouzi is just over 100 kilometres from the modern Mongolian border. We drive in convoy out of Jining, then made our own pace.

Immediately, the Spyker and Itala roar into life as the drivers realise they are now on a relatively quiet stretch of highway, a far cry from yesterday's tangle of trucks. 'We had a lot of fun running with the Spyker,' Lang says later. 'We had the Itala flat to the boards all the way.' Warren wonders how much fun it would have been to have the same 7-litre engine that propelled Borghese across this countryside almost 100 years ago. Stijnus and Rob had a closer feeling for it as the big Spyker lopes along comfortably all day. Except for some silicone in the tank causing the occasional fuel blockage, the big car is clearly the sweetest and most powerful vehicle of the group, and deserving of its 'Dutch Rolls-Royce' nickname.

The fast cars beat a police roadblock that catches both De Dions. Two uniformed cops, one with a little English, and a shadowy plain-clothes officer haul the drivers and passengers aside and grill them about what they were doing in an area that is off-limits to foreigners. Fortunately one of our Chinese-speaking 'fixers' arrives a few minutes later and smooths everything over. We never find out why the police stepped in like this, and just put it down to China being, well, China.

Chris and I swing the Contal off the highway into a couple of villages just for the fun of it and are invited into someone's house for lunch. We exchange gifts and even play pool at one of the weather-beaten tables outside on the wide dirt footpaths. The table has a horrendous roll and the cue ball isn't round, but none of that matters.

John and Andrew have the longest day but their little De Dion's engine, so fresh when it left Sydney, is now beginning to bed in and free up. Even at this high altitude, John can happily report that the car feels more powerful and responsive, and smoother.

Half of the crew members are very red-faced at dinner thanks to the frigid 20-knot headwind and harsh sun, both of which are almost impossible to escape in veteran cars. But every face breaks into big grins as we recount our adventures. We've seen camels, strange little rodents, a raptor, and some people even think they've seen a wolf. We can't wait for what's coming up in the next few days over the Mongolian border.

We initiate two periodic awards tonight: the Borghese Award for outstanding heroism and the Godard for more dubious acts. The inaugural Borghese goes to Andrew Snelling, who repaired the blue De Dion's broken exhaust manifold with a soft-drink can and two hose clamps. The ABC TV crew's director, Peter George, has for months been promising to arrange for the Contal team to run out of fuel in the Gobi Desert so he can film us dying and capture the suffering that Pons and Foucault went through. And today, in the barren wastes of northern China, Peter ran out of fuel himself, alone, and was rescued by the Contal riders. For this he earns the first Godard.

LEFT: AS THE EXPEDITIONERS HEADED INTO OUTER MONGOLIA (STILL IN CHINA), WHERE THE LAND BEGINS TO FLATTEN INTO DESERT, THEY PASSED THREE OF THESE INDESCRIBABLE VEHICLES.

RIGHT: PHOTOGRAPHER BOB BARKER TAKES HIS LIFE INTO HIS HANDS TO SHOOT THE SPYKER (L) AND ITALA (R) AS THEY DRIVE PAST HIM.

ABOVE: AFTER THEIR CLOSE CALL WITH BOB, THE TWO CARS TAKE A BREAK.

RIGHT: WARREN AT WORK ON THE ITALA WITH LANG (VISIBLE THROUGH THE WHEEL) AT THEIR HOTEL IN SUNITEYOUZI. THEY ARE BEING SUPERVISED BY THE DOG, CHRISTENED RUFF — BECAUSE, SAYS BOB, HE IS THE ONLY KNOWN DOG WHO ACTUALLY BARKS 'RUFF'.

DAY 5

Suniteyouzi to Gobi Desert

Mick: Driving to the Chinese border, we bear the brunt of the same chill wind that fought us yesterday. We make an early start, aiming to hit the border when its gates open at 9 a.m. because the whole complicated process of exiting China can take hours. The closer to the border we get, the more the road deteriorates, until it peters out into a potholed dirt track — but right alongside it are thousands of Chinese roadworkers building a new highway.

Erlian, the border town, feels quite cosmopolitan after the past few cities. Erlian is also known as Erinhot, the name used in 1907. We regroup in the railway square and begin transferring gear from our CAA support vehicles into our own trailers. We have other vehicles waiting in Mongolia for us, but first we have to drag everything across the border to them. An hour later we are ready — and Stijnus has lost a bag full of paperwork and photos, including precious records of his Spyker's history. This is the first theft we've suffered.

The border crossing takes three hours — not too bad compared with what we anticipated. The Chinese take our driving licences from us and then, in an irritating act of token graciousness, return them as souvenirs. These licences cost us thousands of dollars and we feel we have a right to them. After a few false starts we are waved through the gates and out of China, none of us unhappy about it.

And then a posse of Mongolian vehicles that want us to turn back confront us in no-man's-land! We are already too annoyed to face more petty bureaucracy, and are getting angry when the Mongolians climb out of their cars ... the district governor, a small military band and five beautiful girls in traditional costume. Our faces light up and our mood turns completely. This unexpected and genuinely friendly welcome makes our day and sets us up for what we know will be a wonderful experience in Mongolia.

Zamyn-Uud has all the look of a frontier town, like something from the Wild West except with *gers*, the traditional Mongol tent, as well as ramshackle wooden buildings. It's dusty and chaotic, exactly what you'd expect to find with the Chinese border behind and the Gobi Desert in front.

The road is actually a series of tracks wandering vaguely in all directions through the enormous emptiness of the Gobi. Sometimes you can look across and see, say, a De Dion away off in the distance. Then it disappears behind a rise so imperceptible you can't even make it out, but the little car will suddenly pop up again even further away. Then its path might cross yours. Our main guides are the telegraph lines to our left and the railway to the right, both running roughly parallel a few kilometres apart. Some sections are sandy, some corrugated, some covered in stones. Always there are the telegraph lines ... but then you lose them! The rugged terrain demands full concentration as the old cars bounce along, and it is easy to forget about watching the lines. The same problem occurred in 1907. We too could cut across country to find the lines again, but many of us also have GPS satellite-navigation equipment to rely on.

As usual the two big cars, the Spyker and Itala, make ground quickly. The Contal can maintain a good pace on the smoother sections of track but slows dramatically in the rough. Keith averages about the same pace as the Contal in his De Dion, while John's blue De Dion makes slow but steady progress.

Karakorum Expeditions — run by Australian Graham Taylor, now a resident of Ulaan Baatar, the Mongolian capital — will look after us for the duration of our Mongolian stay. We arrive, one by one, at a fabulous camp centred on a *ger* with a hot meal and Aussie champagne. But by the time darkness swallows the Gobi's vast space, John and Andrew still haven't arrived. We aren't worried, though, because Henry Pang and Robert Rosenberger are with them in the mothership — Henry's four-wheel drive towing a trailer — and they have all they need to camp out.

We sit down to eat when someone calls out, 'John's coming in!' And sure enough, the blue De Dion putters into camp after a long and gruelling drive. We've all made it. The five Peking to Paris cars survived their first day in the Gobi Desert without mishap.

LEFT: STIJNUS SWAPS HATS WITH A GUARD
AT THE CHINA–MONGOLIA BORDER.

RIGHT: YOUNG MONGOLIAN WOMEN
MAKING A PRESENTATION TO THE
DRIVERS JUST AFTER THEY ARRIVE IN
MONGOLIA, TO WISH THEM GOOD LUCK
FOR THE TRIP.

ABOVE: KEITH AND WARREN CELEBRATE
THE EXPEDITION'S ARRIVAL
AT THEIR FIRST CAMP SITE IN THE
GOBI DESERT.

RIGHT: WARREN FILING A STORY AT THE
CHINESE BORDER IN THE SHADE OF THE
YELLOW DE DION, AS LOCALS LOOK ON.

Warren: The border between China and Mongolia opens at 9 a.m. sharp. The plan is for the Expedition vehicles to arrive right on opening time and so a 6 a.m. departure from Suniteyouzi is scheduled for the 100 kilometre drive to the border town of Erinhot.

We drive across an arid landscape, dead flat in every direction. Our first real confirmation of the approaching Gobi is the sight of a herd of shaggy bactrian camels blocking the highway. Erinhot's skyline gradually comes into view and soon we're in its bustling streets. To our surprise, Erinhot is an oasis in far-flung Inner Mongolia. Like most Chinese border cities, it is designed to appear very impressive, its streets are wide and clean, its architecture modern — as far removed from the squalid surrounds of Suniteyouzi as you could imagine.

We marshal near the railway station before heading the few kilometres out of town to the border. The Chinese side of the border is an impressive eight-lane driveway over which an enormous steel arch painted like a rainbow gives the impression that there must be a pot of gold at the end of it. There is for somebody: our official government minder receives his last payment and we are allowed to leave China.

We are to take delivery of our two support vehicles, a light twin-cab truck to tow the trailer and a van bought second-hand in Mongolia when Lang visited on the reconnaissance trip two months before. Up to the border the CAA supplied two Jeeps with drivers whom we now have to say goodbye to — they have become great mates on the trip through China.

Once we've officially crossed the border, a convoy of black four-wheel drives bounce along the road toward us. What now? There's going to be some problem for sure. The vehicles pull up, the doors open and out falls a host of Mongolian officials and a military brass band. Clutching an array of panel-beaten E-flat horns, cornets and euphoniums, the band strikes up an ear-splitting rendition of the Mongolian national anthem. This surprise welcome has been organised by the Mongolian Australian Society, better known as the Mozzies — a group of Mongolian nationals who have studied in Australia as part of an aid program. Our host is a young Mongolian named Batsurii, who

1907

GOBI DESERT

Godard organised for fuel to be sent back to Pons, leaving himself short of what he'd need, and then everyone carried on in the morning into the worst of the Gobi Desert. The Itala managed up to 100 km/h sometimes, and vanished ahead. The Spyker's tanks were bone dry by the time it was less than a third of the 280 km to the next resupply point, at Udde. Cormier gave Godard a token amount of fuel then carried on, promising to send more back. It was 47°C in the shade, and Godard and du Taillis, waiting with their car, had almost no food or water, and no shelter. Pons and Foucault were even worse off: they were sick, having drunk water from a puddle, and were dehydrating badly. Only the Itala reached Udde on this day.

completed a Master's Degree in Canberra and who, in a few weeks, will take the position of Mongolian Ambassador to Thailand. The local governor welcomes us to Mongolia as five girls in wild-pink traditional costumes present the drivers of the five vehicles with bright blue sashes for the Expedition's good luck. These exquisite girls climb aboard each car, and we then proceed behind the convoy of four-wheel drives through the local village. The girl sitting next to me in the Itala welcomes me with a well-rehearsed greeting: 'Welcome to Mongolia — home of Genghis Khan'. The Mongolian people's love of the great Genghis Khan startles me — even after last century's tug of war between Soviet Russia and communist China over Mongolia, the locals' adoration for their mightiest figure remains undiminished. If old Genghis was anything like the Mongolians we've just met, he's been getting an unfair rap for centuries.

For the first time we see the distinctive *gers*(what the Russians call *yurts*), the circular felt-covered homes of the Mongolian nomads. They lie on the peripheries of the town, the main centre being a series of decaying, sand-swept Soviet-built apartments. The road through the village is made simply of large cement slabs lying in the desert sand. The four-wheel drives pull up where the road abruptly stops at the village outskirts, the brass band firing up another number. I ask Batsurii about what's happening. 'They are wishing you luck for your journey across the Gobi,' he says.

Before us is a harsh, gritty desert stretching as far as the eye can see. This is the Gobi — where Auguste Pons and Octave Foucault almost perished when the Contal ran out of fuel, where Godard and du Taillis were forced to drink the water from the Spyker's radiator in order to survive. What would be in store for us?

Lang and I decide to remove the Itala's quivering mudguards for the desert crossing and set off following one of countless dirt tracks. There is no sealed road in the Gobi, just an endless web of rough camel tracks that converge and diverge across a broad-swept, almost featureless landscape. The Itala hammers along the original Peking to Paris route, following the overland telegraph line. These ancient telegraph poles, preserved in the Gobi's dry, cold climate, are very likely the same ones that cast shadows over Prince Borghese's Itala as he tore along these tracks. We overtake the Contal — Mick and Chris are struggling with the tiny machine as it flounders in the sand. All they can do is take their time. On the horizon we can see John's De Dion Bouton following the railway. By following either the telegraph or railway lines we will reach our first camp site, some 100 kilometres away.

The Itala parked near a *Ger* and a more Western tent in the Gobi Desert.

The Itala rounds up some camels near the Chinese border.

DAY 6

Gobi Desert via Saynshand

Mick: Dawn in the Gobi Desert is glorious: a long, pre-dawn glow that erupts into a blazing orange sunrise. Then suddenly the sun is blindingly white and heat seeps through the chilly air. We wake early despite the late finish last night — sunset wasn't until almost 10 p.m. — and are soon on our way.

The two De Dions go on ahead while the other three cars attend a re-enactment of the time the Spyker was towed by camels after running out of petrol. Two local camels are brought in and hitched to the Dutch car. The beasts moan their displeasure at pulling over two tons of recalcitrant car behind them, but once they get some momentum up they do a fine job of moving it across a few hundred metres of desert. We also hitch up the Contal to one of the animals, which plods along effortlessly under the light weight of the little three-wheeler.

We follow the railway towards Saynshand, the region's capital city. After yesterday's thrill of entering the desert, of discovering new territory, we now look at the landscape's details; the Gobi is full of them. It looks more barren than the outback, with almost no plant life except grass. We see two stunted trees before Saynshand, the last for hundreds of kilometres. And yet the desert teems with life: thousands of horses, camels, goats and the Mongolians who tend them. Their *gers* are never far away and we often see horsemen in the distance. Wells are now quite common, probably much more so than when Borghese, Cormier et al came through in 1907. We also see plenty of vehicles, although it's a far cry from Pitt Street.

Not far from camp, Keith's De Dion breaks an axle after struggling through a patch of deep sand. Anthony Eden, our talented and tireless mechanic and sweep driver, hauls it onto the trailer and finds a welder in Saynshand to attempt repairs. He and the Brodies stay there until late in the evening, reaching camp after dark with the French car repaired but still on the trailer to save time.

Saynshand appears across the desert on the edge of a low ridgeline. The town is dusty and slightly run-down but, inevitably in Mongolia, friendly. Teenage girls walk around in short skirts and stiletto-heeled boots, a fashion that turns out to be popular all over Mongolia. We get fuel and some supplies, then follow the railway line out into the desert again.

Again, there is a choice of many tracks to follow, or we can simply carry on over virgin ground. Where the ground is not covered in grass tussocks, it is smooth and we can travel quite quickly, but the most consistently good route is the service track for the railway. Apart from Anthony towing the yellow De Dion, Chris and I are the last ones in, and the sun sets while we are still almost an hour from camp. The long twilight gives us fading visibility until about 10 kilometres out, and then we cover the last stretch in full darkness (our spotlight is in a support vehicle that is already in camp), crawling along in the knowledge that there is nothing to run into out there in the Gobi.

Warren: Luigi Barzini, the Italian journalist travelling with Prince Borghese, described the Gobi as being a 'place of death and agonies'. It is, in fact, a place of startling, unbelievable beauty. It has an almost lunar landscape; its lack of vegetation, except for miniscule outbreaks of desert grass, gives the place a dramatic, breathtaking appearance. Tracks meander here and there, and of course there is the telegraph line and the railway through to Ulaan Baatar, but apart from that the Gobi is a vast, empty place. The air here is incomprehensibly dry. You can feel any moisture in your skin being sucked into the desert. Our camp site has been set up by Graham Taylor and his Mongolian staff, who have constructed a *ger* and a field kitchen — a most welcome relief to find a bit of shelter, hot water and some local tucker at the end of the day.

LEFT: THE YELLOW DE DION, ITALA AND SPYKER IN CONVOY THROUGH THE GOBI DESERT.

RIGHT: THE PASSING ITALA AND SPYKER FAIL TO IMPRESS LOCAL GOATS.

ABOVE: THE SPYKER BEING TOWED BY CAMELS IN THE GOBI DESERT, IN A RE-ENACTMENT OF A 1907 EVENT.

RIGHT: TIME FOR REST AND REFLECTION AFTER DINNER IN THE *GER*.

Not far away from the site, Stijnus and Rob are having the Spyker pulled along a sandy patch by a team of camels. Some of the local tribesmen have hitched up a pair of bactrian camels and, after some considerable strain and wheelspinning, 'rescue' the big Dutch car from the Gobi's clutching sands.

Today is a 120 kilometre drive through to the sandswept town of Saynshand and another 50 kilometres to a designated camping site. The Itala, the yellow De Dion and the Spyker stick together for some distance but the stark difference in engine power means the 2-cylinder car has to travel at its own pace. The bigger-engined 4-cylindered Spyker and Itala match speeds of around 60 kilometres through the desert. The Spyker's 4.6-litre engine certainly has more grunt than the Itala's 3-litre, particularly when climbing hills — a novelty for Stijnus, who normally drives the car around dead-flat Holland. There's surprisingly little time to take in the amazing scenery the cars are belting across; there is only head space for the next pothole to negotiate, the next washaway, which gear to select.

It's easy to tell when you are approaching a town: the road deteriorates and pollution increases. The entry to Saynshand is through the garbage tip, a place awash with plastic bags and filled with clapped-out industrial equipment — old electrical cables, burnt-out trucks and twisted metal lying half-buried in sand. The town itself is a no-nonsense frontier town. There's a curious mix of Asian tradition and the reminders of the old Soviet presence here: on top of a hill sits a T34 tank-based self-propelled gun as a well-kept monument to Russia's occupation of Mongolia.

The locals in Saynshand are delighted to see the cars. The brass horn becomes a crowd favourite to the point where it's difficult to extricate the cars from the growing throng of children who are by now piled ten high on top of them.

The Itala and the Spyker arrive at the camp site only to hear that Keith and Louise's De Dion has broken an axle. Lynne Shaw and Bev Kidby in our admin vehicle are in the town teeing up a welder to assist. Keith and Louise may have to stay in Saynshand for a few days.

The Contal boys are still missing; it's getting dark and we're growing concerned as to their whereabouts. They eventually turn up, having driven nearly 50 kilometres through the deserted Gobi in total darkness with no headlights. An hour later, Anthony arrives with the De Dion on the trailer. We have everyone.

DAY 7

Gobi Desert

Warren: We are all becoming seriously filthy. And I mean filthy. In the Gobi, there are no showers or running water. The cars, having no roofs, windscreens or doors, leave us all well and truly exposed to everything under — and including — the sun. Each day is an onslaught of dirt, exhaust, oil, insects, cold, heat and an incessant searing wind that diminishes only when you hit the brakes. The wind has cracked my lips, which now have the look and feel of the Dead Sea scrolls. My nose is starting to peel from sunburn — or is it windburn? Both, I think. My face and forearms are evenly smeared with 40/50 weight engine oil, my hair is matted with a grease/dirt mixture and reeks of petrol, the corners of my eyes and mouth are black with molydisulphide grease. The Gobi's air is so cold and dry, the skin on my neck has the crinkly patina of a seventy year old. My clothes are now so ingrained with gear oil and grit from the desert that I've had to surrender to a grimy, smelly existence for the duration of the Expedition.

Today we are to test the speed of the Itala and the Spyker against Mongolia's famous horses in a *naadam* festival. Keith and Louise Brodie invite me to make the run into the *naadam* in the newly repaired De Dion. For Keith, the little car has been a vertical learning curve — he learnt to drive the thing in Beijing and then moved on to how to change a tyre in the Gobi. Ambling along a rutted track on the edge of the Trans-Mongolian Railway, Keith bravely invites me to drive. The 2-cylinder De Dion with its straight-pull gearbox and vertical steering column is a completely

different experience to the Itala. It's a shuddery, juddery, noisy, grindy, jolty machine that I could never imagine anyone driving to the corner, let alone across two continents.

We hammer along the sandy track for about a kilometre when the car suddenly seems to fall out of gear, just revving in neutral. Looking underneath, our worst suspicions are confirmed: the axle's broken again. There's nothing to do but wait for Anthony and the support vehicle. Here's the lesson for trans-Gobi motorists: don't let me drive your car.

And the *naadam* ... I'm told it's not to be missed — after I miss it. As part of the yellow De Dion crew, I arrive on a trailer just as the wrestling and the car and horse race finish. The Mongolian wrestlers appear particularly fearsome — they're built like the proverbial nuggetty, not-to-be-messed-with, invade-one-third-of-the-world Genghis Khan-style blokes. Mongolian wrestling doesn't seem to have a time limit: it goes on until someone touches the ground with their hand or backside and loses. Nor does Mongolian wrestling have a designated area in which to wrestle — one minute you can be particularly relaxed on a folding stool sipping Mongolian tea and the next a pair of 200 kilogram wrestlers have crashed in a clutch of fighting fury in your lap.

As for the car and horse race, Lang and Bev Kidby in the Itala and Stijnus Schotte and Rob Spyker in the Spyker line up their cars 3 kilometres away in readiness to race a pack of horse-mad Mongolian kids on horseback. The race begins — and the Expedition's most powerful cars are left behind as if they're standing still. The open ground's so rough on the cars that they bounce around on the uneven course; it's little wonder the traditional riders whipped the motorists, with a five-year-old boy on a white horse belting across the finish-line like a one-fifth scale Mongolian ruler under full steam. Genghis would be pleased.

The drive to our designated camping spot follows the railway line, passing through some of the roughest country we've encountered. The first village we crawl through looks positively menacing: miserable grit-swept streets empty except for a few stray dogs. Grim, ramshackle timber houses puff smoke from their chimney pipes, peppered by harsh desert sand flung in the dry wind, the odd decaying Soviet building and jerry-rigged ex-Russian Army trucks sitting beneath the never-ending line of telegraph poles.

The further we go, the sandier the track becomes, meaning the Itala is really struggling in places, so we opt to drive cross-country. This proves much better, and we soon find ourselves racing alongside a herd of white-tailed antelope. In the evening twilight we arrive at our chosen camp site racing another pack of local animals — a wild herd of Mongolian horses.

Mick: No desert is completely featureless, but this little piece of the Gobi is as close as it comes to being in the middle of nowhere. Daylight opens up a 360-degree view of flat, sandy horizon. A few hundred metres to one side the railway line comes and goes into infinity. There is an endless parallel line of telegraph poles another few metres away on our other side. Some people would wake to this scene and feel helpless and alone, but there's not one of us — not even Stijnus, who's never experienced such desolation — who doesn't revel in the freedom of the landscape.

This freedom is home to the Mongolians, who have a strong sense of community. Today, there's a *naadam* being held just a few kilometres up the track. A *naadam* is a sporting festival featuring the nation's three main sports: horse racing, wrestling and archery. We join in, racing our Itala and Spyker against the locals' horses. We don't win the cross-country dash, but the cars don't disgrace themselves either.

The Mongolians have no qualms about climbing all over our old cars and playing with every control and button. The kids, especially, go to town on the vehicles and there's nothing we can do about it short of standing guard and physically dragging the little blighters away — but we're not keen on being such thugs when we're being treated so warmly. Besides, it's far better to take our chances that nothing will be damaged than to miss the *naadam*. However, when Chris and I return to the Contal, all Chris's water has been drunk and my helmet's strap is torn, but we shrug it off. It's impossible to be angry at these laughing kids.

People are beginning to mine the Gobi and we travel through tailings from small-scale operations. A local woman complains to us that the place has gone to hell because of the mining; we can only hope the big companies don't move in with open-cutting equipment and complete disregard for the Gobi's majesty.

LEFT: LANG KIDBY PREPARES TO RIDE — DRIVING GOGGLES PROVED INVALUABLE IN THE DESERT.

RIGHT: THE 45 HORSEPOWER SPYKER RACING A MONGOLIAN HORSE DURING THE *NAADAM* FESTIVAL.

ABOVE: MONGOLIAN WRESTLERS, PART OF THE *NAADAM* FESTIVAL.

RIGHT: THAT NIGHT, ANDREW SNELLING CATCHES UP ON HIS DIARY.

VETERAN CAR, VINTAGE CAR...

To many people, any funny old car with a crank handle, an upright brass radiator, free-standing headlights and running boards is a vintage car. But the Peking to Paris cars are actually veteran cars, a distinction that would be driven home by any handlebar-moustachioed purist. According to the Veteran Car Club of Australia, veteran cars are classified as any motor vehicle built prior to the end of 1918. Vintage cars are those built from the beginning of 1919 until the end of 1930. The first veteran car club in Australia was formed in Adelaide in 1934 and a similar club founded in Melbourne later the same year.

In one tiny village by the railway we cross a new, wide and smooth road gouged through the desert and some of us veer onto it. It sort of goes the right way, but after 10 kilometres or so it becomes obvious that this road — made for trucks on a specific mission between some distant operation and the rail — is taking us away from our route. No worries, we simply turn left on a compass bearing and head back to the railway and telegraph lines. Sometimes we find little tracks to follow; other times we make our own.

Chris and I ride through a small valley dotted with half a dozen *gers*, flocks of goats, some camels and a couple of herders busy at a well. The men hardly bother to look up as our strange contraption motors past. We see marmots everywhere, dashing to their holes ahead of the dust they kick up. A few gazelles sprint across a hill.

In camp that evening we watch train after train rumbling towards China. They begin going back the other way on the single line, and run all night, but we sleep so deeply after our long, hard days that they don't disturb us. A few of us are now sleeping in the *ger*, where it's warm. A few more sleep under the stars with a tarp wrapped around their sleeping bags, but most are happy in their tents.

DAY 8

MAY

S	M	T	W	T	F	S
1	2	3	4	5	6	7
8	9	10	11	12	13	14
~~15~~	~~16~~	~~17~~	~~18~~	~~19~~	~~20~~	~~21~~
(22)	23	24	25	26	27	28
29	30	31				

Gobi Desert to Ulaan Baatar

Warren: The reminders of the Soviet occupation of Mongolia that pop up every now and then in the Gobi seem totally incongruous with the ancient Asian traditions of Genghis Khan and Mongolian pride so ingrained here. With the collapse of the Soviet Union in 1991, the Russians simply walked away from Mongolia, leaving this new democratic society with a whole host of vacated buildings and countless tonnes of machinery and materiel.

Crossing the top of a gentle hill we find the former Soviet garrison town of Choir (pronounced 'Choya' rather than 'Choir' in the style of the Mormon Tabernacle), once a full-blown bustling military town with paved roads, offices, sporting fields, modern multi-storey apartments for soldiers and their families, schools and services — a thriving example of Soviet colonial success. But Soviet success departed Choir on the back of a T-72 when the empire collapsed. Choir army base is now a vision of destruction on a post-apocalyptic scale — abandoned, ransacked and destroyed.

The once busy streets on which Russian military traffic rolled are cracked and split, and strewn with thousands of tonnes of rubble. The grand barracks are stripped bare, the concrete walls torn apart, the steel reinforcing within ripped out for scrap. Unravelled in the ruins lie the scratched and bleached remains of an 8 mm home movie: a woman holding her new baby shyly to the cameraman. In the background a *babushka*, a grandmother, is peering from a corner. We wonder who these

people were and what has become of them. How would they feel about a bunch of strangers finding this very personal film of family life in Choir among the ruins in the Gobi?

Still defiant in a sea of collapsed walls, a bust of Lenin surveys the culmination of his life's work laid out in the acres before him — a mighty Soviet garrison, smashed apart and left to perish in the desert.

Nearby are the remnants of an equally derelict Soviet air base, the only sign of an aircraft being the shell of a 1960s jet fighter perched as a statue on top of a concrete plinth — once a prized display, and left to survive intact because there's no money in aluminium scrap. Before leaving we line up the Spyker and the Itala on the 3 kilometre runway to see which car is the fastest, in a kind of crazy Edwardian Great Race way. Of course we have the reverse situation to 1907: Godard's Spyker had a smaller motor compared to Stijnus's, and Borghese's Itala's motor was more than twice the size of our 3-litre. There's much pushing of the cars, revving of engines and moustache-twirling. A local elder drops his hat to the ground and the race is now officially on, the two cars belting along neck and neck, Stijnus's lead foot and raw horsepower eventually triumphing over the 4-speed gearing of the Itala.

We are heading for higher country this evening and press on to the green hills which envelope the grand city Prince Borghese knew as the Mongolian capital of Urga, now Ulaan Baatar.

Mick: Mongolia was long ago split in two — Inner and Outer Mongolia — and Outer used to be part of the sprawling Soviet Union. The Soviets set up military bases here and cities to support them, but when Mongolia became a democratic state of its own in 1990, the Russians walked away and left all these desert communities to the Mongolians. It was like leaving a brewery to teetotallers: the Mongolians are generally nomadic, besides which the new nation lacked the resources and infrastructure to maintain central heating, plumbing and other essential services. The Russians cities were mostly abandoned, and fell apart.

This morning we visited one of them, not far from last night's camp. The former military town has a few remnant blocks of stark Soviet-era apartments, of

LEFT: ONE DE DION ON THE ROAD, THE OTHER ON A TRAILER — THE BRODIES' YELLOW CAR GETS A LIFT.

ABOVE: MICK AT THE WHEEL OF THE CONTAL IN THE TOWN OF CHOIR; THE ITALA AND SPYKER CAN BE SEEN IN THE BACKGROUND.

ABOVE: EXPEDITIONERS INSPECTING AN IMPOSING STATUE ERECTED DURING THE SOVIET ERA.

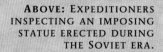

RIGHT: THE 8 MM MOVIE FOOTAGE FOUND IN THE RUINS OF CHOIR ARMY BASE.

which just a handful still have windows and occupants. The remainder of those still standing have been gutted of everything useful, while the best part of the old town was torn down years ago.

A massive statue of a stern, paternalistic figure who doesn't quite resemble Stalin overlooks an old parade ground while leaning on a shield with the inscription 'What was built by The People must be defended'. There is no one left to defend it and no people left to care.

The whole place sums up communism's fate: it was a dismal failure that now lies in ruins. We reflect on the irony that Borghese, an Italian prince, had strong socialist leanings and sympathised with the beliefs of those who would, when he came through in 1907, shortly set off a revolution that would dramatically change the course of world history. What would he have thought if he could see it now?

The group then becomes separated as we head an hour or so away to a former Russian air force base. The Spyker and Itala are to race on the old runway. Half the group follows a guide directly to the site, but the GPS coordinates we were given are wrong, so those who became separated trek cross-country to ... absolutely nothing. The coordinates put us in the middle of a massive, featureless prairie. We all arrive individually too, increasing the confusion as we each try to find out what's wrong.

Chris and I on the Contal — which is comparatively slow when the ground isn't good — are last. We ride to high ground, see Soviet-style buildings in the distance and eventually find ourselves cut off from the Expedition by the airfield's barbed-wired perimeter fence that runs to the horizon. We aren't going to ride all that way, so we pull out a set of pliers. We can now boast that we've cut our way into a Russian military installation.

We arrive just in time to miss the Spyker's victory over the Itala. In lieu of Champagne, someone hands Stijnus a small bottle of Coke that drenches him in sticky fluid as he celebrates his win.

From there we follow the railway line along an appallingly rough and long stretch of roadworks towards Ulaan Baatar. Eventually we reach tar for the first time since China and speed into Mongolia's capital, smiling at the first trees we've seen in days and enjoying the greener, lusher countryside. On one hand it feels good to be closer to familiar things, but, then again, we will miss the glorious Gobi.

DAY 9

MAY
S	M	T	W	T	F	S
1	2	3	4	5	6	7
8	9	10	11	12	13	14
~~15~~	~~16~~	~~17~~	~~18~~	~~19~~	~~20~~	~~21~~
~~22~~	(23)	24	25	26	27	28
29	30	31				

Ulaan Baatar

Warren: There is a handful of places in the world with exotic names that instantly conjure up mystery and adventure — Timbuktoo, Zanzibar and Morocco are just a few of the usual suspects. But I think, namewise, Ulaan Baatar tops them all. What an absolute ripper of a name. No doubt the original crews of 1907 felt the same sense of anticipation and excitement even when Ulaan Baatar was known by the equally exotic name of Urga.

Their arrival at Urga was a great relief — it marked the end of the Gobi's sands, regarded then as the most torturous part of the Raid. In 1907 Urga was actually made up of three cities — Chinese, Mongolian and Russian — which lay some miles from each other in a triangle. Today, Ulaan Baatar (or UB, as the locals call it) is a crazy melting pot of Soviet Occident and Mongolian Orient, a bustling city of about a million people. From what I can see, the inhabitants are some of the friendliest people you'd ever meet. The streets are filled with trucks overloaded with steel scrap plundered from derelict Soviet factories and installations. The Russian influence is still very much here — nearly every car is a Lada or a Gaz four-wheel drive and almost all signage is in the Russian Cyrillic script. The city lies on the floor of a broad valley ringed by spectacular green hills, the highest ones peppered by pine trees — and trees are something we haven't seen for a while.

We're greeted by the Consul General for Mongolia in Australia, Peter Sloane, and his wife, Jocelyn, who have flown from Sydney to meet us. Peter has been a great supporter of the

1907

ULAAN BAATAR

Godard, despite fever and exhaustion, pulled off an incredible feat, driving from Udde to Urga in one hit. He drove 617 km in 23 hours, through the night and often across country.

He could hardly speak when he arrived, and the Raiders' hostess, Madame Stepanoff, cried over the pitiful state he and du Taillis were in.

Borghese had reached Urga more than a day ahead of the De Dions and had left before Godard arrived. The Raiders were all fêted, fed and asked to give joy rides to the few important people in Urga, a town which was made up of three distinct and somewhat distant groups: Russian, Mongolians and Chinese.

Expedition from the word go — 'I wouldn't have missed it for quids,' he tells me.

Today is scheduled as a day off for the crews — but forget it. The Gobi has taken a terrible toll on the cars and every spare second is spent repairing as many of the broken bits and pieces as possible. The Spyker has had an ongoing steering problem which has been difficult to rectify; the car hasn't been able to maintain constant wheel alignment and is in serious danger of destroying all its tyres. Keith Brodie and Anthony have removed the yellow De Dion's broken half-shaft and taken it to an engineering works to be welded. The plan is to pick up whatever is needed for the cars by scouring, locating and bringing back armfuls of incredible once-in-a-lifetime bargains from the local markets.

Ulaan Baatar's markets are something to behold. The 'Black Market', as it is known, is made up of hundreds of stalls selling all sorts of fascinating bits and pieces. If you want Russian army boots, they're for sale here by the hundreds of thousands; we find hats, worse-for-wear flintlock rifles from the 1700s … and I pick up the bargain of all bargains: a suit made from hessian. What a find! Sure, it's a bit prickly, but geez it's a fine cut. But the real eye-opener is the market's food hall, a vast hangar-like building clogged with people buying all sorts of local produce. Mountains of vegetables, fruits, cheeses and meat. Being a vet, Rob Spyker is able to give a running commentary on what sort of beast has just been slaughtered and is now being dissected by an army of blood-soaked, butcher-knife-wielding Mongols. 'This is horse … I think,' says Rob, his mind ticking over, trying to recall pictures from *Gray's Anatomy* in his university days …

DAY 10

MAY

S	M	T	W	T	F	S
1	2	3	4	5	6	7
8	9	10	11	12	13	14
~~15~~	~~16~~	~~17~~	~~18~~	~~19~~	~~20~~	~~21~~
~~22~~	~~23~~	(24)	25	26	27	28
29	30	31				

Ulaan Baatar to Mongolian border

Mick: The Mozzies are a group of Mongolians and Aussies (hence: Mozzies) who foster the strong ties that exist between both nations, encouraged by the Australian Consul General, Peter Sloane. They see us off from Ulaan Baatar with an official farewell on the edge of the city's main square, with a grand statue of Genghis Khan overlooking us. A traditional Mongolian string quartet, a throat singer and a soloist play beautiful music, including a 'blessing for the road' and a delightful tune about the power and strength of fast horses that has a rhythm we drivers could easily relate to.

Not far from Ulaan Baatar the road begins to rise. We are climbing to higher altitudes and the temperature drops steadily. It is 10°C with a vicious wind-chill factor when we pass a river that runs for a while under a large slab of thick ice. Some of us stop for a photo of this rather novel sight, not realising what's about to hit us.

Chris and I are well ahead of the group as the temperature plummets to 5°C and snow clouds engulf the sparse, windswept landscape. We shiver and brace for the onslaught but luckily come upon a cosy roadside café just in time. We dash inside as snow streams horizontally through the air.

The others drive into the bitter cold and snow. We watch the Spyker and Keith's De Dion drive on. John sensibly finds shelter in the trailer behind Henry's Nissan.

And then the weather clears. The front blows over and soon we are driving under blue sky again. What a relief, particularly as we plan to camp tonight. We'd already done more than half

LEFT: THE SPYKER AND ITALA PARKED OUTSIDE THE TRUCK-STOP CAFÉ, BEFORE THE SNOWSTORM.

RIGHT: MONGOLIAN MONKS BLESS THE EXPEDITIONERS' JOURNEY BEFORE THE CARS LEAVE ULAAN BAATAR.

ABOVE: PERFORMERS AT THE FAREWELL CEREMONY ORGANISED BY THE MOZZIES.

RIGHT: LANG LOOKS ON AS WARREN AND ANTHONY PREPARE TO TAKE THE ITALA BACK ON THE ROAD AFTER THE SNOWSTORM. THE CAR HAS A PROTECTIVE BAG ATTACHED TO THE GRILLE, AND SNOW COVERS THE HEADLIGHTS.

the day's 270 kilometres when we sought refuge in that café, so the rest of the day's journey is effortless for all of us. It still feels like a long way, though, and we are all happy to find the camp, an idyllic flat beside a river with steep hills above. We have hours of daylight left and take advantage of it, climbing the hills for the views, exploring up the valley and buying the entire stock of beer in the local area — which amounts to just two cans per person, if that.

Herders come for a look and join in as our Karakorum hosts erected the *ger*. Buddhist monks appear from nowhere and conduct a blessing for us inside the *ger*. John returns the favour by taking them for joy rides around the flat in his De Dion, and the monks can't get the grins off their faces.

We express to our hosts our delight at spending our last night camped in such a tranquil and beautiful part of Mongolia, only to be told there are even more perfect places in the country's western districts. If the Gobi and these northern pastures are second best, the top spots must be better than the Garden of Eden.

Warren: Our brief flirtation with civilisation has come to an end — we're back on the road. The Mozzies have organised a farewell for us in the main square, complete with a traditional Mongolian string quartet. Interestingly, there is an old car of 1930s vintage parked beside ours. It's a 1940 Gaz, a Russian car that is pretty much a dead-copy of the old '30s Ford V8 saloon. But this car, the oldest in Mongolia, has an amazing history. In 1940 Joseph Stalin presented this car to the then ruler of Mongolia, Marshal Choi Balsan, known in his day as the 'Mongolian Stalin'.

Soon our cars are shuddering their way among the local trams and trucks, heading north to cross the mountains. Our mechanic, Anthony, is with me in the Itala and Lang is driving the support vehicle to give Anthony a breather from picking up and fixing wounded cars. The climb upward is proving to be a very long haul. The Itala appears to have lost a bit of its punch — it doesn't seem to pull uphill as well as it did. It's not burning a drop of oil and the engine runs as sweetly as ever, but somehow it's just missing a bit of zing.

It's a long, slow climb out of Ulaan Baatar and the weather ahead looks appalling. Dark clouds are draped along the mountain line, the highest points completely shrouded in a bleak grey mist, everyone bracing themselves for what lies ahead. We are now about to drive over the highest mountain range in Mongolia.

Around a bend we find the Spyker parked beside a roadside café and Rob and Stijnus inside eating mutton soup and drinking coffee. We're all apprehensive about the weather we're about to confront. Back on the road, it's Anthony's turn behind the wheel. The higher we go, the more the Itala is struggling. Top gear here is useless. Put the clutch in, rev the engine, pull back the gear lever, slot it into third, release the clutch, keep the power on. It's still not pulling. The same procedure for second gear. Useless — it's first gear all the way.

I look at Anthony and he's beginning to shiver. The temperature has dropped dramatically and I can feel the first few drops of rain hitting my face; the higher into the mist we go, everything seems to be getting darker. The Itala is only just puttering along — we're really crawling and the engine is running rough. The car is backfiring, as if it is running on only 2 cylinders. Is it the altitude? The points? Magneto? Ignition leads? Fuel? We don't dare switch it off to find out.

The cold is agonising; it is well below zero degrees now. The wind is relentless and knifes clean through every piece of clothing. The rain is now hitting my face horizontally and it's starting to really sting. I look down at my lap and the oilskin coat is covered in ice. It's sleeting! The lens sills on my goggles bank up with ice. Anthony's beard is now ice-encrusted and he is shivering badly. We need to get out of this — hypothermia is suddenly shaping up as real problem. I shout to him that if we see any sort of shelter, a *ger* or a building, we'll stop and get out of the diabolical weather. The cold is getting much worse and the wind-chill is cutting through us like a rapier. Now we're losing vision — it's starting to snow. The blizzard worsens, the Itala running slower and slower until the car finally rolls to a stop. We both get out to have a quick look under the bonnet. Lang turns up with the breakdown truck and we figure out what's wrong: the magneto has been seriously drenched. Pull the ignition leads off, wipe them dry, get back in the car, keep going.

We know that we've broken the back of the mountain range because we're slowly descending. Anthony is silent, shivering but still maintaining complete control of the car as it presses on through the snow. Another hour and we're belting along the floor of the valley with the town of Bahruun Khara in sight, nestled in the mountains ahead of us. The first truck-stop café we see has some Expeditioners outside waving us inside. I have never been so grateful to wrap my hands around a cup of hot coffee in my life.

MAY

S	M	T	W	T	F	S
1	2	3	4	5	6	7
8	9	10	11	12	13	14
~~15~~	~~16~~	~~17~~	~~18~~	~~19~~	~~20~~	~~21~~
~~22~~	~~23~~	~~24~~	(25)	26	27	28
29	30	31				

DAY 11

Mongolian border to Gossinasersk

Mick: Mongolia turns on a glorious morning for our final few hours in this beautiful country. We drive through hazy valleys flanked by receding rows of mountains, all of it tinged various watercolour shades of blue in the cold, moist morning air. Just before the Russian border we see trees on either side of the road — a first in many hundreds of kilometres — and even though the trees are small pines made sparse by indiscriminate logging, after the past week or more it feels as though we are travelling down an avenue of oaks.

And finally we reach a vast, undulating plain that goes on and on with a few low sand ridges in the middle and ragged hills fringing the horizon. This will be our last and lasting impression of Mongolia, and most of us feels pangs of regret knowing we are almost gone from such a wonderful country.

No border crossing is ever easy, it seems. Leaving Mongolia isn't too bad, although we encounter some difficulty with surly officials — but the Russians are more difficult. Half of us go through, half are held back, and then everything stops for lunch. Those in Mongolia play cricket on the border — hitting a boundary is a worry — while those in Russia either continue or wait for those who are meant to be travelling with them. We waste hours. When everything is settled, we have little daylight left and the group will be split in two tonight because those delayed at the border could only make 100 kilometres before having to find a place to stop.

Kyakhta, the border town, is distinctly Siberian, full of houses made of dark wood. The whole landscape changes once we cross the border, and while there are still some sections of bare hills, most of the ground is forested in pine. There's a stark contrast between Russia and Mongolia, and Earth provides a natural boundary between the whole countries. We are never in doubt about the fact that we've entered a new nation.

And to back it up, the road is appalling. It is full of lumps, bumps and car-destroying potholes. Trouble is that, unlike the Gobi, the tar seal gives an impression of security that encourages higher speeds, meaning we hit savage bumps much harder than before. It's an uncomfortable ride and the cars take a pounding.

Splitting the group creates some confusion. The blue De Dion and the Spyker make it all the way to the planned stop at Ulan-Ude, but not without minor mechanical trouble with John's car; meanwhile the sweep vehicle is called back to the rearguard group. Eventually John and Andrew make it to the hotel with Stijnus.

The rest of the Expedition halts almost 100 kilometres short at a small town with a single, run-down hotel. It hasn't seen Westerners since 1999, when an American delegation came through. The town's high school students are celebrating the end of the school year, so hundreds of teenagers are out partying. As the Itala and Contal pull up outside the hotel, a score of young girls come screaming out and swamp us as cameras flash left, right and centre. The local police provide secure lock-up for the two cars and find the yellow De Dion on its way into town, guiding it to safekeeping immediately.

The weird thing about the police is that they keep six of us 'detained' for hours until they locate an English teacher to translate — whereupon it is clear to all that we are harmless and that the police are doing us a favour. We made nervous jokes about free accommodation in the cells until the translator arrived ...

In the end it turns into a huge night for our first experience in Russia. Despite the decrepit state of the hotel, the food and service are excellent and we persuade half the staff to drink with us as we party into the wee hours. Ah, but we underestimate the vodka and things get messy. I must admit, I outdid myself and apparently am carried in from outside by two security guards with my feet dragging limply behind.

We have weeks in Russia ahead of us. Already we are learning about it the hard way.

EXPEDITION PHOTOGRAPHER BOB BARKER AND SOME LOCAL CHILDREN IN RUSSIA,
NOT LONG AFTER THE CARS CROSSED THE BORDER.

A MAGNIFICENT — AND RARE — SHOT OF ALL FIVE CARS TOGETHER AS THEY
LEAVE THEIR LAST MONGOLIAN CAMP FOR THE RUSSIAN BORDER.

Warren: The clash of cultures at the Mongolia–Russia border isn't so much a minor confrontation — it's a head-on collision. The buildings in the border town of Kyakhta are not in the tonnes-of-concrete-Soviet-military-style we've seen in Mongolia, nor are there any *gers*. They are the first examples we've seen of old-world Siberian rural architecture: rough-hewn, skewwhiff timber cottages with incongruous ornate wood lace-work around the windows. Just how old these cottages are is impossible to determine — they could be twenty years old or they could have been scheduled for demolition when Borghese shot through. The metal spire of Kyakhta's Orthodox church across the Russian border glints in the sun, exactly as it did when the 1907 motorists saw it. For them, the glimpse of the church spire in the distance made them homesick. It was a tiny hint of Europe — an indication they were actually progressing west.

There is little difficulty for us in 2005 getting across the Mongolian side of the border, but the Russian part of it proves more problematic. The veteran cars go through easily, but, of all things, the trailer attached to Anthony's support vehicle is refused because it doesn't have the correct paperwork. The border guards' hands are tied — if the paperwork is incorrect, then the trailer isn't allowed across the border. It is becoming clear we might have to turn around and go back to Ulaan Baatar to reapply. Big problem: we now don't have visas to get back into Mongolia. As the guards try to find a way around the hiccup, those of us stuck here in the no-man's-land between borders realise we are in for a long wait. So what do Australians do when they are forced to sit around for a few hours? Play cricket. From somewhere a tennis ball materialises and soon it's on. Some hours later, the border guards eventually figure out how to help us and we're allowed across.

We are now on the very edge of Russia, only metres from Mongolia, but the scenery is so very diferent — these strange timber houses are in their hundreds lining the haphazard streets that crisscross Kyakhta. There's no way we're going to reach our destination of Ulan-Ude tonight — the border delay has cost us about four hours — so we decide to change our plans and pull into Gossinasersk, a hard-core industrial town positioned by a lake. The locals stare in disbelief as the Itala and Contal roll through the town together. We ask a local truck driver to guide us to a hotel — the only hotel in town, as it happens — outside of which a crowd of schoolgirls celebrating the end of school surround the cars as if we've just liberated Europe. As we climb out of the vehicles a police four-wheel drive pulls up and two officers approach us. One gives a slow smile revealing a treasure trove of silver teeth. He thinks it's a good idea for Mick and me to follow him in the cars to the police station. The cars will be safe there.

The police station is a grim Soviet two-storey concrete block house to the left of which is a set of solid steel gates topped with a scrambled mess of barbed wire. A policeman opens the gates from the inside and indicates that Mick and I should drive the Contal and the Itala into the compound. The compound is an oily, black, muddy square, one corner of which is piled high with burnt-out artillery cases. We park the cars where the policemen direct, suddenly hearing loud voices emanating from a small, barbed-wire-strewn, deep-set window in the police station wall.

Grimy faces press against the thick iron bars of a cell window, calling out some sort of abuse. The officer whacks the bars with his truncheon and the faces disappear. 'Will the cars be safe here?' I ask. The officer points to a policeman leaning against a truck holding an AK47 with a folding stock. I guess they'll be safe. Mick and I are escorted into the police station, a dark, evil-smelling building that no doubt was host to some diabolical events during Soviet times. We are told to wait in a small, dank, spartan office containing two desks, two typewriters, two desk lamps, two filing cabinets and an ancient photocopier. A grim, matronly policewoman, fresh from the James Bond school of grim, matronly policewomen, enters the room and asks for our passports. She sits down at one of the desks and starts copying the details on a piece of paper. Mick and I attempt to explain what we're doing in Russia, but she doesn't understand and clearly isn't impressed. Another policewoman arrives and, after a lengthy discussion, they start making telephone calls and photocopying our passports. The door opens and four more undesirables from the yellow De Dion and sweep vehicle are ushered in: Keith, Louise, Anthony and Bob Barker, our photographer.

'What's going on here?' asks Keith. 'No idea — take a seat,' is all I can say. An hour later a small, middle-aged woman in civilian clothes enters the room and sits down with us. 'I am an English teacher from a school in the next town,' she tells us. 'I am here as your translator.' Astonished to learn we are Australian, she tells us she has never met an Australian before. The police are equally surprised to discover that we are on some sort of historical re-creation and eventually find the idea of driving these crazy old cars to Paris amusing. Happy we aren't some CIA operation intending to overrun Siberia with five 100 year-old cars, they release us to check in at the hotel and say we can pick up the cars at the compound whenever we like tomorrow.

MAY

S	M	T	W	T	F	S
				1	2	3
4	5	6	7			
1	2	3	4	5	6	7
8	9	10	11	12	13	14
~~15~~	~~16~~	~~17~~	~~18~~	~~19~~	~~20~~	~~21~~
~~22~~	~~23~~	~~24~~	~~25~~	(26)	27	28
29	30	31				

DAY 12

Gossinasersk to Lake Baikal

Mick: Vodka is a serious problem. If anyone needs proof, they would only have to look at me lying comatose in the back of Anthony's truck. Last night destroyed me. Poor Chris — who is not at all well — will ride the Contal alone for the day. He isn't the only one struggling as we drive through Siberia and try to reunite the scattered Expedition.

We have some sobering moments along the way. We see three serious road accidents — one of them certainly fatal — and begin to realise that not only are the Siberians fatalistic in general, they are bad drivers. Chris expresses genuine fear.

Siberia has a run-down look about it that's interrupted occasionally by beautifully painted and decorated wooden houses, snowcapped mountains, forests of birch that close you in then release you onto open farming land, and spectacular Lake Baikal, the world's largest freshwater lake. Part of our route takes a short detour through several old-style Cossack villages where everything is made of wood.

Siberians are famous for their woodwork. Many of them produce very fine and intricate ornamentation for their log houses. Often the houses are painted either green or blue, with white highlights creating a very pretty effect with the dark grey of the unpainted sections. Yet these houses are also fire traps — we see burnt-out shells on a regular basis. The black soil that defines the entire countryside doesn't provide a solid foundation, either, and some houses are tilted at comical angles. The quality of construction can't be criticised, though.

The roads are as bad as ever. The Contal breaks a main leaf spring about midday. Chris manages to communicate the need for repairs to a passing villager, whose eyes light up as he points to a house just 20 metres away. I've recovered enough to rouse myself from the sweep truck, and we wheel the Contal around and watch as the Siberians take over. They remove the spring, drag out the most rudimentary stick welder we've ever seen, use some lightweight spring steel as a support and weld our broken leaf back together. All in less than an hour. To cut through the metal, the welder uses maximum amps through the stick to blow through it — simple but effective. I don't know what the Siberians called it, but we'd call it brilliant bush engineering in Australia.

We are the last in to the resort on Lake Baikal which has been chosen as tonight's stop. 'Resort' is a loose description. Sure, it has the right basic idea behind it, but the service is woeful, the layout confusing, the water cold and brown as it runs out of the taps — and we have to provide our own toilet paper. Siberia has a long way to go before it catches up with Western concepts of a leisure industry.

1907

Ulan-Ude

Roads — and, more importantly, bridges — had almost fallen into nonexistence in this area since the Trans-Siberian Railway had been built. For several days Borghese slithered along the muddy roads and crossed bridges that collapsed behind him, until he realised that the railway line was a better option. He gained permission to drive on it, was given a policeman to escort him and, later, was written into the timetable. He left word for the following motorists that the roads were impossible. As a result, they decided to load their cars on the train to Irkutsk — and there found themselves just a day behind the Itala again.

Lake Baikal

Warren: There's clearly a growing fascination with the cars from the Russian police. And there is a never-ending supply of them waiting to flag us down and start firing questions. The police are everywhere — they man checkpoints and sit squashed in their police Ladas at every available intersection. The police experience generally goes like this: as your car putters over the crest of a hill, a uniformed policeman at a chicaned checkpoint is twirling a black-and-white-striped truncheon — as you can imagine, the veteran cars leap out of the dull, everyday Russian traffic diet of banged-up Moskvitchs, droopy Volgas and diesel-exhaust-belching Gaz trucks. 'Allo 'allo 'allo, here's a bit of colour and movement for the bored policeman, who suddenly sobers up, snaps his arm out and waves the truncheon, indicating he is hauling you in. The policeman, who is generally no older than seventeen, swaggers over with the truncheon resting on one shoulder and an AK47 slung off the other and makes a remark in Russian, which is probably something to the effect of, 'Okay comrade, what the hell is this all about?' The answers to whatever questions are thrown to us in Russian are as follows: (1) 'Hi — Australian. *Nyet Russki.*' (2) '1907.' (3) 'Beijing, Mongolia, Gobi Desert, Siberia, Russia, Paris.' (4) 'Four cylinders.' (5) 'About 80 kilometres per hour flat out.' (6) '*Dos vidanya.*'

Lang and I are driving along the road that snakes its way around the edge of Lake Baikal and we slow down in the village of Babushkin. Somewhere near here Prince Borghese put the Itala on the tracks of the Trans-Siberian Railway because the roads had deteriorated to such a state that they were undriveable. The Itala attracts a blue Volga sedan, which follows us for a while and then proceeds to slowly overtake us. The car is packed with enormous policemen — five in fact, the one in the passenger seat waving at us to pull over. He gets out and puts on an enormous peaked cap: he's a Captain of Police. Grinning and shouting, he obviously loves the car. He obviously loves vodka too — I am terrified he'll light a cigarette and his 400-octane breath will make him spontaneously combust. We explain to him that we are looking for a camp site near the lake and he unflinchingly demands to escort us. We offer for him to ride in the Itala and I'll squeeze into the already packed Volga police car. Sitting wedged in the back seat between two burly coppers, I have to tilt my head awkwardly to the left — the muzzle of the AK47 held diagonally across the policeman's lap to my right is pretty much pressed into my face. All terrifically friendly, they offer me cigarettes, slip a cassette of Russian techno music into the tape deck and turn up the volume full bore.

We arrive at a camp site on the edge of Lake Baikal, where the captain asks us if we'd care for *chi*, or tea. One of the policemen starts building a campfire while another opens the boot of the Volga, producing loaves of bread, pickles, dumplings, tea and two bottles of vodka. With a cigarette hanging from his mouth, the constable with the AK47 saunters over to me. He opens the machine gun's breach, removes the magazine to show me it's now unloaded and hands me the gun. 'Kalashnikov — very good,' he says, smiling and revealing a mouthful of empty gums sporadically dotted with teeth, resembling the middle octave of a piano. He proceeds to show me how the gun operates until the captain, who up till now has been totally immersed in unscrewing the cap of the first vodka bottle, suddenly pushes him aside and proceeds to draw his pistol from the holster, slamming the gun into my hand. 'Forget the Kalashnikov — this is what Captains of Police use' is what I think he is trying to say. I try to explain to the captain that somewhere around here a century ago, an Itala like ours had driven along part of the Trans-Siberian railway line, and showed him the photograph of Borghese and Guizzardi in the Itala on the railway by Lake Baikal. The five policemen crowd around the photo, pointing back towards where we've just come from and arguing with each other — they know exactly where the photo was taken and it's only about 2 kilometres away.

The police pile back into their blue Volga and we follow them in the Itala and the Spyker, bouncing along the rough service track that meanders alongside the

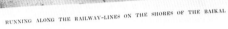

RUNNING ALONG THE RAILWAY-LINES ON THE SHORES OF THE BAIKAL

LEFT: THE ORIGINAL PHOTOGRAPH OF PRINCE BORGHESE'S ITALA ON TRAIN TRACKS ON THE SHORES OF LAKE BAIKAL.

ABOVE: NEARLY 100 YEARS LATER, WARREN AND LANG RE-CREATE THE IMAGE IN THEIR VERY OWN ITALA.

ABOVE: LOCAL WOMEN IN A TOWN NEXT TO LAKE BAIKAL.

RIGHT: THE SPYKER POSES BY THE STILL-ICY LAKE.

Trans-Siberian. Eventually the police car stops and we walk through some grass, only to stumble onto a disused broad-gauge railway line running parallel to the modern standard gauge line. This is the original Trans-Siberian line! Grinning wildly, the captain points to where we have come from and aligns the original photograph. This is exactly where the Prince and his mechanic stopped to photograph the Itala on the edge of Lake Baikal, and it's a once-in-a-lifetime opportunity.

We put the Itala on the tracks and re-create the photo of 1907. As I look at the scene before me, the hair on the back of my neck bristles.

This is why we're here.

Mick: We sleep in this morning because we only have a short, 50 kilometre drive to our destination for the night. After nearly a fortnight on the road with only one day off — and the day in Ulaan Baatar was actually not very restful at all — we are more than ready to lie in. Some of us walk to the lake while others have a leisurely breakfast at the resort. Then suddenly it is after midday and we fall back into that so-familiar routine of packing the cars, pulling on gloves and goggles, cranking the engines and putting more miles under our wheels.

Trees block our view of the lake for a while before the road veers within sight of the massive body of water. We look over the Trans-Siberian Railway, over the low roofs of a Siberian village, and out to the last of the winter's ice floes. Many kilometres of water stretch beyond it to grey–blue hills lining the other side of this part of Lake Baikal. Further on we'll see water right to the horizon.

I follow John and Andrew out to the edge of the water, the Itala close behind us both. Chris and Andrew go straight down to the ice and gingerly step out on the semi-mobile chunks butting against the shore. John spots a seal way off in the distance — a tiny black dot on the white ice. We trudge along the pebbly beach past wooden dinghies, some of them in good condition and others holed and abandoned.

It is strange to reflect that only a few days ago we were in the middle of one of the world's greatest deserts, sweating in the midday heat, and now here we are on the chilly banks of the world's greatest freshwater lake.

1907

UNSCHEDULED STOP AROUND LAKE BAIKAL

When a train was due to pass Borghese had to leave the line, of course. On this day, when doing this, he followed a path and came to a dangerous-looking bridge. He drove onto it anyway, but the policeman escorting him jumped off in fear — a good move, because the bridge collapsed under the Itala's back wheels. The car plunged down through the falling bridge, taking the three Italians with it. It came to rest on its rear, jammed on the remaining timber beams. Miraculously no one was seriously hurt, though Borghese cracked some ribs and Barzini was badly bruised and covered in hot engine oil. Gangers used ropes to drag the car back to the road. Astonishingly, the Itala restarted and was none the worse for its near disaster.

We will be camping tonight, so we want to stock up on various supplies. We stop in a village called Mamushka and find the central business district — a bunch of little wooden huts reminiscent of the small shops you'd have found in an Australian country town of the 1930s. One sells basic foods, another washing and beauty products, while others serve their own specific purposes. Our bunch of veteran cars causes a minor stir, but mostly life goes on without any change, despite the Aussies wandering around and standing out like sore thumbs.

We buy smoked fish, bread, cheese and other snacks. The only one that doesn't go down well later with most of us is the salami, which is worryingly raw and far too fatty for our palates. The fish, which is very oily, is great according to most. I buy a 300-gram tub of caviar for the equivalent of just $10.

We are a bit put out to find that the camp is an abandoned dock on Lake Baikal, made more uncomfortable by a biting wind coming off the lake and clouds that make no bones about their intention to rain on us. We pull out our food and have a picnic in the grotty ruins of the dockyard. It isn't a Mongolian camp by any stretch of the imagination, and when local youths full of vodka and bravado join us, we grit our teeth and try to make the most of a very unusual situation. One young bloke, who's either taken a big knock on the head or killed half his brain with alcohol, makes a serial menace of himself and keeps returning, despite being taken home five times.

Not that it's all bad. We watch a long and gorgeous sunset over the water. Some Russians came with a balalaika — a sort of three-stringed guitar — and entertain us into the evening. While it's still daylight, Chris dives into the lake and discovers a whole new level of cold. Andrew, sloshed on vodka by 2 a.m., strips and dives in too, then wakes the camp with his screams as he sprints back to the fire.

DAY 14

Lake Baikal to Irkutsk

Warren: Lang's arms are outstretched, directing the Itala, which is dangling in mid-air above him, creating the most amazing silhouette in a blood-red dawn. Tied in a sling, our car is being lifted by a massive gantry crane to be loaded aboard the *Valeria*, a ship which arrived at the lake port of Klukva at midnight last night. There is, of course, a precedent for this: in 1907, Prince Borghese loaded his Itala aboard an ice-cutting steamer, the *Baikal*, to cross the lake for Irkutsk. Earlier this morning, no one was sure whether the crane would actually operate — rumour had it that the driver was notorious for not paying his electricity bills and most probably the power had been cut off.

The crane driver's credit reference wasn't the only questionable part of his reputation: he arrived to undertake the great hoisting of our car emitting a fragrance I can only describe as Cologne du Vodka.

The hook holding the sling moves suddenly skyward, taking up the slack as the Itala's wheels leave the ground. The car is now suspended 10 metres above the water, the gantry rolling forward towards the *Valeria*. Suddenly, those looking on from the shore start shouting in panic: the gantry is moving way too fast and the airborne car is being swung toward the ship's bridge, clearly out of control. 'STOP!!! STOP!!!' shouts Lang, but it's no use. The Itala swings over the ship's deck, clearing part of the superstructure but not all, the front right corner smashing full-bore into the wheelhouse, bending the mudguard and cracking a window on the ship's bridge. Lang, now on the deck of the *Valeria*, is still screaming at the crane driver, but he has the situation under control. The car is gently lowered, Lang turning the Itala around in the sling until it lands neatly on the ship's deck.

Bev and I climb on board the ship, dreading the damage report — but, to our relief, it's really only the mudguard and the window that have suffered in what seemed to be a most catastrophic, jaw-dropping exercise.

The voyage across the lake from Klukva to Port Baikal takes three hours. On reaching the port, the Itala is placed carefully ashore by the ship's own onboard crane — a manoeuvre that, in hindsight, might have been wise in the first place.

Now we only have a brief 80 kilometre run to Lake Baikal's premier city, Irkutsk. With Lang next to me in the passenger seat and Bev in the 'Barzini seat' in the back, it should be an easy run into town. Before me is a long, gun-barrel stretch of road that rolls spectacularly downhill and then belts up the other side. I'm about to reach the crest, having thundered uphill, when there is a tremendous *bang* that explodes somewhere beneath the car. The Itala rolls to a stop and Lang and I crawl underneath. The driveshaft has ripped itself apart where it meets the gearbox. Time to call Anthony with the trailer.

Mick: Things don't go well from the start. The only brightness in the dawn comes from a red sun breaking the horizon though ominous cloud over Lake Baikal. There's also a beautiful rainbow, but we're more focused on the rain clouds behind it — coming right at us from the direction we want to drive in. First, however, we must pack away our tents in the drizzle and watch as the precious Itala is hoisted high over the frigid water and into a fishing boat. Once it's on board the rest of the Expedition fires up and drives on the scenic road skirting the lake. Lake Baikal holds a fifth of the world's fresh water and is geologically unique, a fascinating piece of the world in its own right.

We catch glimpses of it to our right over the Trans-Siberian Railway and through the trees, until soon we reach a point were we can drive to the shore and clamber over the last of the ice that the summer warmth is slowly melting away. The lake stretches to the horizon in places. But the road takes our attention from

LEFT: THE ITALA BEING LOADED ONTO THE BOAT, TO BE SHIPPED ACROSS LAKE BAIKAL.

RIGHT: LANG INSPECTS THE CAR AS IT COMES A LITTLE TOO CLOSE FOR COMFORT TO THE SHIP'S WHEELHOUSE.

ABOVE: WARREN CAPTURING THE EXPERIENCE IN HIS SKETCHPAD.

RIGHT: THE ITALA SAFELY ON BOARD, ONLY JUST CLEARING THE SIDES OF THE BOAT.

it far too often: it is rough as guts and doing damage. John's De Dion has fuel trouble and, after he puts it onto the trailer so he can catch up, the dreadful conditions make the car bounce so badly in its green box that the fuel cap comes loose and litres of petrol splash all over the car, trailer and luggage inside.

Stijnus's Spyker cracks a weld in the steering rods. He feels the wheels wobbling and subsequently finds a local welder in a small town whose appearance reminds him so much of the bearded Siberian who'd fixed Prince Borghese's wheel almost 100 years before. And, fittingly, the roughshod workshop provides exceptional bush-mechanic-style quality in repairing the Dutch car. Stijnus carries on a couple of hours later but the road causes a few punctures before his day is done.

On one of the long, winding climbs through the hills on the way to Irkutsk, Keith's De Dion tears its differential housing apart; it will drive no further this day. While several of us attempt temporary repairs, Sergei, an Irkutsk biker who hails originally from Latvia, turns up. He speaks no English but is so switched on that we communicate easily, and by the end of the day the De Dion is in his Irkutsk workshop and the differential out awaiting repairs. His friends rally around us, too, and we are rapidly discovering what wonderfully generous people some Russians can be when strangers need help.

Anthony is kept very busy in the sweep vehicle rescuing everyone who needs him. Chris and I on the Contal, followed by Stijnus and Rob in the Spyker, take a short detour before Irkutsk to ride an old-fashioned ferry across one of the the 300-odd rivers that feed Lake Baikal. The ferry is made from four pontoons attached to a single cable across the river. The ferry has no engine, just a long tiller which can be set to point the vessel's nose diagonally towards the opposite bank. In this way the current does all the work, forcing the ferry to glide sideways on its cable from bank to bank. Simple, ingenious and flawless. We watch trucks loaded with tonnes of logs come across, then enjoy the wonderful experience of doing something just like it had been done back in 1907.

However, we then get back onto the road and continue around the lake. This was impossible a century ago — now it is the norm.

Our only real dilemma once in Irkutsk is how long it will take to get all the cars back on the road. We add a rest-and-repair day to our Irkutsk itinerary and spend Sunday carrying out work on our cars. Everyone needs the time, and all the cars appreciate the attention.

DAY 15/16

Irkutsk to Sayansk

Mick: Yesterday afternoon we had a drivers' meeting to settle on a plan of attack for today because things aren't going well for everyone. The repairs to the Itala and Keith's De Dion are complicated and couldn't be completed yesterday. I've had no luck with new springs for the Contal's front end. John and Stijnus, though, are fine to go. We can all see an easy solution that leaves everyone with a back-up of some kind: John will go on and make distance while he is on a roll in the slowest car; Chris and I will try to leave after getting springs; and Stijnus will decide on the spur of the moment which of us to go with, while Keith, Lang and Warren will spend an extra day in Irkutsk with the sweep vehicle waiting with them. The support van, Grace (so called because it's a Hyundai Grace), will now officially become the scout car and leave sometime in the morning.

And that's how it happens: John's out early, followed soon after by the Spyker and Grace. Chris and I are taken to a municipal workshop, where a blacksmith forges new springs for the Contal. He is amazing to watch, using skills almost extinct in Australia to craft a spring better than the original. Unfortunately we fail to translate our desire to have two made, meaning we end up with mismatched suspension, one side sagging lower than the other.

The corpulent workshop manager summons me to his office and asks for $US150, an outrageous amount here in Russia. I show my shock and stall by going downstairs for a quick conference with Chris, who hands me a soiled $US100 note that

LEFT: LOCAL GIRLS ENJOYING SPRING NEAR THE RIVERFRONT.

ABOVE AND BELOW LEFT: OLD BUILDINGS WITH RELATIVELY NEW PAINT NEAR THE RIVER.

RIGHT: SUNDAY IN THE SUN BY THE RIVER – IRKUTSK LOCALS MAKE THE MOST OF IT.

the banks refused to accept. Before I again sit down upstairs, the manager drops his price to $US100, and so the deal is done. I wonder if he'll manage to change that note, though.

Disaster strikes as we leave the workshop. The enthusiastic Russians did up the spring shackles too tight, locking the suspension. The 10 centimetre step at the gate sends the Contal skyward with a spine-wrenching jolt and Chris screams in pain. We stop up the road to loosen the bolts but the damage is done: we don't know it then, but Chris has hurt his back so badly that he won't be on the Contal for more than a week.

We detour up a nearby road that the ABC TV crew is sure was the one Borghese used when leaving Irkutsk in 1907. It follows the river but is in appalling condition. The village it takes us through is filthy and depressing; the riverbank is littered with trash. Barzini, who described the beauty of Siberia, would roll in his grave if he saw what has become of some of these places.

John, Stijnus and the crews with them make it to Sayansk after a satisfying drive. They find the best hotel they've seen since the Kempinski back in Beijing — which now feels like a lifetime ago. After our dramas Chris and I don't get that far, pulling up in a village and discovering an ancient wooden hotel that is probably identical to those used by the Raiders in 1907. It is run-down and very basic but wonderfully friendly and charmingly rustic.

Warren: The Itala's broken driveshaft is a real problem — there's no quick road-side fix for this. To explain what the driveshaft does in a kind of ready-reckoner way: the engine turns the gearbox, which then turns the driveshaft — simply a thick steel rod — which connects to the differential, which then turns the wheels. The driveshaft is connected to the gearbox and differential by splines at each end which slot inside mated couplings — universal joints. Instead of starting life as one fat piece of steel machined down to having four raised splines on the end, our driveshaft turns out to be a steel rod with four splines screwed into the metal, meaning eight holes are drilled into the steel around its circumference, securing the attached splines. All these holes mean that the driveshaft has the strength and appearance of Swiss cheese, eventually deciding to give up the ghost and decapitate itself on a long hill somewhere outside Irkutsk.

Keith Brodie has had serious problems too: the little yellow De Dion's gearbox jams, cracking a chassis mounting which took a part of the gearbox with it, leaving a big hole in the side of the aluminium housing — absolutely catastrophic. With the car smoking and pouring oil and metal filings onto the side of the road, Keith is approached by a nuggetty, occasionally toothed, bandanna-wearing bikie who happens to be riding by. It turns out that Sergei — or 'Mutant' to his mates — is the president of the local Irkutsk bikie club and owner of a serious mechanic's workshop. Helping Keith out is now his priority. Welding the aluminium gearbox housing back together requires specialist equipment and Sergei offers his workshop to get the De Dion back on the road.

Lang and I approach Sergei to see if he can help out with our busted driveshaft and he is only too happy to assist. An entire new splined end will need to be machined and welded on the driveshaft, but this will have to be done by specialists. Sergei and his seven-foot-tall and four-inch-wide mate Stas have a few contacts at the local aircraft factory. But it is clearly going to take some days to manufacture the driveshaft and then reinstall — Lang and I will have to do a series of marathon drives to catch up to the rest of the Expedition. Well, even Prince Borghese had a day off in Irkutsk after a substantial dinner party that carried through until dawn … There's nothing we can do but sit around in Irkutsk until the driveshaft is repaired. But what a place to be stuck in for a few days! Once known as 'the Paris of Siberia', Irkutsk is a beautiful, cosmopolitan city filled with magnificent nineteenth-century wooden architecture.

While the others have packed up and moved on, it is time for a bit of Irkutskian retail therapy. Hidden in the back section of a decrepit military building in the main street is an army quartermaster's store. Lang has a sixth sense for finding these sorts of places — he's a sort of flea-market king. This place is an Aladdin's cave of military bits and pieces — enormous Russian peaked caps, medals, waterproof jackets, forage caps — you name it, they sell it. Folded in a pile in one corner I find the hottest fashion accessory in any Soviet army parade: the thick woollen stripey jumpers as worn by Russian sailors and the Volga boatmen. A very fetching bit of apparel indeed — I'll be the envy of every Expeditioner. I have no idea where on earth I'll wear the thing — but when in Russia …

DAY 17

Sayansk to Tumen

Warren: Sacha is the Russian cab driver from Central Casting — a Stalinesque moustache perched above a mother lode of gold teeth. Sacha has been teed up to take me to the factory to pick up our driveshaft. He opens the door of his cab, a droopy Volga sedan typical of the kind of taxis that shuffle around the streets in Irkutsk. I reach for the seat belt but Sacha is hugely offended. '*Nyet, nyet!*' he cries. Wearing a seat belt is the equivalent of telling him he's a lousy driver. I begrudgingly leave the belt to recoil next to me. 'Volga,' says Sacha. 'Russia's Mercedes Benz.' That is drawing a particularly long bow: even a brand new Volga bought off the showroom floor still uses the 1950-designed 3-litre motor ...

The workshop is behind Irkutsk Airport, the end of which seems to serve as a graveyard for clapped-out Soviet military aircraft still bearing their USSR red star and hammer-and-sickle markings. An old man sporting a drooping moustache and a flat cap is hard at work on a lathe, finishing our re-splined driveshaft, turning it, stopping the lathe, hand-filing, starting up the lathe again. His arm features a blotchy tattoo of an unfurling ribbon with the word 'Gobi' written across it. I wonder if he once served at the defunct Choir military base we saw only a week before.

He stops briefly and reaches into his pocket to produce a particularly crude packet of cigarettes, the label of which appears to have been printed with a potato stamp. His fingers pull a cigarette out of the box and he goes through a ritual he's clearly performed hundreds of thousands of times, crimping the end of the cigarette in such a way that it adopts the shape of a home plumbing effort gone wrong. I gesture to him as if to say, 'What on earth is that all about?' He pulls a cigarette out of the packet, crimpes it in three places and hands it to me. 'Papirosa,' he says. 'Joseph Stalin — Papirosa.' Uncle Joe's favourite brand, no less.

The driveshaft is an outstanding piece of work — far superior to what we had before. If we can put the driveshaft back in this morning we can probably drive as far as Sayansk, meaning that a hellish 600 kilometre drive tomorrow will see us catching up with the rest of the Expedition somewhere.

The shaft is back in and we're heading out of Irkutsk. Before us is a minor traffic accident at an intersection, but one of the drivers has gone through the windscreen and is lying in front of his car, his head smeared all over the road. If only he'd worn his seat belt. For the first time, I feel uneasy about being in the Itala.

Mick: 'Service' is a word that doesn't appear to exist in Russian, at least as far as the majority of people behind a counter are concerned. Chris and I try to buy breakfast at a café and despite our best efforts to use our limited Russian, to point and to gesture, we are met with indifference that turns to contempt. All we get is coffee and a snarl. One waitress literally shoves Chris aside when she wants to come past. We sulk, wondering how one lot of Russians — like the Irkutsk bikers — can welcome us with such open arms and generosity while another mob — a mob that wants our money! — can be so bloody rude. It is like this everywhere, all the time, with only a few notable exceptions.

Four young motorcyclists from Tumen had heard that the Contal would be coming through town and they rode out to meet us and ride with us. I pull over when we encounter them and, despite the lack of language, we get on famously and admire each other's machines. The pick of their lot is certainly the 1960 Ural, a bike based on the World War II-era BMW that the German army used; Stalin had ordered it copied for use in postwar Russia. You can still buy Urals here, except now they're more modern — more like a late 1960s BMW than a late 1930s model.

THE ITALA REQUIRED SOME MECHANICAL WORK PRIOR TO LEAVING IRKUTSK;
THE OTHER EXPEDITIONERS WENT ON AHEAD.

MEMBERS OF THE IRKUTSK BIKIE CLUB WHO HELPED REPAIR THE YELLOW
DE DION BOUTON, WITH KEITH BRODIE.

1907

THE GREAT HANDLEBAR MOUSTACHE PHENOMENON

De Dion driver number one George Cormier sported a real beauty. So did De Dion driver number two, Victor Collignon, and the Itala's mechanic, Ettore Guizzardi. Handlebar moustaches were all the rage at the turn of the 20th century. Beards and moustaches were intended to say something about their owners. The handlebar moustache signified sophistication, sportiness and wealth. To mould your moustache into the perfect trailing curl involved twirling the tips with moustache wax, a paste made from beeswax and perfumed with menthol. In 1947 a handlebar moustache club was founded at the Windsor Castle Pub in London, where its hirsute members still meet once a month.

The four try to help us take a tour through a vodka factory in town. After a long wait we're told we can't come in because this is a chemical plant, not a vodka factory. That's a lie, but we all shrug our shoulders and go to lunch instead.

After Tumen there's an atrocious dirt road that slows our pace to a crawl for kilometre after kilometre. We had expected things to improve as we moved west but we keep being disappointed by these punishing stretches. You'd be hard pressed to find a disused back road in worse condition in Australia, but this is life in Siberia.

Our hotel tonight is dreadful and certainly not how we'd have chosen to end a day of poor service, bad roads and official lies. It is a crumbling, unimaginative square block of pure Soviet ugliness. The mood has obviously rubbed off on the staff. Our dingy, stinking rooms have a bathroom — unlike some other hotels we've stayed in — but there is no soap, no toilet paper, no hot water, no toilet seat, no shower head and, most stunningly of all, no drain in the floor! We have to wash in cold water in the sink and all the spillage pools on the tiles with nowhere to go. We've paid a pittance for the rooms but it's still too much.

DAY 18

JUNE

S	M	T	W	T	F	S
			1	2	3	4
5	6	7	8	9	10	11
12	13	14	15	16	17	18
19	20	21	22	23	24	25
26	27	28	29	30		

Tumen to Kansk

Mick: The first day of summer in Siberia is cool, clean and dazzlingly green. I break into song, protected from embarrassment by the Contal's exhaust note. This is what travelling is all about: making miles, being energised by the scenery, breathing crisp air and feeling absolutely free. This is one part of motoring that hasn't changed in these 100-odd years. It has probably even existed since the first day a man set off at a trot on a horse way back in ancient history. It's certainly one of the major factors in the phenomenal success of the motorcar and the world will be a poorer place to live if this isn't available to experience in transport of the future.

Then the Siberian roads cruel the thrill. The good road turns to dirt and the dirt turns to a war zone of craters and trenches. Tar returns sometimes, giving a false sense of relief before the road turns to crap again. Some of the holes are almost a metre deep. This goes on all day.

By lunchtime Chris's back, which he's been nursing since Irkutsk, has copped a hiding up front in the Contal. He tries the rider's seat but that is worse, so he finally relents and climbs into a support vehicle.

Stijnus doesn't have such a problem with the bad roads because his Spyker rides so smoothly over them. This car would make many modern vehicles seem uncomfortable by comparison — quite a remarkable achievement. He forges on ahead.

John soldiers on with Andrew in the blue De Dion after making their usual early start — they now have a habit of being

out by 6 a.m. while the rest of us are happy with a 7 a.m. departure. It is never long before we pass him, and later in the day he loads the little car into the trailer and catches up before unloading again and finishing the drive.

They are all ahead, including Chris, when the rain sets in and I slither around the enormous potholes at a dismal pace on the Contal. It is no fun as the water soaks me, my goggles fogging up and trucks continuing to hammer past in both directions. The rain gets worse and so does the road until the bigger trucks give up — one of them gets bogged. And this is a main route!

I am riding on the very edge of a section of concrete roadway when I feel vagueness in the steering, as if I've dropped a front wheel into the mud. I try to steer back onto the road but the Contal won't respond. I realise with dread that the old Austin steering arm has snapped. I slow down as much as possible before the three-wheeler peels off the road and into the scrub. I bail out, landing gently in the mud, watching my machine mow down lightweight trees, miss a big stump, then come to a dead stop on an abandoned truck tyre which cushions the impact so effectively that no damage is done whatsoever. A miracle.

I get out the satellite phone and discover that the sweep truck is just an hour away. The group we've left in Irkutsk has just about caught up and I will be rescued in no time.

Keith and Louise roll their De Dion off the trailer when they reach me and drive the rest of the way. The day is almost done when we turn up at the hotel, just in time to get the last of the food. Andrew jumps into the breach for me, getting the Contal almost fixed by working into the wee hours, and finishing the job the next day.

Meanwhile, we listen as Warren tells us about the massive accident they narrowly avoided during the day. A Russian driver overtaking the Itala suddenly hit the brakes to take a better look at the old car but the speeding driver right behind him was also watching the Itala instead of the road. The two cars shunted at high speed, the front one flying off the road and rolling many times while the second car spun across the Itala's path and out of harm's way. Lang and Warren were ducking debris as they somehow came through the carnage. In the day's second little miracle, no one was hurt.

Warren: The thing to fear most in Siberia is neither vicious brown bears wanting to slash you into small pieces and chew on your head like a bony chicken nugget with eyeballs, nor bloodthirsty bandits with teeth filed to razor-sharp points who'd laugh heartily as they slowly roasted you over an open fire while divvying up your roubles amongst their mates. No: the most dangerous encounter you are likely to have in Siberia is with drivers ferrying new cars from Vladivostok to Moscow.

Some years ago, the Russian Navy — in an enterprising move to raise badly needed funds — began to load the decks of warships with second-hand cars from Japan. Japanese motorists aren't allowed to own a car older than four years, so a glut of near-new cars began arriving in the eastern port of Vladivostok, courtesy of the navy. Today this is big business in Russia — everyone would prefer a near-new imported car to the locally cobbled-together horror show, the Volga sedan. Car dealers in Novosibirsk and Moscow send hundreds of young, inexperienced Michael Schumachers to pick up these cars in Vladivostok and pilot them back — a distance of up to 9000 kilometres.

What we've termed the 'Vladivostok cars' are easily distinguished from regular traffic: they are always Japanese or Korean cars, right-hand drive, have no numberplates, one driver and are thrown around the highway more or less as a weapon.   More often than not they travel in packs of five or six, tail gaiting each other in a sort of road-going express train that overtakes you in one job lot at phenomenal speed. For the majority of their Paris-to-Dakar-style race across Russia they are completely out of control — overtaking around blind corners, having breathtakingly close shaves with oncoming trucks, hurtling along either side of the road at speeds of up to 160 km/h. These guys are terrifying to share the road with.

It's amazing none of us has been seriously hurt, or worse, due to these psychopaths, for whenever they see any of the veteran cars, one of them will grab his mobile phone to take that crackerjack photo on the move and in the process swerve unexpectedly into our lane. Twice Lang and I have been pushed off the road because of these clowns attempting to photograph us, drive the car one-handed and maintain the speed of sound. It would only take a split second of misjudgment for one of these cars to clip the Itala and it would be all over for Lang and I in an instant. The veteran cars, made of steel and wood with no safety features whatsoever, afford zero protection to everyone on board. Sometimes I sit behind the steering wheel gritting my teeth in anticipation of being cleaned up by a Vladivostok car. This morning I witness my greatest fear.

LEFT: MICK SHORTLY AFTER HIS NARROW ESCAPE, WHEN THE CONTAL'S STEERING FAILED. THANKFULLY KEITH (L) AND ANTHONY (R) WERE QUICKLY ON THE SCENE TO HELP.

RIGHT: LATER THAT EVENING, ANDREW WORKS ON THE CONTAL'S STEERING.

ABOVE: A GOOD INDICATION OF THE STATE OF SIBERIAN ROADS AND THE CONDITIONS FACING THE VETERAN CARS.

RIGHT: THE LITTLE YELLOW DE DION ON THE ROAD TO KANSK.

Just after six o'clock I am driving the Itala along the highway across a broad plain when the daily Vladivostok-to-Moscow onslaught clocks on, the first groups of these cars already starting to overtake us. We are travelling at a leisurely 70 km/h when six of these cars, packed so close to each other it is as if they are welded together, overtake us at blinding speed. I can see the lead driver's face looking at the Itala when he passes, realising he's overtaking some sort of interesting car. His brake lights just flicker and it's all over. The second car hits him so hard from behind that the first car spins off the road in front of me, bumper bars, glass and trim raining all over the highway. The other car is by now rolling end on end down the road, the windscreen in a million pieces, parts of the car spinning in mid-air. I keep the Itala moving in a straight line as debris ricochets off the road, bouncing past either side of the car. It is a miracle something doesn't land square on top of Lang and me. The guy in the second car has to be dead. We've seen someone killed on the roads in a minor collision — but it was nothing like this.

I stop the Itala and we get out; the second Vladivostok car has landed where its wheels should be. To Lang's and my amazement, the young driver climbs out the passenger side window, gets to his feet and then collapses on his knees, sobbing into his hands. The other Vladivostok cars have pulled up in every direction, the drivers sprinting towards him, shouting. He is okay — but it only reaffirms our fears about how dangerous the Trans-Siberian Highway can be.

On top of that, our day is becoming a miserable aquatic nightmare: the rain has now really set in, we're soaked to our rotten old underpants and the Trans-Siberian Highway has dissolved into a long, brown cavitied slurry full of farmer-driven ex-Russian Army trucks clunking about on both sides of the road and dumping mud on us. We arrive in a town where the Cyrillic lettering spells TANWET — quite appropriate, as both our tans are seriously wet. The highway runs through the town as a normal suburban road, but it is easily one of the worst stretches of earth we've encountered so far, the Itala crashing up and down from canyonous pothole to canyonous pothole.

Through an unforgivable navigation malfunction (mine), we are convinced we have only 60 kilometres to go in our 600 kilometre odyssey to the city of Kansk. 'I'll just check with a local,' I say to Lang, confronting a bewildered pedestrian shuffling about in the rain. 'Kansk?' I ask, drawing the letters 'km' on the bonnet of the Itala. '*Da!*' he responds, writing the numbers '180' next to the 'km'. 'That can't be right,' I say apprehensively. 'I'll ask another bloke. Kansk?' His response is written up as '185'. 'I prefer the first quote,' says Lang, putting the Itala back into gear.

JUNE

S	M	T	W	T	F	S
			✗	②	3	4
5	6	7	8	9	10	11
12	13	14	15	16	17	18
19	20	21	22	23	24	25
26	27	28	29	30		

DAY 19

Kansk to Krasnoyarsk

Warren: The Trans-Siberian Highway can be rated in three ways during the summer months: Shocking, Appalling and You're Mad if You Don't Take the Train Instead. Lang and I were faced with a deep-breath-taking 600 kilometre drive in order to catch up with the rest of the Expedition after waiting a few days in Irkutsk to repair the Itala. It was an early, crack-of-dawn-Prince-Borghese-reveille-bugle start — we were going to drive a half a day, 300 kilometres, each.

When we left Irkutsk, the highway was an impressive piece of multi-lane bitumen, but it soon deteriorated into a muddy, two-lane morass a mule would baulk at. 'Have we somehow strayed off the route?' 'No, this is it.' 'This can't be it ...' 'This is it ...' This perpetual roundabout of 'Is it or isn't it?' is how one naturally thinks while driving the Trans-Siberian. Just to add a little spice to the whole journey, a bit of rain makes the whole filthy track an absolute waterlogged shocker, the water filling potholes just large enough to float a warship the size of the USS *Nimitz*.

The highway's problems really stem from the conditions of the winter months: permafrost below and a dramatic melting of snow in the spring creating unimaginable quantities of water that tear the road apart like tissue paper. The problem for the veteran cars, of course, is that they have rudimentary, uncooperative and unforgiving steering, suspension and brakes, the inadequacies of which leap to the fore every time they hit one of these infernal potholes that create that surface-of-the-moon look for Russia's trans-continental road. The cars just crash into the never-ending supply of open-cut mines that litter the highway at least 14 times per minute, the sound of leaf springs crying for mercy, of chassis who want to go home, of tyres who are preparing a class action against reckless and culpable drivers.

When I'm driving I'm actually more conscious of Lang in the passenger seat, who's most probably adding up a score of potholes and botched gear changes which will culminate in presenting to me in Paris a hessian sack full of broken springs, stripped gears and punctured inner tubes.

All in all, the Itala's really giving me the ... well, annoying me. I know it's a century-old car but now, in the middle of Siberia, isn't the time to start pulling attention-seeking stunts like breaking down. The belt for the specially fitted alternator has decided to remain somewhere on the highway in Siberia, meaning our battery won't charge. On top of that, the car has decided it won't idle. The beauty of this is that when you pull up to an intersection in neutral, unless you do a bit of fancy Fred Astaire work with the accelerator, the clutch and the brake, the car will stop and the little bugger won't start. Fabulous. 'How big is Krasnoyarsk?' I ask Lang, who visited the city on the reconnaissance trip. 'Oh, from what I remember it's like a big country town — probably about the size of Dubbo.' Driving the nonco-operative Itala through the massive industrial city of Krasnoyarsk, it becomes apparent that the city is more or less like Dubbo — and Melbourne and Adelaide combined.

Mick: Many of us wake this morning to very sobering, disturbing Russian martial music piped into our rooms over a small, plastic, single-channel radio stuck to the walls, bang on 6 a.m. Bizarre. Was this how everyone was inspired to get up in the morning under the Soviet regime?

Travelling almost every day, living with the grease and grime of veteran cars, speeding along without windscreens or roofs, living in tents and bad hotels, and existing on the barest essentials, it's impossible to stay clean. Like most of the Expeditioners, today I pull on the same clothes I've been wearing since Irkutsk.

The front of my jeans are brown from oil and dirt, the back of them grey from dust. My shirt collar is black and the rest of the shirt not much better. The oilskin jacket now matches the Siberian soil. At least I still have clean socks and jocks, but the supply is dwindling. I give my boots a polish and feel better for it, but the fact is that you get used to dirty clothes.

And at least we've only gone a few days without clean stuff — in 1907 most of the men went for weeks. Or longer. To make it worse, they encountered bed bugs, lice and other creatures in most of the inns they stayed in, while we've not had any of them — thankfully.

The low cloud and cold air persist after yesterday afternoon's rain. We drive on reasonable roads to Krasnoyarsk with little distraction today. Only Stijnus has any problems, with the silicone that has been clogging his fuel system giving him no end of grief all day. Each time the lines block he has to stop and clean them out. By early afternoon it's happening every few minutes, and we laugh quietly when he climbs out of the car singing about 'silicones in the fuel, silicones in the fuel' in his heavy Dutch accent before breaking out into a series of curses. Later in the day the swearing becomes part of the song.

Krasnoyarsk is the biggest city we've seen in a long, long time, with wide avenues full of traffic that, like city traffic all over the world, is intent only on getting somewhere else, quickly. It is a shock to us on our slow and cumbersome cars with poor brakes, but we manage.

The locals knew we were coming and whenever any of us stop to check our directions we have a good-willed person coming up and telling us what hotel we're going to and how to find it.

Not everyone in Russia is so friendly. Later this evening someone walks into my hotel room, giving the impression he is a hotel employee, and while I have my back turned for a few seconds he snatches my money belt before smilingly making his way out the door again. I am suspicious, but not quick enough to react, and by the time I realise what has happened, he is gone. We were warned that we'd be targets for thieves and frauds, and now we have no doubts.

DAY 20

JUNE

S	M	T	W	T	F	S
			✗	✗	③	4
5	6	7	8	9	10	11
12	13	14	15	16	17	18
19	20	21	22	23	24	25
26	27	28	29	30		

Krasnoyarsk to Itatski

Mick: We are in a muddle leaving Krasnoyarsk. I take several wrong turns until a Russian bloke called Sasha (a third of the male population seems to be named Sasha) drives alongside and waves me to follow. He leads me halfway out of the city, indicates that I can just follow my nose from there on and waves goodbye. Once again, there's that incredible Russian hospitality. As I prepare to get going again, the Spyker and Itala drive past in the opposite direction. This is a one-way street ...

We eventually sort ourselves out and somehow most of us meet up the road for breakfast. John has moved on ahead of everyone, driving directly to Tomsk with the De Dion in the trailer and putting himself two days ahead of the group. He wants to spend a day there doing some serious maintenance and figures he would be better off doing this than waiting for whenever the next rest and repair day might be called. Perhaps everyone should have done the same, for as it turns out we will arrive a day after John and need a second day ourselves. But we can't have foreseen that.

Stijnus has more trouble with silicone in the fuel but now a few of the more mechanically minded Expeditioners begin to wonder about the validity of the silicone theory. Some things just don't add up. Chris, an electrical engineer and a bloke who knows engines pretty well, is riding with Stijnus today and begins nosing around in the Spyker's electrics. Andrew and Anthony join in, and after another couple of breakdowns the penny drops:

LEFT: WARREN SPORTING THE FRUITS OF HIS RETAIL THERAPY IN IRKUTSK: A RUSSIAN SOLDIER'S CAP AND STRIPED SAILOR'S TOP. HERE HE MUGS FOR THE CAMERA WITH KEITH AND MICK.

RIGHT: WARREN ATTEMPTING TO LIGHT A RUSSIAN CIGARETTE.

ABOVE: OLGA RECEIVES A KISS FROM WARREN AFTER BRINGING THE EXPEDITIONERS A FEAST.

RIGHT: BREAKFAST THAT MORNING AT A TRUCK STOP — BLINEYS AND EGGS.

this has nothing to do with fuel. The modern ignition system is failing … and then it dies. The Spyker goes for a ride on the trailer.

This is a bit spooky. Back in 1907 the Spyker's ignition failed before Tomsk and the car had to be entrained and sent to Tomsk for repairs. Tomorrow we'll be in Tomsk — repairing the Spyker's ignition.

Either the local radio station has been talking about us or truckies have spread the word over the CB radio, because now, more than ever, we're getting enthusiastic waves and toots from truckies and even car drivers as we motor along. It has happened before, but not to this degree. This will last for another few days, too. It makes us feel welcome and we return the greetings with feeling.

Our camp tonight is an experience in itself. First we spot the Brodies coming down the road being buzzed by an even smaller car of almost identical yellow. When it gets close enough we realise it is an old Fiat 500. The comical pair of cars looks hilarious. The Fiat is being driven by two Italian blokes, Fabrizio and Danilo, who are driving from Turin to China and having the time of their lives (find out more at www.europaasia.it). We yarn for a while and argue about who is more insane before they continue to Krasnoyarsk.

Then Olga and her sons appear from Itatski, the village a couple of kilometres away. The boys were here earlier; they'd taken photos and then gone. They return with calendars printed out with the photos they took, while Olga has a Russian feast for us — fresh milk, boiled eggs, the best cottage cheese we've ever tasted, a massive jar of gerkins, bread and more. And her own home brew that she insists isn't vodka and makes even her wince. We have a great evening.

JUNE

S	M	T	W	T	F	S
			X	X	X	④
5	6	7	8	9	10	11
12	13	14	15	16	17	18
19	20	21	22	23	24	25
26	27	28	29	30		

DAY 21

Itatski to Tomsk

Warren: Over the past week or so the Itala's been growing increasingly more difficult to start. Every bush mechanic here has had a crack at a diagnosis and checking the ignition points is high on the Top 5 list of ignition problems. To do this on the Itala means you need to remove the magneto. About 130 kilometres outside of Tomsk, the Itala throws a hissy fit and begins behaving like a hairy goat. The car was running like a steam train 5 minutes ago — the birds were singing, the sun was shining, everything was right with the world. Lynne Shaw and I were motoring along on the beautiful back roads to Tomsk with speed demons Keith Brodie and Andrew Snelling in the 8 hp, 2-cylinder yellow De Dion. But just to put a dampener on the day, the red car decides to start wheezing and coughing and shuddering. Suddenly the Itala stops dead — no warning, the engine just cuts out and the car rolls to a standstill.

'I told you — it's the points,' says Andrew, our resident electrical genius, leaping out of the De Dion and hoicking the Itala's bonnet open. 'I'll pull the maggie out and do them properly.' The magneto is one of those car parts that's earnt a charming nickname, like a dizzy (distributor) and the jenny (generator). Modern cars, mercifully, don't have magnetos — they have been replaced as a car's spark-creating gizmo by the distributor, the coil and the alternator.

Andrew removes the magneto and cleans the points; the car starts like a little ripper but within a few minutes has reverted to backfiring, convulsing and falling unconscious.

'I don't understand it,' says Andrew. 'It should be right. Maybe it's a tooth out.' Here is where the whole world as we know it comes apart. You see, the magneto is driven by gears that engage, turning the whole thing over, and if you don't align the teeth on the mating gears exactly how they were before you separated them, then all the timing to ignite the petrol and release the exhaust will be out of whack — so you might as well book a retirement village now, because it'll take an ice age to get the thing running again.

We try to start the car one more time — more explosions emanate from the exhaust. Andrew wipes his forehead and takes a deep breath. He tries and retries to get the Itala going, removing the magneto, repositioning the teeth on the gears, moving the sequence for the spark plugs. Still no go. After three hours Keith and Lynne need to leave for Tomsk in the De Dion, so Andrew stays with me to try to sort out whatever is wrong with the car. The engine will run, but only as if it is operating on 2 cylinders, so if we don't do something we'll be stuck out here all night. We'll make a run for it.

Andrew sorts out the electricals enough to make the car go for about 5 kilometres, then it simply dies, rolling to a stop on the edge of the road. Andrew won't give up, though: he is determined to keep the car on the road. But finally we're faced with a steep hill several kilometres long. It's all over — the car is never going to make it. Slugging it up the hill, backfiring and losing momentum, the Itala coughs and coughs until it dies. At 10 p.m. Andrew is still fighting with the car like a possessed surgeon pounding cardiac compression on a deceased patient. 'Mate, time to let it go,' I say to him. 'Time to call Anthony and put it on the trailer.' He slumps over the steering wheel. The magneto has won.

Mick: There's maybe two or three hours of real night at this time of year in these high latitudes, and it is fully light at 5 a.m. However, most of us are feeling weary and, in some cases, seedy enough to roll over and go back to sleep until after 6 a.m. That feels like sleeping in, but you can get away with that when you're camping because it doesn't take long to get organised and on the road. The Spyker speeds on ahead — lashed onto the sweep vehicle's trailer. It will need as much time as possible in Tomsk to sort out its ignition problems. The Itala and yellow De Dion follow without the security of Anthony's back-up, but Andrew, who didn't go ahead with John yesterday, rides in the Itala with Warren and can offer plenty of mechanical assistance if necessary.

While everyone else hits the road to catch John in Tomsk, Chris and I have a slower start. Chris is in the Contal for the first time since hurting his back in Irkutsk but within half an hour is in pain again, so we pull into the next village to discuss what to do. Locals gather to look, as usual, and when one offers to replace a couple of bolts that have dropped out of the Contal, we follow him to his house. This turns into tea inside his home, which turns into a meal, then a *banya* with a neighbour, followed by lunch. We can't believe it. Mind you, we have the ABC's Kim Traill to thank, because she is able to translate entire conversations for us — and the ABC is also keen to arrange the *banya* for its documentary.

A *banya* is a Russian sauna-bath. Part of the cleansing process involves being whipped with big bunches of birch leaves, so there are Chris, the ABC's Paul Costello, old Ivan and I naked, sweaty and beating each other. Not your everyday Aussie experience ...

The Brodies coax their De Dion all the way through Marinsk to Tomsk, but the water jacket on the engine is corroded and the leak is getting worse all the time. Keith also thinks his clutch, which howls in protest every time he gets moving, is growing noticeably worse and is likely to fail somewhere not far up the road.

As Stijnus points out, whenever you do 1000 kilometres in a veteran car back home, something will go wrong. We've done that distance many times over on this trip already, through conditions that most enthusiasts would flat-out refuse to inflict on their old cars, and the punishment is showing. We call another day of R and R — not rest and recreation, but repair and rebuilding.

John has had his R and R day already, so he elects to carry on tomorrow while the going is good, although Andrew stays back to offer assistance to those doing repairs. The rest of the Expedition gets busy on their cars. And wouldn't you know it — one of our biker mates from Irkutsk is in Tomsk and helps us no end with sourcing parts and finding assistance. Brilliant!

We award Borghese and Godard badges of honour in Tomsk. The Borghese goes to Chris, Paul and I for our stoic heroism in braving the *banya* and then admitting to the kinds of things that Aussie blokes just shouldn't do. The Godard goes to Kim for enthusiastically filming a bunch of naked men.

LEFT: LOCAL CHILDREN IN TOMSK, SIBERIA.

RIGHT: STIJNUS BREAKFASTING ON BLINEYS AND COFFEE WITH LOUISE AND ANTHONY IN AN ORNATELY DECORATED TRUCK STOP.

ABOVE: THE MAIN STREET OF TOMSK, WHERE THE STATUE OF LENIN DIRECTS TRAFFIC.

RIGHT: THE SPYKER ON THE TRAILER IN TOMSK, WHERE ITS IGNITION WAS REPAIRED – EXACTLY THE SAME WORK THAT WAS CARRIED OUT ON THE 1907 SPYKER IN TOMSK. LATER, THE ITALA JOINED THE 2005 SPYKER IN THE WORKSHOP.

JUNE

S	M	T	W	T	F	S
			✗	✗	✗	✗
⑤	6	7	8	9	10	11
12	13	14	15	16	17	18
19	20	21	22	23	24	25
26	27	28	29	30		

DAY 22

Tomsk

Warren: Tomsk: the university town where Charles Godard was forced to wait for six days while the Spyker's magneto was repaired; and by the look of things a century later, so might we. Godard, who knew nothing about things mechanical, went to the local university, which advised him that they were able to resurrect his clapped-out electrical gizmo by rewinding the coil. For us it seems possible to repair our magneto without having to go these extraordinary and expensive lengths — it's specialist stuff. But in order to check where our ignition timing is at, we need to find somewhere to buy a timing light — or, as they call it in Russian, a 'stroboscope'.

There's a curious practice in Russia of being able to flag down a private car, negotiate a fare and use it like a taxi to wherever it is you want to go. Standing in the middle of the street, I am eventually able to do this, somehow or other convincing a driver that I need to go to an '*avtomart* for a stroboscope'. We hit as many *avtomarts* as we can find but no hide nor hair of a stroboscope whatsoever. Eventually the driver takes me to an auto electrician, a quiet and patient fellow who understands no English but is able to communicate with me through a translation program on his office computer. If we can get the Itala to him, he can check the timing for us.

Running on only a couple of cylinders, the Itala flatulates along the few kilometres through Tomsk's back streets to the workshop. Before long, Andre, the auto electrician's boss, pulls up in a fresh, out-of-the-box V8 Toyota Land Cruiser and

CHRIS BOYLE IN THE 'RINSE'
CYCLE OF HIS HOTEL BATHROOM
CLOTHES WASH.

BACK TO FULL HEALTH, THE MAJESTIC SPYKER IS PARKED OUTSIDE THE MAGISTRAT HOTEL IN TOMSK.

somehow extricates himself from the driver's seat, looking like a golf ball going through a garden hose. Andre the giant takes a look at the magneto and utters to Sergei the diagnosis made in Tomsk twice every century: 'Your magneto needs to be rewound.' Tomsk must generate some sort of electrical field that causes magnetos to blow up on approach. Or, more likely, it's a good indicator of how long a magneto will last — from Peking to Tomsk. The maggie can be rewound at a specialist factory ... tomorrow. Tomorrow. Another delay for us; another massive drive of 600 kilometres or more to catch up with the rest of the Expedition.

Andre is a generous sort of bloke and not only in physical proportions. Standing in his workshop, a large garage with hydraulic hoists and workbenches, Andre invites Lang and me to a *banya*. Lang and I look at each other. Now, I like Lang — and I'm sure he likes me — but for a split second myriad disagreeable images flash before our eyes ... of the pair of us sitting around in the bollocky launching into each other with a fistful of sticks. A *banya*? Why not! When in Tomsk ...

Andre suddenly disappears through the greasy cement floor, climbing down a checkerplate steel ladder to the mechanic's pit beneath. This dark subterranean world which only mechanics doing oil changes and gearbox removals are privy to is the usual grease-monkey's pit of drums of sump oil, engine blocks and broken pistons. We follow Andre's massive silhouette through a maze of undersized corridors, finally arriving at the bottom of a set of stairs. Andre unlocks a heavy steel door and ushers us inside. Before us is a sparkling Shangri La of spotless tiles from floor to ceiling, potted palms, a deep swimming pool and the clean timber doors of the sauna. Mercifully, Andre spares us his leviathan presence in the sauna and leaves Lang, Sergei and me to it.

A *banya* is fundamentally a sauna with which another ladle of water on the coals brings the room to a temperature only slightly lower than that of the surface of the sun. Sergei knows how to use the birch, hauling it out of a vase of water. You don't pussyfoot around with the old birch. Nooo ... you gently flail the patient across the shoulders and down their back and legs and then swing your arm back and whack the living daylights out of them. After 10 minutes of this I feel like I've done five rounds with Kostya Tszyu inside a blast furnace. 'Now you go for a swim,' says Sergei. I collapse in the pool — it feels wonderful. A great calm has arrived. Lang and I put our clothes back on and we float up the stairs and ladders to the world above ground. All the worries and hardships of the past few weeks have disappeared.

JUNE

S	M	T	W	T	F	S
X̶	⑥	7	X̶	X̶	X̶	X̶
12	13	14	15	16	17	18
19	20	21	22	23	24	25
26	27	28	29	30		

DAY 23

Tomsk to Novosibirsk

Mick: Fixing the Spyker hasn't been too difficult because we were able to source suitable coils and tweak the system to work more efficiently, so it lines up in the morning with the Contal and yellow De Dion. The blue De Dion is a day ahead again but the Itala will lag behind once more, thanks to major problems with its magneto and the spare one. Warren gives us a smart salute as the three cars ease into Tomsk's morning traffic and head for a hotel just the other side of Novosibirsk.

Today is the anniversary of the day Lang and Warren came up with this whole Peking to Paris concept, and here's Lang, getting ready to head back out to the Tomsk workshop where the 1907 Itala is being repaired, and Warren in his black boots, khaki jodhpurs and jacket (the handlebar moustache is just starting to come good, too), watching a 1907 Spyker, a 1907 De Dion and a replica of a Contal lurching up the road in pursuit of another De Dion bodied just like the original Raid's had been.

We've often been stopped by the police at the dozens of checkpoints on Russia's roads; usually they're just curious and wanting a look and, truthfully, we've begun to tire of it because it slows us considerably — we can lose up to an hour a day to the police, for no reason — and we wonder if we'd get away with simply waving and carrying on. But this morning, for the first time, one of them asks for our papers and the stop takes longer than usual.

Stijnus eventually passes the De Dion and presses on. He likes to get in his car, wind up its loping engine and blast along

LEFT: The Contal and yellow De Dion drivers stop for a picnic lunch.

ABOVE: A pit stop for the Brodies' De Dion. The *shazlik* cooker and its woodpile can be seen in the background.

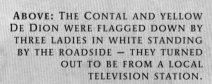

ABOVE: The Contal and yellow De Dion were flagged down by three ladies in white standing by the roadside — they turned out to be from a local television station.

RIGHT: A study in size — the largest vehicle on the expedition, the Spyker, trails the three-wheeled Contal and the 2-cylinder De Dion.

at a comfortably quick pace. The Spyker is never happy when held back with the slower vehicles. Chris is up in the De Dion with Keith while Louise rides with me on the Contal, and the two vehicles potter along together for most of the day.

One of the delights of the journey has been to add a small diversion to the day. Today the four of us stop in a village to buy food and then find a shady spot in a paddock to enjoy a picnic lunch. Somehow it is almost free of mozzies and other biting creatures, and we relax and laugh in the pasture, eating our bread, salami, cheese, eggs and other typically Russian foods.

We have an uneventful drive to the hotel, which turns out to be a dismal little motel-style place opposite an abandoned factory and the local airport. And here we pay the equivalent of $20 for a bed — prices are definitely climbing now that we're getting closer to the more populated western part of Russia.

We learn that the Itala will be on its way tomorrow and that John's De Dion has reached Omsk with a cracked radiator and ignition problems. John will get these things fixed and carry on.

Warren: The Expedition is leaving without us today. Walking back from a café, I see Mick and Chris aboard the Contal leading Stijnus in the Spyker and the yellow De Dion Brodie-bunch heading out of town. I can't help but feel proud to be part of such a crazy event — all those guys have come this far and are still pressing on. I give them a salute and they salute back — they know the Itala's in a dire state and we won't be seeing each other for some time.

Bad news: Lang's returned from the factory — they can't rewind the magneto. They could do it for Charles Godard in 1907, so what's happened in a hundred years that they can't do it now? They must have foreclosed on the Tomsk franchise of Magnetos 'R Us. What a nightmare. We are, however, carrying a spare magneto, but it's in questionable health. Now's the time to see what we can do about cannibalising both to make one a goer.

Lang and our Russian auto electrician mate work solidly trying to utilise interchangeable parts. For hours they try, falling into a horrible pattern of experimenting with a new theory which then requires resetting the timing and

1907

NOVOSIBIRSK VIA KEMAROVO

The sun came out for the Itala but it made the mud even worse, turning it from a thick soup to a glutinous mass that held bogged cars in an impossible grip. The Itala sank eight times, costing the crew hours every time. Its radiator was clogged with mud and the engine ran worryingly hot. The road was so appalling that the chassis, springs, wheels and differential took a horrendous pounding — Borghese feared it would destroy the Itala (one of the De Dions later snapped a spring here). They didn't make Tomsk until the next morning, and enjoyed the city's hospitality with mixed feelings: its European style cheered them, but the signs of impending revolution were depressing.

shifting the ignition leads, only for the car to run like a chaff-cutter and then having to start all over again. The magneto's working its evil voodoo.

Lang has had enough — like Andrew Snelling a few days before, he is slumped over the steering wheel, exasperated. It's 7 p.m. and things are getting desperate. It's time to try a last-ditch idea. If the magneto doesn't want to behave, then maybe we should bypass it altogether. By disabling the spark-producing mechanism and using the distributor part of the magneto connected to an ignition coil from a modern car, the engine — in theory — should run like a bottler. Last night Lang had a yarn with Andrew Snelling, who drew up a diagram of how it should all work, and so Lang and our electrician fit a Russian Lada ignition coil to the Itala — 1900 technology meets 1930 technology. It's now or never …

The Itala fires up, the coil producing a big fat spark igniting the fuel like a house — or a carburettor full of fuel — on fire. A wave of relief washes over everyone. We're back in the race.

DAY 24

JUNE

S	M	T	W	T	F	S
~~5~~	~~6~~	⑦	~~8~~	~~9~~	~~10~~	~~11~~
12	13	14	15	16	17	18
19	20	21	22	23	24	25
26	27	28	29	30		

From Novosibirsk

Warren: This morning Lang and I are psyched up for the 650 kilometre hell-drive to catch up with the Expedition, which is by now belting somewhere across Siberia. These massive double-hit drives are a serious undertaking, but they were everyday stuff for the motorists of the original Raid. There's no mucking around here: we just steel ourselves and get on with it. We're still nervous about Lang's plan of bypassing the magneto with the coil.

We're on the road before 6 a.m. and I'm behind the wheel, the car heading slowly out of Tomsk. It seems to be running well but it just never pays to be too cocky about these kinds of things; neither Lang nor I talk about it in case we jinx it. I hate the magneto.

Great — the police. We aren't even out of Tomsk yet and we've been flagged over by a policeman, who receives the usual 'Hi, we're crazy Australians who are driving a crazy old car to Paris and no speak Russian' routine. Deciding we're in the too-hard basket, he waves us on and I start the whole process of winding the Itala up to speed through the gears again. A few kilometres further and we see another checkpoint and the silhouette of a policeman sauntering out to the middle of the road, waving us to stop. The whole routine again.

Free to go, it's only a matter of minutes before two police cars overtake us and we find them waiting around the next bend with seven policemen and women beside the road. Flagging the Itala over, a captain of police approaches us as if to read the Riot Act. Suddenly his face cracks into an apologetic smile, his hand holding up a camera. 'Photo?' he asks. The next 20 minutes are spent with the police officers draping themselves in various poses across the bonnet, sitting behind the steering wheel, wearing our driving goggles, cuddling a grimacing Lang. When the photo session comes to a halt, the police captain shakes my hand, wishes us a safe journey and presents us with a bottle of vodka. What is it with Russian police cars being stocked with emergency vodka? Where do they fix the standard-issue crate in the boot — between the AK47 rack and the box of stun grenades? We gratefully accept and place the bottle between us in the front seat.

Another 2 kilometres and we round a bend, only to confront another policeman waving at us to pull over. What now? He circles the car and stops suddenly, raising his eyebrows — clearly unimpressed. He taps the bottle of vodka between driver and co-driver with his truncheon, impatient for an explanation — surprisingly, there is a zero blood alcohol limit in vodka-mad Russia. 'Police! Present! Gift!' we try to explain. If they're not trying to pour it down your throat they're trying to rip it off you. Cautiously he decides to leave the bottle alone, giving me the evil eye. He waves us on.

Now we're on through Novosibirsk, a whopping, gritty industrial city of about 1.5 million people which opens up onto a vast, flat Siberian wilderness, part forest, part sprawling plain. The countryside is a strange mix of tightly bound islands of enormous trees occurring sporadically on a sea of vivid, wild-green grass. It was through here that Prince Borghese's mufflerless Itala terrified the locals and their livestock as they shot through. Kilometre after kilometre we press on, the countryside not changing one iota, the realisation of Siberia's vast expanse becoming gradually crushing — strangely claustrophobic. 'Sibir' comes from the ancient local Altay language and means 'sleeping land', something I can begin to understand as we drive in the afternoon sun. Heading west, both Lang and I are becoming drowsy driving head-long into the warm sun in the long, golden twilight. Lang takes over and to our relief we spy the silhouette of the tent-topped Spyker, the yellow De Dion and the Contal at a solitary truck-stop café. Keith Brodie is in fine form, a cigar clenched between his teeth, offering Lang and I a beer as we climb out of the Itala.

LEFT: WARREN ACTS AS WAITER FOR THE OTHER EXPEDITIONERS, BRINGING THEM DINNER AT A CAFÉ NEAR A LAKE WHERE THEY CAMPED FOR THE NIGHT.

RIGHT: KEITH TAKES SOME DELIGHTED CAMPERS FOR A SPIN.

ABOVE: WARREN STAKES HIS CLAIM ON THE SPYKER, WHICH IS BY FAR THE MOST POWERFUL VEHICLE ON THE EXPEDITION, OUTRUNNING THE ITALA.

RIGHT: KEITH LINES UP HIS DE DION NEXT TO A MURAL DEPICTING AN EERILY SIMILAR VEHICLE; THE MURAL WAS AT THE EXPEDITIONERS' MOTEL.

Mick: We leave our dingy motel outside Novosibirsk in glorious sunshine but have a sobering reminder of the 35 000 Russians who die on these roads every year. The first few kilometres of road are lined with over a dozen memorials to men, women and children who have died on this innocent-looking stretch of tar. This isn't a bad piece of road compared to what we've seen before, nor is it heavily used. There are few corners. We can only guess at the reasons for the carnage: alcohol and fatigue.

Later in the day we pass a crumpled car that rolled off a gentle bend an hour or so ago. The ambulance is departing with no sense of urgency: another memorial will be erected here.

We have lunch in a funny little establishment run by Alexander Tschuvko, a man obviously inspired by the openness and architecture of places like Holland — workers are building a windmill out the front. We have a short tour of the building out the back with its *banya*, pool and bedroom with mirrors on the ceiling. Alexander also tells us that this is the region where a combined US–Russian scientific team found the remains of woolly mammoths as well as the first hard evidence that America's indigenous peoples originated in Siberia before the last Ice Age.

Chris and I, along with Rob Spyker in one of the support cars, go to the nearby village for a haircut while the others carry on. The Itala roars past soon afterwards and is in camp half an hour before we arrive. Warren and Lang did around 600 kilometres today, a terrific effort in a 98-year-old car.

We camp on the shores of a small lake where the excited and laughing local kids are outnumbered only by the mosquitoes. It is a beautiful spot with lush, green grass to set up our tents on and stands of birch trees that filter the blood-red light of sunset over the water.

We contact John by phone and discover that he is now in Ishim, over 600 kilometres ahead. He repaired his radiator but it has broken again, indicating a more serious problem that must be causing these repeated failures. He has also broken one of the trailer's main suspension leaves on the rough road to Ishim and has to source another. Finally, he needs Andrew to catch up as soon as possible to carry out the more troublesome repair to the magneto. Tomorrow I will take Andrew ahead on the Contal and we'll try to do the full distance in one day. Everyone else will head to Omsk, a comfortable 300 kilometre drive away. ༃

DAY 25

JUNE

S	M	T	W	T	F	S
~~5~~	~~6~~	~~7~~	⑧	9	~~10~~	~~11~~
12	13	14	15	16	17	18
19	20	21	22	23	24	25
26	27	28	29	30		

To Omsk and Ishim

Mick: Andrew and I set out on our marathon run and knock over 100 kilometres in just under two hours before breakfast. That's a great run if you're not operating by today's standards, but if we were in Australia with a modern car we'd have been appalled. It's all relative, and we know the day will be a very long one, because we've only done a sixth of the distance we need to achieve.

The early drive has a couple of highlights, including the distant sight of a deer on the edge of the forest and a close encounter with an owl that flies right above our heads for a few seconds, almost close enough to touch, before flicking left and soaring away to the trees. This is one of the joys of not being hemmed in by roofs and windows.

We stop just short of Omsk at a café with two bears in a cage. The bears seem happy and healthy enough but live in filth and don't have much of a life. We get as close to them as we dare but their arms can reach at least half a metre out of the bars, so we're careful.

We press on beyond Omsk. I suffer our first difficult police check. An aggressive cop with attitude pulls us over at a checkpoint and begins loudly demanding something. I can't understand him, and the more I indicate this the angrier he becomes, talking louder and faster. I produce all the paperwork I have but it's not enough. I can't do any more than that, though, and eventually the guy gives up and sharply waves me on.

Trouble is, as much as I'd like to escape right away, I can't — my clutch cable snapped as I pulled up. I push the Contal up the

THE CONTAL BLAZES ITS OWN TRAIL THROUGH THE RUSSIAN COUNTRYSIDE.

THE RIVER BEACH IN OMSK, A POPULAR DESTINATION FOR LOCALS — AND THE OCCASIONAL EXPEDITIONER.

road a little and we hastily bodgy up the cable to work at least as far as Ishim, where the spare is waiting.

By now it's well after lunch and we're just past halfway there. I'm getting tired and the road deteriorates badly. The going's hard, no doubt. Finally we reach Abatskoe, one of the last towns before Ishim, a pretty place surrounded by floodwaters and protected by levees. We stop for dinner then tackle the final hour's travelling into the slowly sinking sun. Just up the road, though, something goes snap and the bike shudders. I pull over ... and find another broken spring.

Andrew has a splint for just this problem and, using a bit of tree branch as a spacer, gets us going again within half an hour. He's a genius and after a 16-hour journey we pull up in Ishim, where John's waiting to greet us at the hotel.

Warren: Rob Spyker is behind the wheel of the Itala today, piloting Lang and I into Omsk. This is a big city full of trams and trucks, and Rob pushes our Italian car through dense traffic towards our hotel. Borghese and Barzini nearly imploded in Omsk due to delayed exhaustion, the pair of them collapsing — Barzini doing so on the street, where people assumed he was just one of the incalculable number of vodka-soaked drunks sleeping it off.

Omsk is a beautiful city in the summertime, sporting its own Bondi Beach, a large stretch of sand on the edge of the Irtysh River. Most of the Expeditioners decide to go for a swim where hundreds of the locals pack the beach. Contrary to what cartoonists think, Russians aren't overweight, monobrowed, Leonid Brezhnev lookalikes sitting on deckchairs on grey pebbly beaches in greatcoats and slippers. We in the West have been given a stereotype of old Soviet-era Russians that is so far from the truth it's not funny. And sadly, from a cartoonist's point of view, it's not funny. Everybody on the beach is fit and good looking, unlike the Expeditioners, who would frighten a bat out of a cave. Particularly me, who ventures into the water in my underpants — a move that is guaranteed to panic everyone greater than any shark alarm. Stupid move: for some reason Lang and Rob think it's funny to crash-tackle me in the water and steal my undies. How childish. Mongrels. I wish I'd thought of it first.

JUNE

S	M	T	W	T	F	S
			~~4~~	~~5~~	~~6~~	~~7~~
~~1~~	~~6~~	~~7~~	~~8~~	(9)	(10)	11
12	13	14	15	16	17	18
19	20	21	22	23	24	25
26	27	28	29	30		

DAY 26/27

Omsk and Ishim to Tyumen

Mick: Andrew and I sort out the problems in our respective vehicles, getting springs made for the trailer and Contal at the local municipal depot where, as in Irkutsk, there's a blacksmith. We must buy the spring steel but this time there's no other charge and certainly no corruption. The guys there are great. And throughout the day the rest of the Expedition catches up after runs far less eventful than the Contal's. It's a successful day for all.

Russian hotels haven't been kind to us on many occasions and now we have a new challenge: heat. The digs in Ishim are the usual ancient and ugly Soviet-era holes and in this case they don't even include communal showers, let alone a bathroom in each room. And now the heat and humidity are stifling, and the rooms unventilated — unless you can stand the hordes of mosquitoes that swarm in through open windows. Many of us get little rest before waking for a 7 a.m. start.

And to make it worse, kids have been playing on the Contal, despite the tarp over it, and they not only figured out how to turn on the ignition, they left it on all night — so the battery's flat. And they stamped so hard on the brake pedal that the activating rod has snapped clean in two. So Chris and I are delayed, repairing and re-firing the machine; we then set off in drizzling rain. We're already in dismal moods and now we're being covered in a spray of filth off the road — and it is putrid. Russia has a long way to go with public hygiene.

We only cop the edge of the main storm, though, while a merciless downpour soaks everyone else in their first hour out of town.

LEFT: A WOMAN RIDING DOWN THE TRANS-SIBERIAN HIGHWAY IN THE BACK OF HER HUSBAND'S THREE-WHEEL MOTORCYCLE TRUCK.

RIGHT: THE CHANGING FACE OF TRANSPORTATION — A CENTURY-OLD DE DION BOUTON BY THE ROADSIDE, EXPERIENCING A MINOR BREAKDOWN, AS A COLOURFUL TRUCK FLIES PAST.

ABOVE: MEMBERS OF THE OMSK CAR CLUB AND (RIGHT) A LOCAL CHILD ESCORT THE EXPEDITIONERS FROM THEIR CITY.

Chris's back is still not good but he struggles on in the Contal's front seat. We're cruising in front of the sweep vehicle, staffed today by Louise Brodie and the ABC's Lynne Shaw, when they get an SOS. The Itala has broken off one of its spring mounts, a major disaster for the day's drive because it can't be fixed without the help of a good welder. The Italian car is loaded onto the trailer and taken to tonight's stop, Tyumen, where the men of a local workshop happily work almost right through the night to fix it.

Today's a long day, just over 300 kilometres, and the De Dions motor on for many hours. John is able to give his a midday rest by using the trailer but the stricken Itala spoils Keith's chances of taking the same option. Stijnus speeds on as usual, way out in front and doing it comparatively easily.

Chris and I get lucky again. The ABC has discovered mineral baths just off the route and we are the only ones to come past at the right time. We ride down a winding track to find an outdoor pool with muddy sides and a building containing bathtubs. Dozens of kids from a summer camp are there too, so we wait patiently for them to finish before sliding into the warm, saline water ourselves. The nurse tells us it is reputedly great for bones and contains bromide to promote relaxation. Maybe the waters help Chris's back, but they don't calm him: he splashes and larks about like one of the kids. Afterwards we both feel great, as much for the clean feeling as anything. It makes our day and changes our moods dramatically.

Warren: We've just left the town of Ishim and it's pouring. No, it's actually bucketting down — the very day our photographer, Bob Barker, decides to come with us in the Itala. I'm behind the wheel again, pushing our car through torrential rain. Our oilskins are not proving up to the task for such bad weather: I'm soaked through, sitting in a pool of freezing water that's trickling down the inside of my boots into my already waterlogged socks. This is hard going and the bleak weather ahead of us doesn't suggest that it's going to get any easier.

It's difficult enough to keep the Itala on the road at the best of times, but today is shaping up to be one of the most difficult. There's very little conversation you can have in these old cars: the buffeting and relentless wind noise makes it almost

LEFT: KEITH BRODIE TAKES A NAPOLEONIC STANCE WHILE HIS CAR IS BROKEN DOWN. BOB BARKER SAYS THAT 'BREAKDOWNS ARE OFTEN A TIME FOR HIJINKS, ESPECIALLY AFTER SITTING IN AN OPEN CAR DURING TORRENTIAL DOWNPOURS – THEY'RE A CHANCE TO WARM UP, DRY OUT AND UNWIND.'

ABOVE: WARREN GETTING SOAKED AS HE FIXES THE LOOSE MUDGUARD ON THE ITALA.

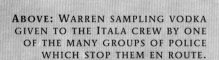

ABOVE: WARREN SAMPLING VODKA GIVEN TO THE ITALA CREW BY ONE OF THE MANY GROUPS OF POLICE WHICH STOP THEM EN ROUTE.

RIGHT: DE DION AND ITALA AT A BREAKDOWN STOP. SHORTLY AFTERWARDS THE ITALA WAS LOADED ONTO THE TRAILER – SOMETHING WHICH BOB SAYS THE DRIVERS HATE TO DO – AND TRUCKED OFF FOR REPAIRS IN THE NEXT TOWN.

impossible. Add some blasting rain and it becomes totally impossible. So Lang and I sit side by side, silently facing the oncoming rain peppering our faces at 60 km/h. The sky is black; the rain and oily slush from passing traffic smear the lenses in my goggles, making the road even more difficult to see. There's a service station ahead — it's time to fuel up.

Back into the car — back into the diabolical weather. It's strange: my mind is so incredibly focused in these conditions, it's working triple time watching for potholes, anticipating oncoming traffic, my foot acting as a tremor meter on the accelerator, alert for any change in the engine's performance.

It's time for breakfast, and through the drizzle I see a gathering of ravenous semitrailer drivers parked in a feeding frenzy around a café, chowing down on kafe and blineys. Blineys are fundamentally a pancake, or a crepe, or a big pikelet — whatever you like to call it — filled with either cottage cheese, meat or jam. We eat them every morning for breakfast. If I eat another one, I'll explode.

Lang, Bob and I stagger into the café like three drowned rats. Before long other Expeditioners pull in, including Bev in the support vehicle. 'Well, Bob,' says Lang, putting his wringing wet oilskin back on after breakfast. 'Are you going to stay with us for the rest of the day or will you opt for comfort and cowardice?' Talk about a heavy ultimatum. For Bob, there was never any question — he is going to see the day right through. The rain outside is getting heavier as we're about to leave, and we notice that a rear mudguard has shaken itself loose and nearly collapsed on the tyre. Ever since we remounted the mudguards in Ulaan Baatar, they have continually rattled themselves loose. I have to get under the car and lie flat on my back to tighten the thing up; as I lie in an enormous puddle, I wonder what the hell I am doing here. We should just remove these mudguards altogether like Prince Borghese did with his car.

We're on the road again, barrelling through the rain. After a few hours the sky begins to lighten and the bad weather eases off. Suddenly I hear a *ping* from somewhere at the back of the car and a slight twitch through the steering and the accelerator. 'Something's happened,' I say to Lang, hauling the car up on the edge of the highway. And it has: the steel pin holding the end of the right rear leaf spring has sheered off from the chassis, leaving the spring in mid-air. It's lucky it didn't punch a hole clean through the fuel tank — only the mudguard bracket I tightened up this morning was stopping it. I take back everything I thought about removing the guards. Time to call Anthony to come and get us with the trailer — we need to get the suspension fixed in the next town.

DAY 28

JUNE

S M T W T F S

~~12~~ ~~13~~ ~~14~~ ~~15~~ ~~16~~ ~~17~~ (11)
12 13 14 15 16 17 18
19 20 21 22 23 24 25
26 27 28 29 30

Tyumen to Yekaterinburg

Warren: There was no problem fixing the Itala's busted spring shackle pin. A mechanic's workshop placed neatly next to our hotel in the oil-rich town of Tyumen had the problem fixed overnight and we are now fighting fit for the run to Yekaterinburg. We're almost in the Urals now; the dreamlike monotony of an endless Siberia is, finally, coming to an end.

After a few hours' driving, we round a bend to find the familiar multicoloured shape of the Spyker parked beside a run-down country café, with Stijnus and Keith Brodie sitting at an outdoor table. We pull the Itala in and are immediately greeted by a moustachioed gentleman sporting very few teeth — and those he does have are solid gold. He places a can of beer in each of our hands and slaps me on the shoulder, obviously delighted to see the cars. 'What's going on here?' I ask Keith. 'Blowed if I know,' he laughs. 'We just arrived and this fella raced up with a few beers.'

The man fires up the barbecue — a 44-gallon drum sliced lengthways filled with coals. '*Shazlik?*' he asks. '*Da, da,*' we chorus — we are growing quite accustomed to the local kebabs. He brings out a plate of impressive diced meat on skewers and places the kebabs on the barbecue.

It's damned satisfying to have crossed Siberia. There is a genuine feeling of accomplishment and it seems okay for once to relax. Stijnus is very much the life of the party and any kind of captive audience is enough to fire the starting gun on an endless repertoire of jokes. It is an absolutely beautiful afternoon, cloudless and warm, a cool beer and the smell of the kebabs cooking. The *shazlik* are, of course, delicious and by the time we are ready to leave, our host's entire extended family has arrived, and they're looking at the Spyker and the Itala and checking out these strange jodhpurred motorists. A small girl wearing a distinctive scarf and a pale blue, full-length silk dress comes up to look at me. I understand now — they're gypsies. The café is owned by gypsies.

'I'll go inside and get the bill,' I say, wandering through the front door. The man's wife, a seriously wide *babushka*, starts to tally up what we ordered. She speaks to herself, writing down all sorts of strange numbers with a pencil on a slip of paper, and eventually arrives at a figure. My eyes widen — this adds up to about $US95! It's thousands of roubles! For four kebabs and a few cans of beer we didn't ask for! 'I'm sorry, this can't be right, madam.' I've just pulled the pin on a hand grenade. The woman explodes, violently throwing her hands in the air and shrieking before collapsing forward on the counter, her head buried in her hands as she wails and sobs.

'Look, I'm sorry, but I don't think the bill is correct.' More screaming and howling in Russian, her hands outstretched as she looks up at either heaven or mould on the ceiling. 'Just stop for a minute ...' She is back on the counter, wailing at maximum volume. Her husband flies through the door, snatching the bill out of her hand and pushing it onto my chest as he fires a volley of Russian expletives at me. Aaaah ... he's not so happy now.

'I'm not going to pay this amount,' I tell him. The woman is by now convulsing on the counter. I wonder if every poor diner in this place gets to see the matinee session. The family has started to filter inside through the back door. This is becoming ugly — I need to get out.

'Look, this is all I have,' I say, rifling through my pocket and producing a few 20-rouble notes. The man launches into me again as I turn around and stride to the door. There is a small crowd milling outside who can hear something going on, and they don't look pleased. Lang already has the Itala idling; the man stands at the café door, shaking his fist in the air and shouting abuse. 'Let's get out of here,' I say, leaping aboard. Keith and Stijnus have already sussed the situation and the Spyker is now well and truly putting the kilometres under the wheels. Farewell, Siberia ...

OBVIOUSLY FRIENDLY POLICE POSE IN FRONT OF THE DE DION ON THE TRAILER — MANY POLICE STOP THE DRIVERS WANTING TO CHAT OR HAVE PICTURES TAKEN WITH THE CARS.

MECHANIC ANTHONY EDEN AND A YEKATERINBURG MECHANIC INSPECT THE SPYKER, WHICH SNAPPED ITS DRIVESHAFT JUST OUTSIDE OF TOWN.

Mick: We're all excited about getting to Yekaterinburg, a city we expect to be more cosmopolitan, more familiar and even romantic after our weeks coming from the east. The road out of Tyumen promises an easy trip, too — dual carriageway, wide lanes, smooth tar. It lasts just a few kilometres, though, and then suddenly Yekaterinburg seems a long way away as the road deteriorates to an abysmal stretch of potholes that give the cars constant short, sharp hits. Just when we think we've seen it all, Russia manages to throw up a completely new road-surface nightmare.

One reason it is so bad is that it is unrelenting. There are no smooth sections on which to rest, just unending toil for the drivers. The Contal, with its rigid frame, is horrendous here.

But eventually the road improves. Then the police take over. In some places the cops are thicker and more active than in others, and this seems to be one of the busy places. Many of us are pulled over at checkpoints, by random patrol cars and by officers carefully positioned at places where drivers frequently break the law. It's hard to know precisely what's right and wrong on Russian roads because people flaunt the laws all the time, yet, perversely, insist that the laws must be obeyed.

As has become our habit, we try to ignore the police when they wave us down because we're sick of the wasted time, but Chris and I have a few encounters today. The first is a road-side patrolman who is very forceful about pulling us over. His mate wanders around the Contal with his finger glued to the trigger of his automatic rifle. During the second episode the armed officer keeps his weapon pointed directly at Chris, who walks in circles to avoid it while the barrel follows him.

Our third encounter is more worrying. I overtake a truck in what turns out to be a no-overtaking zone. The cop indicates that he could tear up my licence. I try to look contrite while Chris tries to make them laugh. It works and they wave us on.

A mass of coal-black cloud swallows the land ahead in the final run to Yekaterinburg. The rain pelts down, blinding us and drowning our wet-weather gear until we're all soaked to the skin. But the storm passes by the time each of us finds our way into the city and our hotel opposite the main railway square.

Less than five minutes from the hotel, the Spyker snaps its driveshaft. The offending piece is a modified VW component — as usual, it's the modern mods that let us down. Stijnus strides up the road to an automotive workshop, arranges a tow and gets the Dutch car settled in with the enthusiastic mechanics, who jump straight into the job.

DAY 29

Yekaterinburg

Mick: We've called another day of repair and restoration, so after we awake we get stuck in. Most of us knock over the essential work in the morning and spend the afternoon touring the city, visiting the site where Tsar Nicholas II and his family were murdered; a cemetery full of very capitalistic headstones (he who dies with the most toys wins?), and a memorial to thousands killed in Stalin's purges. Russian history is full of death.

We hear little news from Stijnus until mid-afternoon, when the familiar rumble of the Spyker fills the street and we see the red, white and blue machine pull into the car park. Another major breakage overcome.

Warren: Two years before Borghese roared across Russia, a squadron of Imperial Guards opened fire on a 200 000-strong industrial protest march in St Petersburg, killing several hundred men, women and children. This kicked off the 1905 Revolution against Tsar Nicholas II which, although it was ultimately put down, simmered away until it reached critical mass in 1917. At the time of the original Peking to Paris Raid, Russia was well and truly on the road to dramatic political change.

It's amazing how historical perspectives can move full circle. Last night in a restaurant in Yekaterinburg, the indefatigable Lynne Shaw struck up a conversation with a charming local couple, Sergei and his wife, Dasha. They both spoke terrific English and offered to take a few of the Expeditioners around the city today on a personal tour. It makes all the difference talking to the locals instead of professional guides, who give plenty of information but not much from the heart.

Yekaterinburg is a beautiful city — it was Nicholas II's favourite retreat. But it's more infamous as the place where the Tsar and his family were imprisoned and then later executed.

Since the fall of communism, Russians seem to have been going through a painful revisitation of their twentieth century history. Communist education programs painted the Tsar as an incompetent, pompous fop, but since the fall of the Soviet Union there has been a groundswell to almost deify him and his family. The fact that in 1917 many Russians were glad to see the Tsar go, after ploughing two million troops to their deaths in World War I and the tragedy of millions more starving, doesn't seem to pop up on the revisitation-of-history radar. Still, after so many years of crazy communist claptrap about their history, Russians today are glad that they can make their own judgments.

The site where the Tsar and his family were murdered is today an extraordinary shrine to the Romanovs. The timber house in which they were imprisoned stood for many years until the then governor of the region, Boris Yeltsin, ordered it to be bulldozed. Now an enormous cathedral stands on the site, a bronze statue of the Tsar and his family placed near the entranceway. Within the cathedral are numerous depictions of the family as religious icons: gold halos radiate from their heads and they're posed as though they are medieval saints. Photographs of the Tsar, the Tsarina and their extraordinarily beautiful children fill the walls, their composure candid and relaxed.

Sergei and Dasha are quite vocal about their respect for Russia's murdered royal family. 'A terrible crime, a terrible crime happened here,' says Sergei, shaking his head. 'The Tsar, he is like Christ — he did the right thing for the people and he was killed by the people.'

DAY 30

JUNE

S	M	T	W	T	F	S
~~12~~	~~13~~	~~14~~	~~15~~	~~16~~	~~17~~	~~18~~
(13)	14	15	16	17	18	
19	20	21	22	23	24	25
26	27	28	29	30		

Yekaterinburg to Kungur

Mick: Europe at last! Just outside Yekaterinburg we reach the border between Asia and Europe, where a replica of a verst pole marks the same spot where the French component of the 1907 Raid celebrated with Champagne. We follow their example, cracking a bottle of bubbly by the pole with our cars crowded around us. We feel we've achieved so much, that we've beaten the odds by getting all our cars here despite their age and all the physical, political and personal hurdles that have stood in our way. Yet we've done it easy compared with the men whose exploits we are honouring.

When you travel each day, one at a time, without looking too far ahead (for it will only become too daunting to consider), you lose sight of the bigger picture at times. When a milestone comes along — the Mongolian border, the Russian border, now the Asia–Europe boundary — the magnitude of the Expedition comes back to us and forces us to reflect on it. So we have a closer insight than ever before into how proud those men must have been.

And then onwards again. There's always more distance to cover and we can't stand around feeling good about ourselves for ever. More appalling road hinders progress and the weather continues its grey and drizzly ways until, around lunchtime, the heavens open in a downpour that drives each car to shelter at the nearest café.

We often wonder how many of the people we're passing heard stories from their grandparents about those cars that came through in 1907. In the picturesque little village of Kisalevo

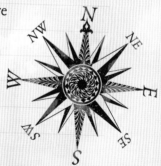

we're introduced to such a man, Vasili. Chris, the Brodies and I stand by a tiny wooden bridge listening to Vasili describe how his grandparents, who lived right *here*, watched in fear as supernatural carriages roared past and disappeared up *that* hill where the road still goes today. His grandparents had crossed themselves as protection against whatever evil it was that they had witnessed. We are fascinated. Vasili turns to Keith's De Dion.

'No, the cars my grandparents saw weren't like that,' he says firmly. 'They were much bigger.' We smile. Like all good stories, this one had grown in the telling.

A group of young Russians on holiday are frolicking around the *banya* out the back of Vasili's house. They invite us to join them, and naturally Chris and I accept. We steam, we beat each other with birch leaves and then plunge into the 5°C stream flowing from a spring just a few hundred metres away. The Russians smear us in the creek's therapeutic mud, which they say is sold for exorbitant sums to resorts, and by the time we've finished we feel cleaner than we have in weeks.

We all end the day in Kungur, a dirty, dilapidated town full of unemployment, vodka-dulled youths, surly barmaids and potholed roads. Again, Russia shows us her highs and lows all in one day.

Warren: I can't believe it — we're here. Actually here at the border that divides Asia from Europe. This is the exact point where Cormier and Collignon's De Dion Boutons were photographed either side of the standard Russian distance marker, a black and white verst pole, the drivers clearly relieved that the endless horizons of Siberia were now well and truly behind them. We're in the Urals now, and stepping inside Europe for the first time. Further, I can't believe we still have all five cars running, despite the catastrophic breakdowns, the appalling weather, the shocking roads and some of the worst gear changes I've ever heard.

This is the moment to replicate the photograph. Keith Brodie and John Matheson place their De Dions on either side of the pole; I'm fairly certain the last two De Dions to do this were headed for Paris as well. And it's time for the Champagne. I don't think any of us have consciously thought about actually reaching such an important milestone — or a verst pole — as this. We've just been

LEFT: THE DE DIONS RE-CREATE AN IMAGE TAKEN OF THE 1907 DE DION PAIR (BELOW) AT THE BORDER BETWEEN ASIA AND EUROPE.

ABOVE: ALL OF THE VEHICLES LINE UP TO MARK THE HISTORIC CROSSING AT THE VERST POLE.

RIGHT: (L TO R) KEITH BRODIE, ANDREW SNELLING, JOHN MATHESON AND ROB SPYKER RELEASE THE CHAMPAGNE.

1907

EKATERINBURG

While Borghese drove in a northern loop via Ekaterinburg on better roads, the De Dions took the more direct southern route through the Urals. The prince had over a week's lead, and it grew larger as the Frenchmen slithered on muddy tracks in the rain. Borghese enjoyed a fêted welcome and banquets on his route, while Cormier's team was reduced to stays in minor inns infested with lice. When Collignon awoke one morning (if he'd managed to sleep at all) his body-belt was so infested with vermin that the others immediately ran outside.

following the route, metre after metre, pothole after pothole. Like Cormier and Collignon standing in this spot a century ago, John and Keith aren't quite puttering along the Champs Elysées yet. There's a hell of a long way to go.

The weather and the road deteriorate in a miserable partnership that makes driving an absolute nightmare. The highway is a shocker. Trucks throw up oily spray, blurring all vision, and on top of that there is more road surface missing than there is road. The rain makes the increasing number of enormous potholes nearly impossible to see and I'm doing my absolute best to hit every single one. The problem with the old cars is that the mechanical brakes on the rear wheels aren't exactly the liveliest; when that's coupled with the high centre of gravity, it makes the car handle like a kitchen table. And on top of that, the need to keep momentum up means that, try as I might, I can't seem to avoid crashing the car into holes, with some appalling jarring and jolting.

I'm over this. It's one smashing blow to the car after another. I can feel the shock of the timber wheels crashing in and out holes, telegraphed through the shuddering steering wheel. Lang is bracing himself — every time the car smacks into a hole, his realisation of what damage is being done increases. It's some hours before we reach the outskirts of Kungur, a town with a sprawling vista of a fetid prison, atop which is a vast entanglement of barbed wire. Imagine being inside.

Bang — the biggest pothole I've hit so far and there's metallic noise from the front of the car. Lang swears. There goes the headlight: the stand has snapped off. What a great way to finish the day.

DAY 31

Kungur to Ochansk

Warren: John Matheson's sitting in the blue De Dion grinning from ear to ear — the car's just stalled in the bottom of a muddy water-filled hole, up to the axles in slop. This is what it's all about: being out in the wilds. We're trying to navigate a route along some muddy back roads through a forest in the Urals, to reach the ferry for Ochansk. It's not often we get the opportunity to take the cars seriously off the beaten track — the potholed, truck-filled highway is off the beaten track enough anyway.

A local in the village gave us gave us a few directions, a sort of vague gesturing with a smattering of Russian followed by a broad grin revealing a tremendous set of gums. We've followed two wheel ruts that meander into some seriously rough country. The question on everyone's mind: how on earth are the cars going to handle this? The answer: amazingly well. When these cars were new, most roads were like this — nothing more than abominable cart tracks that turn to chocolate mousse in the rain. So when you look at these old cars, you realise they were built with features that are ideal for off-road conditions: high ground clearance, a wheel on each corner for an excellent angle of approach, and low gearing.

John's car is push started and he takes another charge through the hole, this time belting up and out the other side. Then it's Keith Brodie's turn, the little yellow car fishtailing its way through the mud, Keith holding the steering wheel with the same teeth-gritting determination as Washington crossing the Delaware. You can see how the light chassis is capable of twisting with the changing conditions. Stijnus, of course, uses the Spyker like a Panzer and crashes the big car through the worst conditions as if it's nothing at all. Poor old Mick and Chris on the Contal are doing it tough, however, the spidery little machine bellying out on a ridge of concrete-like compacted mud. We have to lift the moto-tri off so that they can continue their death-defying slip-sliding along the track. In the Itala, it's Lang's turn behind the wheel.

The old local in the village said something about the track linking up to an old military road made from cement blocks that will lead us to Ochansk. We've found a road that fits the description and according to the compass it's heading roughly in the right direction. Rounding a bend, we confront an enormous truck; we ask the driver if this road leads to Ochansk. He looks uncomfortable and crosses his arms — the road is blocked where he comes from. He points to the way we've come from and says, 'Ochansk'; we need to turn back. There's a bit of argy-bargy amongst the Expeditioners because the map and the compass suggest otherwise.

The truck crawls past, under some serious weight. It's overloaded with concrete slabs from the road — this bloke's actually stealing the road! No wonder he doesn't want us hanging around.

The slab road is remarkable, built to withstand tank traffic, but it's our deserted expressway through the forest. For 20 kilometres we hammer along the concrete until we find a crane loading another truck with slabs from the road. The crane operators and the truck driver are initially suspicious, but as we squeeze the Itala past them, they climb down to have a look. We explain what we're doing and they relax, giving us a loaf of fresh bread and milk. They're the most generous road-thieves I've ever met.

A little further on, Bob Barker, sitting with his usual *laissez-faire* style in the back of the Itala, is photographing Stijnus following us in the Spyker. The cars are deep in the pine forest, hammering along the road nose to tail. Bob's voice cuts in over the engine noise in a loud yell. 'The Spyker — it's gone over!' We stop the Itala and run back along the track toward the big Dutch car, which is poking skywards from a deep culvert on the edge of the road. Stijnus put a wheel over the edge and the whole car went crashing down the hole, with only the front right-hand wheel barely hanging onto the road. Rob, in the passenger seat, leapt out of the car as it speared off the road into the ditch, neatly pirouetting to safety.

Stijnus is in shock — this is his father's car, his most valuable possession, and this extra-rare and valuable machine is now down some hole in a forest in the backwoods

LEFT: THE SPYKER MAKES DRIVING
THROUGH THE MUDDY ROAD FROM
KUNGUR LOOK EASY – BUT NOT THAT
EASY, FOR IT FALLS INTO A CULVERT ON
THE EDGE OF THE ROAD (BELOW) AND
HAS TO BE TOWED OUT BY THE TV
CREW'S VAN.

ABOVE: LANG AT THE
WHEEL OF THE ITALA.

RIGHT: THE BRODIES LEAD THE
BLUE DE DION AND SPYKER.

of Russia. Stijnus wanders around in disbelief, but, to his absolute credit, he doesn't explode or implode. This is our equivalent of Borghese's Itala crashing through the bridge in Siberia — it looks dramatic, but from what I can see, the car should be okay. It's a big car, though — how on earth are we going to get the thing out?

The film crew has a four-wheel drive Toyota Hi-ace van — hardly a Kenworth wrecker, but the only thing around that might stand a chance of hauling the old Spyker from its premature grave. With a tow rope we hook the Hi-ace up to the car and every spare pair of hands is placed behind the Spyker. The Hi-ace rolls forward to take up the slack in the rope. With everyone blowing a foo-foo valve from the strain, the Spyker begins to shift, the running boards ploughing the soft black soil. It's out. And it's okay. I can't believe how easy it was to get the car out; Stijnus can't believe it either. Mind you, it was a lot easier getting it in.

Mick: Our concrete road 'shortcut' costs us hours; we'd have made far better time taking the main road, but the back way was more interesting.

We cross the Kama River on a ferry that loads from the side, making for a long and fiddly boarding process complicated by our pair of trailers. Somehow the ferry master gets us all on and half an hour later we are on the other side at Ochansk. We are so far behind schedule that we elect to camp here tonight and find a serene camp site on the Ocher River just up from its junction with the mighty Kama. We look out from a high bank across flat water that flows gently past perfectly green pastures and stands of pine and birch. It is the most beautiful camp since Mongolia.

Many of us have a swim in the cool water, feeling so much cleaner for it. We have the usual visits from locals, all of them friendly and few of them bombed on vodka. A group of youngsters plays guitar and sings nearby for a while and we watch the long, long sunset change the water from blue to purple to red before the light fades after midnight.

Chris and I go for a walk before hitting the sack and get talking to three Russians. We think they offer us a lift back to camp but instead they drive us to their place for a *banya* ... where we stay until 4 a.m. They drop us back at the river and we manage an hour's sleep before the Expedition stirs again.

DAY 32

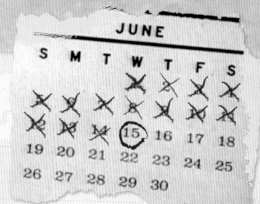

JUNE

S	M	T	W	T	F	S
X	X	X	X	X	X	X
X	X	X	X	X	X	X
X	X	X	(15)	16	17	18
19	20	21	22	23	24	25
26	27	28	29	30		

Ochansk to Syusi

Warren: Journalist Luigi Barzini was quite specific in his 1908 book *Peking to Paris* about how you locate Nikolai Petrovitch, the shovel-bearded blacksmith who made a wheel for the Itala. Nikolai had a local reputation for creating miracles with timber and wood and, particularly, in constructing wheels for *telegas*, little carts with iron rims on wooden wheels. He was recommended by an old man in the village of Dobrovo.

Barzini recounts the directions to Petrovitch's workshop: 'Where does this man live?' asked Prince Borghese. 'Six versts away. You go this way. You find a little white house. To the left of the house there is a slope down and then a little bridge. You go over the bridge and you are at his door. You can't make a mistake.' Okay, here we are on the edge of the village of Dobrovo; if we head back east for about 6 kilometres, which is near enough to the old Russian verst measurement, we'll see if we find a little white house.

The drive back through the open countryside does land us fair and square in a cluster of three or four ancient timber cottages. None of the houses appears white, but, then again, a lot can happen to clapped-out old dwellings in rural Russia over 100 years. We look at a little house that could have been white once — it should have a path down the side. I swing the Itala through the grass, onto a path running neatly alongside the house. With a copy of Barzini's book in his lap, Lang instructs: 'Okay ... now, there should be a river ...' 'There's a river ahead,' I respond, the Itala bouncing down the path. Lang continues: 'And it says here that there should be some houses over the other side ...'

Suddenly rooftops come into view. 'There are houses here!' I can't believe it. 'And a footbridge over the river to get to the houses,' says Lang. Before us is a beautiful scene of a fast-flowing 40-metre-wide river spanned by a simple timber footbridge. This is it — this is where Borghese found Nikolai Petrovich to help repair one of the Itala's wheels.

Lang walks up to the edge of the footbridge. When I say bridge, it is really a ricketty series of long single planks as wide as your foot connected to posts driven into the river bed. He stretches out his arms like a Barnum & Bailey tightrope walker and places his foot on the first plank. The whole plank bows under his weight, nearly disappearing beneath the water. Lang swings his other foot in front and begins the slow and delicate process of crossing the river, raising his arms up and down, balancing with precision until his foot eventually touches the other side.

My turn. I place my weight on the plank. Not only does the plank bend under my weight, it swings violently from side to side only millimetres from the water, which is travelling under my feet at what seems like 500 km/h. 'Struth, Lang, I'm going to fall in here,' I say to him, noticing the entire bridge actually swaying due to my attempt to cross it.

'Don't look down,' says Lang. Easy to say when you've already crossed the river and you're standing on the other side waiting for your mate to fall in the water.

Lang is on the other side with his arms folded, impatient that I'm wasting time. The river is belting along under me. 'I'm going in ... I'm ...' I can feel myself falling forward, an overcorrection — I'm in the river. I hang on to one of the bridge posts, my legs floating downstream. I come up squirting water, and somehow manage to hoick one of my waterlogged boots back over the plank. I climb back onto the bridge. Lang rolls his eyes and we walk up to the timber house, knocking on the door.

An old dog built like a beer keg standing on toothpicks barks with a raspy baritone at my watery strides. A woman in her 40s cautiously answers the door — she is confronted by Lang, with a beard in the style of King George V, and me, some near-drowned bloke in water-filled knee-high boots and wringing wet jodhpurs. We have a copy of Barzini's book to show her the photograph of Borghese with Nikolai Petrovitch holding the newly repaired wheel for the Itala,

LEFT: A GORGEOUS IMAGE OF THE YELLOW DE DION LEAVING THE RIVER CAMP FOR ANOTHER DAY ON THE ROAD.

BELOW: MICK TUCKS INTO A LOCAL DELICACY — TWO TYPES OF CAVIAR!

ABOVE: A LOCAL MAN APPEARS TO BE STANDING GUARD BY THE ITALA AS THE DRIVERS INSPECT THE WRECKED CHURCH.

RIGHT: THE ITALA PARKED BESIDE SOME EXPEDITION TENTS — WARREN, AT LEAST, WOULD COME TO PREFER CAMPING TO HOTEL ROOMS.

and through every method of communication — mime, drawings, diagrams in the mud — try to find out whether she knows anything of him. Eventually she comes to understand what we're talking about, but sadly she has only lived in the old house for 15 years. But in that time, she tells us, whenever they have dug the soil around the house, they have invariably found old tools, hammers, nails, rusting horseshoes and pieces of iron.

In the corner of the yard, Lang spies a pile of rusting, ancient iron scrap. 'Look at this,' he says, wrenching at an old circular band of iron. 'This is the metal tyre that goes around the wheels of a *telega* — and look, it's been beaten closed by a blacksmith — not welded.'

We smile in astonishment. This is the place.

Later on we pull into a remote village to buy some food for dinner. The gist is to buy enough grub for everyone back at the camp site. There are three shops in the village, the first of which has very little other than some tinned food and a few bottles of vodka and beer on the shelves. The second has even less and so does the third. I figure that between the three I could probably put together enough for a meal for everyone with a bit of salami and some bread ... but the girl in the shop refuses to sell me the bread. It is genuinely like rock — it is days old. Okay, the salami — I'll have one of those ...

Sergei the interpreter takes me aside, looking quite embarrassed. 'Don't buy too much,' he whispers. 'There'll be nothing left for the villagers to eat. They'll starve.' This is a Russia I have not seen until now.

Mick: Today we are travelling completely on secondary roads, avoiding the heavy traffic of the highways. The area is like a graveyard of derelict churches, and the Brodies stop at one to find out more. This one was built in the 1800s and had a congregation measured in thousands in its heyday in the early twentieth century. In 1937 Stalin ended it all, turning the church into a storage yard for tractors, partly gutting it in the process. All its gold was looted, of course. A local man remembers that his school desk was made from one of the icons that had once decorated the church's walls.

What's left of the building is disappearing as locals take the bricks to build their own houses.

A group of nurses from the area's sanatorium invite the Brodies to lunch afterwards, laying on a feast for them and talking about the sanatorium's history. During World War II it housed children rescued from the murderous siege of Leningrad; afterwards it was converted into a mental institution. It now has 200 inmates and 100 staff.

The nurses look disapprovingly at Keith's dirt- and oil-encrusted clothing (and, apparently, approvingly at Keith) and say he'll probably scrub up pretty well in a clean outfit. They insist that they should take his clothes away and wash them — he can wear a hospital gown while he is waiting — but Keith still has a long way to drive and can't wait. He and Louise offer their thanks and hit the road again.

Warren and Lang take the Itala on their detour in search of Nikolai Petrovich's old workshop while the rest of us carry on, trying to make up ground after yesterday's early stop. John went on further last night and is now well ahead. Late in the day he discovers that the tar ends suddenly, replaced by a slushy road made slick by fresh rains. The De Dion slides wildly and at one point spins 180 degrees. It takes John over two hours to drive the 40 kilometre length of road. Eventually he reaches the end, and then discovers that the rest of the group is making camp way back at the other end of this arduous drive. He opts to go all the way on to Kazan and have a rest day there while we catch up.

Chris gets back into the Contal's saddle for the first time in way too long. His back isn't perfect but he has a huge grin on his face the whole way, despite copping some showers. Stijnus spends most of the day travelling with the Contal and we all team up with Grace, the scout van — and I wimp out by jumping in there and catching up on sleep.

We camp tonight near Syusi, a small village just off the road. For the first time since we started camping in Russia we have almost no visitors, making our own fun by sitting around telling childish jokes and eating bread and cheese, drinking wine and beer and relaxing. Perfect.

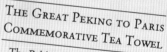

1907

THE GREAT PEKING TO PARIS COMMEMORATIVE TEA TOWEL

The Peking to Paris Raid of 1907 was one of the first sponsored motorsport events in the world. Companies such as Shell, Dunlop, Pirelli, Michelin, Bosch and Louis Vuitton jumped on the sponsorship bandwagon for the very first time, their brands plastered on postcards, commemorative crockery — whatever they could attach their names to. All sorts of Peking to Paris memorabilia surfaced: inscribed pewter ashtrays, silver cigarette holders, etched glassware, cushions ... all to immortalise a great motoring event. Prince Borghese's winning Itala became such an institution in Italy that model kits and scale replicas of the car were being manufactured into the 1980s.

JUNE

S	M	T	W	T	F	S
			X	X	X	X
X	X	X	X	X	X	X
X	X	X	X	(16)	17	18
19	20	21	22	23	24	25
26	27	28	29	30		

DAY 33

Syusi to Kazan

Mick: Departure time isn't until 8 o'clock this morning — a real sleep-in after our efforts over the past month or so. Most of us had an early night, too, and are up well before we had to be, but a few keep snoring till they have to be gently nudged into life with a size 10 boot. Still, it beats the buzz of an alarm clock, particularly when you wake to the glorious morning we see today. There isn't a cloud in the sky.

Keith services his De Dion up on the main road, after deciding last night that crawling around under the little battler is not much fun when the grass is damp and the ground soggy. John is already in Kazan, so the rest of us pack away our dew-soaked tents and motor onto the main road again. We run on good roads for a while before the fun starts.

At first, when we cross into the territory of a poorer shire, the road is just the usual rough and rutted ribbon of Russian torment. John warned us last night that the tar ends 'suddenly', and he wasn't wrong. Over a crest the blacktop falls away into a nightmare of unmaintained dirt road. Our saving grace is that it isn't wet; John must have copped it so much worse yesterday.

The Spyker bends its soft rims several times, the Contal crawls at its slowest pace in many days and Keith's De Dion plods along without any major damage. However the Itala breaks its right-side rear main suspension spring, right up at the front mounting point. Yes, the same mount that broke a few days ago. Closer inspection reveals that the spring-securing bolt was done up way too tightly, preventing the spring from pivoting in the right place, so of course it broke.

And of course the Russians can fix it ... or not. For the first time, we encounter Russians who refuse to help. The workshop Warren and Lang stop at is closing in 15 minutes and the guys won't wait around. Meanwhile, Warren comes up with an ingenious temporary fix. All they have to do is rig the tyre levers into the spring set-up to act as supports, and away they'll go. Who knows how far they'll get? Either way, it's worth a shot. The Itala eventually makes it all the way to Kazan under its own steam — an admirable effort.

Keith and Louise have a great day, driving until they meet the Itala crew hard at work on their emergency repairs. The two cars, with Anthony in the sweep truck, have a long wait at the ferry crossing for Malmish, so they settle in for a picnic lunch on the river banks.

Further on the road takes us into Tatarstan, a much richer area with its own government and a much wealthier Muslim community. The buildings are neater, the colours brighter and the people obviously that little bit prouder. Small, sharp-spired mosques are in all the villages. Best of all, from our point of view, the road is a revelation: smooth, well maintained and a real joy to travel on. We knock over the final 100 kilometres to Kazan in excellent time, the big Spyker flying at 90 km/h. That might not sound fast to most people, but in our cars, after the roads we've experienced, that kind of speed seems incredible.

We call a rest day in Kazan for Friday. Only John, who's had his day off already, motors on. The rest of get stuck into servicing, washing and repairing — our usual routine of 'rest'.

Warren: The road through the forest is one of the better ones we've seen. Lang is really putting the Itala through its paces this morning — we're trying to reach the ferry to cross the Vyatka River for Malmish before 9 o'clock and he's not wasting any time. We overtake Keith and Louise, who are slogging away on a long hill in the little yellow De Dion. Rugged up, they wave as we shoot past. We're now only 10 kilometres from the ferry and its 8.40 — we should just make it.

LEFT: THE YELLOW DE DION FREQUENTLY NEEDS A PUSH – HERE LANG AND WARREN GIVE IT A SHOVE TOWARDS THE FERRY TO MALMISH.

BELOW: (L TO R) WARREN, ABC DOCUMENTARY PRODUCER PETER GEORGE AND THE BRODIES REST WHILE THE CARS ARE ON THE FERRY.

ABOVE: THE UNSUNG HERO OF THE EXPEDITION – ANTHONY'S SWEEP VEHICLE AND TRAILER, LEAVING THE FERRY.

RIGHT: IN BOB'S WORDS, 'LANG KIDBY REVERSING ONTO THE FERRY WHILE WARREN BROWN WATCHES AND WINCES IN THE BLOWING DUST.'

Suddenly there's a loud bang and a violent knock from the rear of the car — what now? Lang pulls the Itala up and we circle the car to find out what's happened. This looks catastrophic — the top leaf of the rear right-hand spring has snapped in two, the whole busted spring freely pointing skyward. I don't think we'll be on the 9 o'clock ferry.

We can do one of two things: put the Itala on our support trailer or jerry-rig some makeshift repair and keep going. Searching through whatever bits and pieces we have, it looks like our two spring steel tyre levers could be pressed into service to brace the spring. By loosening the spring U-bolt, the tyre levers could slide underneath, hook under the spring bolt at the other end and brace the spring. Lang gives it a go, the tyre levers fitting perfectly, using a few steel and brass drifts as extra bracing and then tightly wrapping the whole splint in fencing wire. Well, it looks like it should work, and if it can hold until we find a replacement spring, we're laughing.

The wait at the ferry crossing is frustrating — there is a time-zone change from one side of the river to the other, and even though the ferry is due to depart at midday, what with lunch for the ferry's crew in whichever time zone they desire — which probably means both — the ferry doesn't shuffle across the river to pick us up until about 4 p.m.

Once on the other side we search the town of Malmish for someone to help repair the spring and discover a blacksmith's workshop, the forge in full swing, sparks showering as the blacksmiths hammer flat lengths of glowing cherry-red steel. They all down tools to have a look at the Itala and its broken spring, but it's late in the afternoon and they can't start work on it until tomorrow. One of the locals produces a second-hand truck spring, which, amazingly enough, resembles the Itala's. If we can press on to the Tartar city of Kazan we might be able to find a spring-maker or, at a pinch, use the truck spring.

1907

KAZAN

Godard caught the De Dions at Kazan after an epic drive from the point at which the Spyker's magnetos had failed. In 14 days he covered about 5500 km, driving till his hands were raw. The De Dions had taken 32 days, and Borghese had taken 21 days. In one 29-hour run Godard covered a calculated distance of 865 km, a record that couldn't be confirmed, as the distance couldn't be accurately measured. He often drove through the night with no lights. He lost almost a day to a broken spring, was briefly lumped with a motherless baby, and diplomatically brushed off a huge, alcoholic countess. Meanwhile, he was found guilty in a Paris court of fraud after his dubious money-raising efforts.

Kazan

Warren: Kazan, the capital of Tatarstan, is one of the most extraordinarily beautiful cities in the world. Founded in 1005, it was ravaged by Ivan the Terrible, who forced the ruling Khan to become Christian, and ever since the region has survived as a curious mix of Muslim and Christian cultures.

These days Kazan is undergoing a major restoration program and within a few years it will be a showpiece for Russia. This modern and sophisticated city possesses a magnificent Kremlin that is an architectural and historical marvel. But for Lang and me, our stay in Kazan will be spent trying to sort out the Itala's broken spring. Yesterday's makeshift repair worked amazingly well and still shows no sign of shifting. In an emergency situation, the repair would probably last until Paris, but we still have an enormous distance to cover and the car needs to be roadworthy at all times.

We've been given the use of a large empty garage in the compound of the local gas company, where we jack the car up, remove the spring and dismantle it. The idea of finding someone to make us a spring is more or less thrown out the window as the local guys at the gas company shake their heads — no spring makers in Kazan. We have to use the second-hand truck spring given to us in Malmish and somehow have it altered to fit the car. It never fails in Russia — someone at the gas company knows someone's wife who is friends with the uncle of someone who knows somebody who works in the local aircraft factory. In Russia it's not who you know, it's how many people you know who know other people.

We give them what's left of the original spring and the second-hand truck spring and by mid-afternoon the spring returns ready to fit. They've done a pretty good job of resizing it but on closer inspection it's apparent that the centre hole isn't in the correct spot, which means the spring won't line up on the axle properly. Lang has smoke belching from his ears.

We approach the blokes at the gas company too see if they have any drills suitable for piercing spring steel. Three fellas continue three different conversations between themselves as to how the hole should be drilled. Eventually one arrives with a set of drills and begins winding one into the drill chuck. Hang on, these are masonry drills — they're meant for drilling cement, not steel. Even on the packet it says 'masonry drills', but since none of these three blokes can speak nor read English, no amount of protest can make them understand. We decide to let them go.

One of the three puts his weight behind the drill and squeezes the trigger, the whole drill skating off the spring and busting in half. Lang's looking into space, trying to keep his blood pressure somewhere below molten lava as the masonry drill exercise continues until the entire packet is broken. Unable to help, the three gas company experts apologise and retreat out the door, wishing us luck.

Since our cordless drill is now completely flat, Lang and I decide the only option is to hand drill a hole with the only metal drill bit we can find, a process whereby the spring is wedged hard vertically into a corner of the room, the drill bit clenched in the jaws of a pair of vice-grips and turned under full body weight, very slowly biting into the steel. This is last-ditch stuff. After an hour of taking turns holding the spring and turning the vice-grips, a hole is eventually drilled, the spring is fitted to the car and we're ready for the road tomorrow. I wouldn't have believed it if I hadn't seen it.

1907

CHARLES GODARD AND HIS BEARD

At the turn of the 20th century, a beard indicated wisdom and solid wealth. That's why when you see an old photograph of a company's board of directors, they're standing bolt upright disporting an impressive array of shovel beards which are intended to say 'Invest with us, we know how to handle your money because we have the biggest beards'. Interestingly, serial con man Charles Godard was the only 1907 Peking to Paris participant with a beard: a handy device when convincing all and sundry to give you some money.

JUNE

S	M	T	W	T	F	S
			✗	✗	✗	✗
✗	✗	✗	✗	✗	✗	✗
✗	✗	✗	✗	✗	✗	(18)
19	20	21	22	23	24	25
26	27	28	29	30		

DAY 35

Kazan to Makarevo

Mick: Zofar Kadeev and his sister Zulfia — who were incredibly helpful yesterday with ensuring that the Itala's broken spring was successfully replaced before Zofar took some of us out of town for a barbecue and *banya* — join us again this morning to lead us out of Kazan. It will be impossible for us to repay the debt of gratitude we have towards so many Russians, and Zofar and Zulfia have proved that the Tartars can lift the bar even higher. We wave goodbye outside the city and follow the M7, the busiest highway we've experienced since China.

A truck accident has caused a massive back-up of oncoming traffic after the road bottlenecks from dual carriageway into a single lane. There are multiple minor prangs as a result and we dawdle past kilometre after kilometre of frustrated drivers. The Russians ignore lanes when this sort of thing happens and fill every available space with cars. The tar has two or three lines of cars stopped dead while another couple of lines choke the gravel verge. They try to steal the narrow strip of tar left for us while cars and even trucks roar up *our* gravel shoulder. The dust kicked up by the latter blocks visibility and we plunge into it, hoping against hope that there's not a car coming head-on at us. It's frightening and hilarious at the same time.

Later we're making good time on varied surfaces in constant traffic, but this kind of highway is no fun at all on the smaller, slower veteran cars. John, already a day ahead, decides to press on even further to Nizhni-Novgorod. For the rest of us, the plan is to drive to Liskovo, then cross the Volga on a ferry to Makarevo and make camp. Chris and I check the map and discover a much more attractive option: turn off 80 kilometres earlier at Vorotinets and take the ferry from Fokino over the Volga to Mikhailovskoy, then follow back roads to Makarevo.

It's a good choice. We sit on the bank of the Volga for two hours waiting for the ferry, kicking back and watching barges cruise up and down the mighty river. While on the ferry, Leonid Kaznin invites us to dinner at his house in nearby Raznezhe, where he feeds us a delicious ling soup and fresh vegetables and herbs from his garden. Leonid is the professor of philosophy at Nizhni-Novgorod's university. He's home in his family village for the weekend, although his wife, dean of mathematics at the uni, is studying in Moscow.

Meanwhile the rest of the Expedition crosses the river and lands beside Makarevo's incredible walled church. The crew camps almost under its walls with the town on the other side, but the immediate appearance of six very drunk Russians prompts them to pick up and move on down the river. They find a comfortable site and the evening proves very pleasant — apart from the greatest infestation of mosquitoes we've yet had the displeasure to endure.

Warren: Spyker-driving Stijnus Schotte is one of the truly eccentric characters of the Expedition. He's a big-framed bloke with a jolly, chubby face on which sits a pair of spectacles with lenses like glass paperweights. He has a booming voice that is incessantly firing off volleys of totally inappropriate sexist jokes, which over the past month have somehow made him kind of endearing. Sitting on the imposing Spyker, Stijnus is about as close as you can get to Toad of Toad Hall.

We have arrived at the edge of Russia's mighty Volga River and are waiting for a ferry to load the Expedition vehicles on to reach the other side. 'Would yoo beleeve, Mister Brown,' says Stijnus in his unmistakable Dutch accent, 'that I have found a perb up the road?' A perb? Oh — a pub! 'I think wee should go and infestigate,' he continues, 'down't yoo?' I climb onto the Spyker's running board and, with Lynne in the passenger's seat, Stijnus shuffles the big car along a sandy riverside track.

The car climbs onto a long stretch of sandy road and pulls up outside what for all intents and purposes is a Russian pub. For a nation with such a reputation of

LEFT: ANTHONY AT THE WHEEL OF THE YELLOW DE DION, GETTING A WAVE AS HE LEAVES KAZAN.

BELOW: ANTHONY AND KEITH STANDING ON A PARAPET OF THE MAKARIEV MONASTERY ON THE VOLGA RIVER.

ABOVE: 'MONK GEORGE' BLESSES THE ITALA AND SPYKER OUTSIDE THE MONASTERY.

RIGHT: THE STUFF OF LEGEND — STIJNUS WITH HIS SPYKER AND WARREN WITH HIS ITALA MAKE AN IMPRESSIVE SIGHT BY THE VOLGA; THE SIZE OF THEIR ACHIEVEMENT ON THIS EXPEDITION ALMOST DWARFS THAT OF THE BEAUTIFUL MONASTERY IN THE BACKGROUND. IN 1907, THERE WAS NO WAY THE SPYKER AND ITALA COULD HAVE BEEN PHOTOGRAPHED TOGETHER HERE — BORGHESE WAS ALREADY RACING AHEAD TO VICTORY.

putting away ocean-tanker-loads of vodka, there isn't a country town pub tradition like there is back home — which might not be a bad thing. In Australia, every outback town has at least three pubs: The Railway Hotel, The Royal and The Exchange. In Russia's outback, villages only have grimy truck-stop cafés where you can get a particularly ordinary grey-coloured feed and buy cans of local beer and bottles of vodka off the shelf. But, frankly, for unwinding after a long day, Russia's roadside cafés are about as enticing as lunch in the post office.

So it comes as bit of a surprise to find what is more or less a pub here by the Volga. It has a few tables inside, a bar, and beer, for once in a fridge. Cold beer in Russia just doesn't happen. We have become used to drinking soft drinks and beer here at what uncomfortably seems to be body temperature. Beer is only served warm to very warm during the summer months. Why on earth don't they drink it chilled, like the coffee they serve me? So Lynne, Stijnus and I get hold of the first cold beers we've held since … since … some time ago anyway. It's marvellous to have a small break like this — the days behind the wheel have been so gruelling, any opportunity to take our minds off potholes and magnetos is particularly welcome.

The vehicles are loaded on the ferry for the journey across the Volga. It's late afternoon and the old boat putters through a thick maze of trees clumped together in the water, obstructing any vision of the other side. The river is calm and the only sound is that of the ferry's diesel engines echoing among the greenery. The ferry soon breaks free of the tree line and the enormity of the Volga's width hits us like a road train. But it's the vision of what our tiny ferry is heading to that leaves everyone speechless.

Before us is a blindingly white fairytale castle not even Walt Disney could hope to whack his name onto for sheer magic — its gilded, onion-shaped domes shine spectacularly in the low sunlight. It's the Makariev monastery, founded in 1435, put out of business during Soviet times and re-kick-started by a small group of nuns in 1991 whose aim is to restore the monastery to its former glory.

We unload the cars and roll them up the ramp alongside the monastery's thick, whitewashed walls. This is one of Russia's hidden treasures — in a country locked up to the West for the best part of the twentieth century, who knows what's tucked away in its remote regions? We set up camp on the edge of the Volga only a few hundred metres downstream from the monastery and build an impressive campfire. The evening is spent under a full, pale moon watching enormous barges toing and froing along the river.

DAY 36

Makarevo to Nizhni-Novgorod

Mick: Sometimes it's good to just drive without adventures or misadventures, and so it is today. The run to Nizhni-Novgorod is a short one — less than 200 kilometres — so most of us take it easy. John is aiming for Vladimir, where he'll pause till we catch up for the run into Moscow.

All of us heading for Nizhni get lost, though. The Contal, yellow De Dion and Spyker miss a turn and drive for half an hour in completely the wrong direction before realising our error and turning around. Lang loses his way in Nizhni but, as we find soon afterwards, that's not hard with the basic city maps and vague directions we've got, but by mid-afternoon we're all settled into our hotel overlooking the Volga by Lenin Square. All towns have a Lenin Square with a Lenin statue, this one being particularly large and impressive. Lenin is still everywhere in post-communist Russia but there are no signs left of the hated Stalin.

John is pulled over by police as he drives to Vladimir, but it's no ordinary patrol this time. A convoy escorting closed vans — carrying criminals or money or who knows what — flies past at great speed, screeches to a halt and disperses a bunch of armed men. While some flag down the De Dion, others are posted at each corner of each van as guards, their eyes alert and guns at the ready. Any hint of menace is quickly dismissed, though, as the cops smile and pose for photos and even clown around with their weapons.

Left: Locals on the hydrofoil to Nizhni-Novgorod.

Below: (L to R) Warren, Louise, Peter George and Rob on the ferry.

Above: Warren and Rob give Bob a smile.

Right: Anthony gives a local directions on how to play pool.

JUNE

S	M	T	W	T	F	S
				✗	✗	✗
✗	✗	✗	✗	✗	✗	✗
✗	✗	✗	15	✗	✗	✗
✗	(20)	21	22	23	24	25
26	27	28	29	30		

DAY 37

*Nizhni-Novgorod
to Vladimir*

Warren: For me, the day just isn't satisfying enough unless I'm completely saturated at some stage or other. The drive to the town of Vladimir has been wetter than a drive to Atlantis — Lang and I are absolutely soaked. I'm convinced we're all now totally impervious to evil weather — bring it on, I say. I'm immune to passing Volgas packed with faces pressed against the windows, laughing at the two idiots sitting out there in the rain. Motoring for me now translates to being bashed about by the wind, having bugs suicide themselves on my goggles and sitting for hours on end in soggy, cold underpants. For water to actually reach my underpants is harder than Chinese algebra, but somehow it manages to work its way through so that I'm uncomfortable for the entire day.

For wet weather in the Itala, I have worked out the standard ensemble. If you start with me standing in the bollocky, first up it's very thick socks and a pair of undies. Then my shirt and, of course, tie; a pair of jodhpurs and my knee-length boots. Yes, yes — I know: I'm never going to be George Clooney if I wear jodhpurs, but they are the most comfortable thing imaginable for driving.

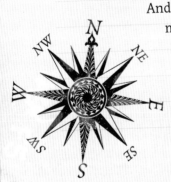

And the boots — never once have I had cold feet, even crossing the mountains in a snowstorm in Mongolia; the knee-high boots keep the icy wind out completely. I then have a three-quarter-length cotton jacket in the very attractive safari-suit style; a knee-length leather coat; and, over the whole lot, an oilskin. On my head I have a leather flying helmet and split-screen goggles and on my hands a pair of leather gauntlets.

Left: Chris Boyle gears up before boarding the Contal after a lunch stop; Mick, in the background, is already aboard.

Below: Keith Brodie makes a phone call in front of the ABC crew.

Above: Spyker and Contal prepare to drive out into the wild wet weather.

Right: A *shazlik* barbecue with the Spyker and Contal in the background.

1907

Nizhni-Novgorod

It seems incredible, but after the few kilometres of metalled road leading into Kazan, the De Dions and Spyker made just 40 km on the first day's drive to Nizhni-Novgorod. The road was so deplorable that they declared it without doubt the worst of the entire journey. Maps indicated a major road; reality produced nothing but mud, because rain had set in again. They were lucky to find a monastery for shelter that night, for they were nowhere near a town of any kind. Borghese passed effortlessly in good weather, but the others were soaked and frozen, and it took them 4 days to reach Nizhni-Novgorod.

All of this weighs a metric tonne, and when it's sopping wet, it's about fifty times that weight. The thing is, when it's raining, water doesn't just come from the sky — it's blasted horizontally into you, it's ricocheted off the road, it's dumped on you from passing trucks. Water sprays up from the wheels and blasts between the floorboards, permeating any weakness there may be in your entire clothing plan.

But the thing I look forward to most at night is to take all this waterlogged gear off knowing that it'll still be wringing wet when I put it all back on in the morning and I can go and sit in the Itala and do it all again. In my next life, I'm going to come back as a fish. You can have the same fun without all the clothing.

Mick: Today it's grey and wet. It's the first time on the road that we cop rain all day and soon we're all soaked. The oilskins haven't been re-proofed and don't do the job now, and no onc has any wax! We've got some coming from Australia but that won't help today. We put our heads down and drive, reaching Vladimir without incident.

John and his crew have a more interesting time detouring north to Suzdal, claimed to be Russia's most beautiful city. It is unspoilt by modern touches, and retains more than its fair share of stunning historical churches and buildings.

DAY 38

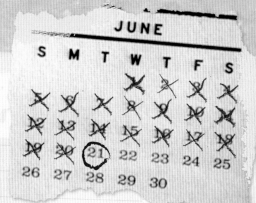

Vladimir to Moscow

Mick: Moscow! Today we reach the beginning of the end of our journey. The hardest work is behind us, the bulk of the distance has rolled under our old wheels and we're now properly entering the familiar Western world we left over a month ago. We're not necessarily relieved about it, because we've had so much fun and don't want it to end ... or even to diminish. Europe isn't quite home to our mainly Australian group but it's familiar enough that we Expeditioners are worried about losing our sense of adventure.

That sense is certainly hiding during the drive into Moscow. Like yesterday, the clouds drizzle on us almost all day. Again we are drenched and today it is colder — down to about 10°C with wind chill on top of it. Not fun.

Our planned convoy into Moscow fails when misguided messages imply that the most distant cars are going to arrive an hour or more late at the rendezvous point. No matter. We cruise in through slow traffic — Moscow is a congested city with seven million cars vying for position — and are astonished at the city's beauty, its many landmarks, its colours and its river. Anyone brought up on Cold War propaganda wouldn't believe that this is the same place as portrayed under communist rule.

Mind you, much of the city — like other parts of Russia — has been rebuilt or refurbished. It now has regained the glory that Borghese, Cormier, Godard and others must have admired so much in 1907.

We tour Moscow but are dismayed to discover we've arrived on the 64th anniversary of Russia's invasion by Germany. Red Square and the Kremlin are closed off for a solemn ceremony. We don't get in till late afternoon but by then the sunlight on the painted buildings, on the golden decorations crowning the spires and bathing the thousands of people walking through gives the whole scene a more magical quality.

1907

Moscow

The Italians were rapt as the Itala sped along a real road. Because they'd judged by past experience, they'd seriously underestimated the distance they would cover, and so arrived hours early for their reception in Moscow. Even so, crowds of cars and motorcycles met them outside the city. This was truly Europe — home. Even Borghese showed 'a vague shadow of emotion'. They spent 4 days here, feasting, resting and enjoying their success to date. The De Dions arrived 19 days later to an even bigger welcome, partly because the De Dion Bouton company turned up in force with both spin doctors and mechanics. The worst was behind the Raiders, and it was all downhill to Paris from here.

Warren: I've had enough rain now. Please stop. We're heading toward the outskirts of Moscow and, once again, Lang and I are sitting in the Itala suffering another deluge. The traffic is clearly getting thicker and the roads are getting wider when suddenly we see the familiar shape of John Matheson's blue De Dion Bouton ahead of us. Andrew Snelling's at the wheel and he waves enthusiastically as we overtake him. John and Andrew had pressed on a few days before to keep in front of the Expedition — making sure the little 2-cylinder isn't lagging behind has been a priority.

Only a few kilometres on we pull up under the sign announcing that we are entering Moscow and wait for the blue De Dion to arrive. A waterlogged Andrew and John leap out, glad to see some familiar faces.

The plan was for all the cars to marshal at the Moscow sign to travel into the city together, but the crook weather and the fact that the Expedition has been stretched out over 100 kilometres means that standing around in the rain waiting for everyone to arrive doesn't have the same appeal as checking into our warm, dry hotel.

LEFT: LOUISE IN THE YELLOW DE DION FOR THE LAST TIME — SHE HAD TO LEAVE THE EXPEDITION IN MOSCOW — AS ANTHONY REVERSES THE TRAILER INTO THE AUSTRALIAN EMBASSY.

BELOW: THE EXPEDITION DROVE THROUGH MANY DAYS OF RUSSIAN RAIN — AND THIS IS ONE OF THEM. HERE THE SPYKER GETS LOST ON THE WAY TO MOSCOW.

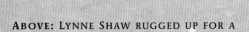

ABOVE: LYNNE SHAW RUGGED UP FOR A DAY IN THE CAR WITH STIJNUS.

RIGHT: OLD CARS IN AN OLD CITY IN MODERN TIMES — THE SPYKER AND CONTAL GET A GREEN LIGHT.

JUNE

S M T W T F S

26 27 28 ㉒ 23 24 25
29 30

DAY 39

Moscow

Warren: Moscow's old, grey Soviet days are well and truly over. Today it's an aggressive, fast-paced capitalist city by any Western standard. The Politburo's iron-fisted presence 15 years ago has been overtaken by a powerful, wealthy elite and there's no better way for them let the world know that Communism's dead and money is king than with the motorcar. Moscow's not a city of sad-faced Volga sedans and puddin'-faced Gaz four-wheel drives like those we'd seen in the east. Moscow's full of black, blacked-out-windowed monstrous-engined Benzs, black Audi A8s, black Range Rovers and black Hummers. These cars aren't subtle.

'Sir, what do you think of the Russian people, sir?' I am being interviewed by Vitaly N. Glazunov for 'Voice of Russia Radio', the third biggest international radio program in the world. Vitaly is a seasoned old smoothie, Russia's radio version of Walter Cronkite, a man approaching 70 with silvery hair and an even more silvery voice. 'Sir, Russia is a great friend of the Australian people, sir, and I would like to know what the Australian people think of Russia?'

Australians have always had a similar anxiety about what foreign nations perceive of their country. I don't know how many times I've witnessed B-grade foreign celebrities arriving in Australia, taking one step off a 747 and getting hit with the question, 'What do you think of Australia so far?' Russia in the twenty-first century is very keen to find out what the Western world thinks of it. As far as I'm concerned, I love the place. Russians and Australians have a sense of humour that is based on hardship — in the same way that Australian jokes more often than not have a 'Dad and Dave' bush element of rural deprivation, drought, remoteness and naivety, Russians relate to food shortages, miserable old *babushkas* and a bleak existence.

There is a great old joke about some poor, hapless bloke standing in a queue at a shop where the shelf is completely bare. He says to the old *babushka* behind the counter, 'Do you have any food?' She replies: 'Yes.' 'I'll have two kilos' worth, thanks,' he says. Be grateful for what you can get in Russia, is the razored message.

The Australian Embassy in Moscow has organised an official reception for us at the Ambassador's residence. Australian Ambassador Bob Tyson has turned over this astonishing, heritage-listed building for a dinner function attended by a who's who on the Moscow social scene, who have come to look at our cars. For me this is an extra-special event, as I meet Moscow's premier political cartoonist, Alexander Umiarov from *Pravda*, the famous newspaper founded by Lenin in 1912.

Despite neither of us being able to understand what the other is saying, we hit it off immediately. This is the amazing thing about cartooning — no words are needed to communicate. Alexander and I understand each other like we've been mates for 20 years. Alexander has arranged for me to meet *Pravda*'s Editor-in-Chief. For any editorial cartoonist, the chance to visit one of the world's most legendary, historic and mysterious newspapers is an opportunity inconceivable to refuse.

Mick: Our cars are parked at the Australian Ambassador's residence, where tonight we're fêted by dignitaries and guests from many different nations. We give dozens of joy rides in the blue De Dion and Contal, much to our new friends' delight, although we suspect we're wearing out our welcome with the Russian guards on the gate. Oh well …

Afterwards we hit the town to farewell Louise Brodie, who's been such a delight to travel with but who must return to Australia. Peter Brown is taking over the passenger seat in the De Dion and on his first night with us he proves he'll fit in easily.

Two full days off in Moscow give us the best rest we've had for the entire journey. We realise, too, that we need it. For all the fun and adventure, the Expedition has been hard work.

Left: Moscow's famous Red Square.

Below: The Expeditioners at the Australian Embassy residence in Moscow, with Ambassador Bob Tyson, who is at the wheel of the Brodies' De Dion. The two Mathesons, Mick and John, sit together in John's blue De Dion.

Above: It took five police to check Andrew's papers after they pulled him up for walking on the grass in Red Square.

Right: Louise and Keith with their daughter Claire, who met up with them in Moscow just before Louise left the Expedition.

DAY 40

Moscow

Warren: Today I meet Alexander Umiarov in the foyer of *Pravda*'s offices. We catch the lift to the office of the Editor-in-Chief, Vadim Gorshenin; Alexander knocks on the open door of a cavernous, timber-panelled room. At the far end, a solitary figure sits behind a massive desk, studiously shuffling layout sheets. Above him hangs an enormous framed photograph of Lenin reading an issue of *Pravda*. We are invited in and Gorshenin, a big man in an open-necked shirt, strides across the room and gives me a firm handshake, his face breaking into a smile. We sit down and soon a silver service of strong Russian coffee arrives.

Vadim explains to me through Sergei, our Russian interpreter, that *Pravda* is preparing a special edition for the next day's commemoration of the end of World War II. They will reprint the front page from 1945 — the very same sort of commemorative idea *The Daily Telegraph* would print back home. He proceeds to explain *Pravda*'s history, showing me a selection of trophies and statues, part of an enormous collection of treasures that were presented to the newspaper during the years of its Soviet monopoly. Still a die-hard communist mouthpiece, *Pravda* doesn't sit comfortably with modern democratic Russia. However, Vadim reckons that if a referendum were held, most Russians would opt for the old communist regime. I'm not so sure about that, but certainly there is a groundswell of older Russians who prefer the communist 'order' over the 'recklessness' of Russia today.

The burning issue for Vadim is Russia's intention to join the World Trade Organisation, a move he considers premature as so many Russians still suffer from food shortages. With a request no cartoonist could refuse, Vadim asks me if I am prepared to draw a cartoon he can publish in the newspaper. The idea of a cartoon of mine being published in *Pravda*, the world's most vilified newspaper, has tremendous appeal — of course I'll do it. In just the same way I would converse with my editor in Sydney, we have a mini editorial discussion about the newspaper's stance on the WTO and the ramifications for Russia.

That evening I sit in the American Bar and Grill in Moscow with my brushes and a bottle of India ink, drawing up a cartoon on the back of a paper placemat. There is a marvellous irony: here I am in Moscow, in a restaurant decked with more stars and stripes than the Superbowl, and I'm working out a cartoon for a communist newspaper about Russia and the World Trade Organisation.

The cartoon depicts a queue in a shop, the shelves completely empty except for a solitary framed certificate announcing that Russia is a member of the WTO. The sad-faced customer is looking hungrily at the certificate, asking the shop attendant, 'How does it taste?' It will be delivered to *Pravda*'s offices tomorrow, to be printed later this week. Hero of the Soviet Union — that's me.

This evening we are to take the five cars out for a tour of the heart of Moscow, around the Kremlin and Red Square. Travelling with me in the Itala is my new best mate, Alexander the editorial cartoonist. The cars are picked up from the Australian Ambassador's residence and are launched in convoy out into Moscow's traffic. We are greeted with cheers, waves and car horns blasting in approval. We drive alongside the red, crenellated walls of the Kremlin and up to St Basil's Cathedral, the cars up at the edge of Red Square and a crowd of school students on their way to their end-of-school formal seize the cars for a photo opportunity.

Stijnus has only one desire in Moscow: to park the Spyker outside the Metropole Hotel, exactly where Charles Godard parked his Spyker in 1907. Godard was photographed here and Stijnus is hell-bent on doing the same. As soon as he sees the Metropole, Stijnus swings the big car into the driveway and pulls up directly on the spot where Godard stopped. I have never seen him so happy; for Stijnus, this is a personal pilgrimage: he has brought his father's car, the great car from Holland, to the very place where the most famous Spyker driver of all, Charles Godard, once stood — the rogue, the charlatan, the brilliant motorist.

Left: Warren takes fellow cartoonist Alexander Umiarov for a spin in the Itala.

Below: A Cossack stands in front of the cars at St Basil's Cathedral in Red Square.

Above: A delighted Stijnus outside the Metropole Hotel with Warren.

Right: All five cars in front of St Basil's.

JUNE

S	M	T	W	T	F	S
			✗	✗	✗	✗
✗	✗	✗	✗	✗	✗	✗
✗	✗	✗	15	✗	✗	✗
✗	✗	✗	✗	✗	(24)	25
26	27	28	29	30		

DAY 41

From Moscow

Mick: A couple of days' rest does wonders for your energy levels but we can't wait to get back on the road today. The addiction of travel has bitten deeply and we have itchy feet as we fire up the cars for the run to St Petersburg. We've elected to take three fairly easy days for the 780 kilometre trip, but we're in for a surprise ...

We soon discover that there are two Russias: one to the east of Moscow, the other to the west. Here in the west the roads are far, far better — though still often far from perfect — and the entire region has a wealthier appearance, a smarter attitude and a fresher feel. The improved roads make a world of difference for us and many of us surprise ourselves with how quickly we can cover distance now. We weren't prepared for such a change.

We also receive word that if we can get to St Petersburg in two days (or at least by 11 a.m. on the third day) we can join a cruise with the Moscow Car Club, a group of old car enthusiasts who happen to be holding their own event while we're in town. We've already spoken to them about hosting a ball so we can live it up like Prince Borghese did in 1907, and it seems there's more fun to be had if we can get our act together.

And so for the first time the group splinters spontaneously. The blue De Dion crew wants to forge on as fast as possible and makes it to a hotel just beyond the night's designated camping spot. The Spyker and Contal are making such good time that they press on almost 100 kilometres further. The Itala and yellow De Dion, though, are happy to take their time and make camp as planned.

Left: The cars leaving Moscow.

Right: Lang plays a trick on Lynne Shaw, who was off shopping for dinner, by hoisting her tent out of harm's way. As Bob says, 'Safe from bears up there.'

Below: A Russian road sign in Cyrillic – a challenge for any English-speaking motorist

Warren: It's 6 a.m. What?! We were supposed to be up at 5:30 and out of here by six! Anthony and I have slept through the alarm and we're in strife. We leap up, into our boots, grab our bags and run for the hotel elevator. Last night Keith instructed me to be up at 5:30 — we have to be out of Moscow before the monstrous peak-hour traffic jam cranks up. Since Louise returned to Australia, the always enterprising Keith has been text-messaging Krysia, his personal assistant in Sydney, asking her to ring him with an early morning wake-up call.

Prince Borghese made a quick 2000 kilometre detour from Moscow to whiz up to St Petersburg, where he famously attended a ball. We're about to do the same. We've picked up the cars from the Ambassador's residence and are heading out of Moscow early. But it seems we've taken a wrong turn. 'Right,' says Lang. 'Do a U-turn here.' 'Here?' I ask in disbelief. 'But it's eighteen lanes wide.' Indeed, the main drag in Moscow has nine lanes each side — it's a serious piece of bitumen. 'Just do it — here.' So I wrench the wheel around to full lock, spearing the Itala across a mighty wave of oncoming traffic. It's not every day that Moscow's motorists are cut off by a 100-year-old Itala — twice a century, at last count.

The rest of the Expedition follows, the mighty Spyker, the Contal and the De Dions cutting a swathe across the centre of Moscow. But we're now on the right track — farewell, Moscow.

And now a side note about Russia and mosquitoes. When I think of mosquitoes, for some reason I think of tropical climes, steaming jungles, swamps, anacondas, tse-tse flies — Dr Livingstone, I presume. I don't automatically think of Russian forests, where there are so many mosquitoes in the air, they need air traffic control for them to land. Our camp site for tonight is situated in a thick fug of these buzzing, insectivourous vampires. The real problem with these nasty things is that they can bite through your clothing — shirts, pants socks and jackets are completely useless. And big! The mosquitoes here are of such a size that we've had to anchor Keith Brodie's De Dion to the ground in case one of them carries the car off. I've been bitten so many times that all the bites have joined together and have become an itchiness collective.

We are deep in a forest situated along the road between Moscow and St Petersburg. Andrew Snelling has been talking to a local who took him to a natural spring hidden in a culvert among the trees. Beside the spring, a drinking cup was placed on a post. The clear, clean spring offered the most beautiful water — a wonderful secret in the forest.

DAY 42-44

St Petersburg

Warren: Sergei, our guide and interpreter, stands before an ancient cathedral, little different to so many ancient churches and cathedrals we've seen in Russia. 'This cathedral,' he says, 'is the heart of Russia.' Sergei has never visited the river city of Novgorod before and is clearly moved by the experience of standing before Russia's oldest church, the cathedral of St Sophia. Completed in 1052, the cathedral of St Sophia has survived a thousand years of ransacking by the best, including Ivan the Terrible and the Nazis. Novgorod was the first permanent settlement of the Varangian Norsemen, who really kick-started Russia as we know it from here. This beautiful city possesses a magnificent Kremlin, in the grounds of which we all sit in the long twilight, eating dinner, drinking Russian mead.

The next day we head for St Petersburg. It does seem peculiar that Prince Borghese would make such a big detour from Moscow to St Petersburg, ostensibly to attend a ball. It was completely out of character for a man who was renowned for his discipline in planning and his steely resolve to accomplish the mission at all costs. Was there really another motive for Borghese to make this detour after slogging it out across Siberia and the Urals?

The road connecting Moscow to St Petersburg is by far the best we've seen in Russia — it's dead straight and in impeccable condition. Lang has a theory that Borghese's long drive north was part of his plan to avoid the appalling muddy roads that continued southwest into Poland. The further northwest he travelled, the more able he was to link up with the excellent German roads in Prussia. Believe me, anything to get off Russian roads makes sense.

St Petersburg is the showpiece of Russia. On a warm summer day the city sparkles, its magnificent architecture, boats gliding along the canals, exquisite restaurants — it's a city that rivals Paris for sheer beauty and wonder. There is so much to take in that our brief stay here will not do it justice.

This evening we are attending a function organised by the Moscow Car Club, which has transported several cars to St Petersburg. The function is to be held at the Konstantinovsky Palace, a magnificent building restored as part of the city's tricentennial celebrations in 2003. For us, it's a time to spruce up a bit — John, Mick and Andrew decked out in dinner suits; for me, it's my first public appearance in the hessian suit I bought in Mongolia. I knew it would come in handy somewhere on this trip.

Mick: Today we continue our separate ways. After a 5 a.m. departure, John makes St Petersburg by late afternoon. The Spyker and Contal have a lazier run and lob into town just in time for a 5 p.m. press conference at the very glamorous Astoria Hotel, where John and his team join us. The sudden entrance of a bunch of oil-stained, road-grimed, unkempt travellers clearly offends the sensibilities of many guests but the staff handle us well, patiently indulging us as we sit down to afternoon tea with their best china. Battered Akubras and oilskins never looked so out of place.

Meanwhile the Itala, yellow De Dion and back-up crew make their way closer to town and, with an early start next morning, arrive at the docks in time for the cruise on Sunday morning. Then things fall apart: we're guests at President Putin's palace but he's just rearranged his plans, which crashes our plans. The cruise is cancelled and half our day is wasted.

We recover what we can of the day by exploring some of St Petersburg, and continue our newfound fascination with the place on Monday. It's the most beautiful city we've seen in our travels and we quickly understand why the single-minded Borghese would have made such a massive detour to go there, even for a single night. We have several days and it's still not enough.

LEFT: WARREN AND LANG IN THE
FRONT WITH ANTHONY AND ROB
IN THE BACK OF THE ITALA,
EN ROUTE TO THE BALL IN
ST PETERSBURG. WARREN IS
WEARING THE HESSIAN SUIT
HE BOUGHT IN MONGOLIA.

BELOW: MICK TEAMS BLACK TIE
WITH HIS BUSHMAN'S HAT FOR
HIS CHAUFFEURED RIDE TO
THE BALL.

ABOVE: JOHN AND ANDREW
LOOKING SPIFFY IN THEIR DE DION
AS THEY MOTOR THROUGH
ST PETERSBURG TRAFFIC.

RIGHT: THE EXPEDITIONERS
LINE UP OUTSIDE THE
KONSTANTINOVSKY PALACE.

JUNE

S	M	T	W	T	F	S
				1	2	3
4	5	6	7	8	9	10
11	12	13	14	15	16	17
18	19	20	21	22	23	24
25	26	27	(28)	29	30	

DAY 45

St Petersburg to Pskov

Mick: Our second-last day in Russia dawns grey and damp but most of us cop little rain all day. For everyone but the Itala, the drive is a straightforward one, hindered only by a few sections of road that can only have been put there to remind us of what we went through in Siberia. Rough and gnarly, these give the cars some hard treatment at a time when the novelty of awful roads has long gone and we're looking forward to smooth driving.

The Itala is pulled over not long into its drive. Our Russian registration has expired and while we had our insurance renewed, we hadn't realised we'd failed to have the other half of the job done properly, and this means trouble. A quick bribe gets them out of trouble but in Pskov tonight we hit the panic buttons, charging around madly trying to sort out registration for all the cars before we hit the border tomorrow. Border crossings can be hard enough without being blatantly illegal when you arrive, so we must have the rego renewed.

Tonight we farewell Russia together. It's the first time we've had everyone in the one place at the one time for a meal since well before Moscow and we laugh as we remember some wild times and great places in the month since we came through Kyakhta. That feels so long ago. For all its frustrations we've loved Russia, and many of us make a pledge to come back.

LEFT: THE TOWN ENTRY SIGN FOR PSKOV, THE EXPEDITIONERS' LAST PIT STOP IN RUSSIA.

BELOW: ANTHONY PERCHES PRECARIOUSLY BEHIND DRIVER CHRIS ON THE CONTAL AS PETER BROWN, WHO REPLACED LOUISE BRODIE IN THE YELLOW DE DION, TAKES THE PASSENGER SEAT.

ABOVE: MICK AND KEITH LOOKING A BIT WATERLOGGED ON THE STREETS OF PSKOV.

RIGHT: A CEREMONIAL GIFT-GIVING OF RUSSIAN DOLLS WITH THE ABC CREW'S RUSSIAN DRIVERS ON THE EXPEDITION'S LAST NIGHT IN RUSSIA.

Warren: It's raining, of course. Another miserable day on even more miserable Russian roads. We are approaching an intersection on the outskirts of St Petersburg when we are flagged down by a policeman holding an AK47. Here we go again.

You can never tell with the police — most just want to have a look at the car, and they smile and wave you on. But not this policeman. He very slowly circles the car, shaking his head in disapproval. I'm doing the usual spiel, explaining what we're doing, when he barks an instruction at me. He wants to see all our paperwork. This is a pain in the neck, as it requires dismantling 500 layers of clothing. Whatever documents we hand him aren't enough. He wants the registration papers, our passports, our drivers' licences, our international drivers' licences, insurance paperwork.

'*Nyet, nyet, nyet.*' He scowls with a face of pure disgust. He repositions the AK47 slung from his shoulder and points to the police checkpoint office. We're being hauled in. He swaggers through the door and drops the machine gun on his desk. Two other policemen stare in surprise at the two soaking motorists wearing jodhpurs, long boots, flying helmets and goggles. He sits down and studiously pores over the paperwork, shaking his head. '*Nyet, nyet,*' he keeps saying.

Suddenly he finds a problem. On a customs document there is an incorrect date. Clearly agitated, one of the other policemen leaps to his feet and holds his wrists toward us as if he's handcuffed. 'Arrest! Arrest!' he shouts in my face. I'm standing next to the iron cage they have in the office ready for hard nosed criminals like Lang and me. The other two police officers leave the room.

'I see,' says Lang, clearly sorry for such an appalling offence. 'Is there a fine we need to pay? Do we need to pay a fine … in roubles … or dollars?' Lang produces his wallet. The police officer's eyes dart around the room at light speed. Without flinching, he whips open an empty drawer in his desk. Lang places a US note in the drawer and it's slammed shut faster than it opened.

The policeman waves us outside and we climb back into the Itala for a quick getaway. 'Get out of here,' says Lang as I put the car in gear. 'That was very well done,' I say. 'That was getting nasty.' 'It wasn't that well done,' snorts Lang. 'That was a US hundred — it was the only US note I had. He'd probably have taken a ten!'

DAY 46

JUNE

S	M	T	W	T	F	S
			~~1~~	~~2~~	~~3~~	~~4~~
~~5~~	~~6~~	~~7~~	~~8~~	~~9~~	~~10~~	~~11~~
~~12~~	~~13~~	~~14~~	~~15~~	~~16~~	~~17~~	~~18~~
~~19~~	~~20~~	~~21~~	~~22~~	~~23~~	~~24~~	~~25~~
~~26~~	~~27~~	~~28~~	(29)	30		

Pskov to Rezekne

Mick: The registration hassles cost us a few hours in the morning and we don't get properly started at the border until around midday. First one then another of us comes through into Latvia and we roll towards Rezekne for the night. We're warned by the Englishmen who've come to take on the driving role for ABC TV's vehicles that the roads here are dreadful and the trucks will run us into the bushes. Within minutes of setting off, though, we have to laugh — these roads are absolutely brilliant after Russia's and the trucks behave like obedient students filing into class. We doubt that anyone will ever really understand us when we try to describe what we encountered in Siberia.

Latvia is a kind of Russo-Europe. It used to be part of the Soviet Union but has recently signed up for the European Union and is remarkably better off for it. The country is cleaner, wealthier and better organised than Russia. Rezekne is not a large town but exudes affluence compared to anything of similar size we've seen in Russia.

Yet the charm hasn't gone, either. The elegant wooden architecture we so admired right through Russia is everywhere here, too. We drive past freshly cut fields of grass with haystacks piled high. Vegetable gardens thrive, even in the small, quaint villages. There are almost no ugly factories spoiling the environment and the hideous Soviet-era blocks of units are often abandoned, waiting to be removed.

LEFT: A Russian lady on her way into town, as the Expeditioners drive out.

BELOW: The last Russian police checkpoint on the highway.

ABOVE: Stijnus and Lynne aboard the Spyker as it leaves Pskov.

RIGHT: The blue De Dion gets a push across the Russian border into Latvia.

And there are still stands of remnant taiga — coniferous forest — throughout the landscape. In 1907 the taiga was an ongoing monotony for the Raiders but there's so little left that it's a pleasant reminder for us of quiet Siberia, diverting our attention briefly from the increasingly busy roads. We smile as we cruise through it.

Warren: We're at a truck stop just before the Latvian border. Mercifully, this is the last time I'll be eating a bliney and drinking 'coffee-mix'. When all the cars have assembled, we head for the border gates and pass through the Russian side before reaching the Latvian authorities. There's no problem with the veteran cars entering Latvia, but there is a problem with Grace and Anthony's Nissan truck because they're on Mongolian numberplates. The Mongolian plates use Russian Cyrillic lettering, which makes them invalid in the European Union.

Rob Spyker hops into the Itala with me and for the first time in five weeks we're outside of Russia. Waiting at the edge of the Latvian border is Peter Tombs, one of the new drivers of the ABC's vehicles; his son, Mark, and his son-in-law, Jacko. Peter is a fascinating bloke — he is what you might call a 'vehicle wrangler' for film and television and has been responsible for the vehicles in *Saving Private Ryan*, *Band of Brothers* and the James Bond film *Goldeneye*, just to name a few.

For some reason, as soon as we cross the border, the Itala starts running like a hairy goat again. It's running on two cylinders if it's lucky. We're heading for the village of Rezekne about 45 kilometres away but the car is not responding, and it certainly looks like a monster storm is brewing on the horizon. I pull the car over and remove the fuel bowl to see if we have a problem with crook fuel. It's flowing well — I reassemble it and we keep going. It's going to be another bloody electrical problem. Magneto, here we come.

The sky is getting darker by the minute and soon the first heavy raindrops start whacking my flying helmet. The rain increases until it's a total deluge, I can't see where I'm driving, and then ... a tidal wave is dumped on the Itala from a passing truck, drenching Rob and me completely. The Itala starts to shut down — that last waterlogging drowned the motor and the car doesn't want to play. We limp to the hotel.

JUNE

S	M	T	W	T	F	S

DAY 47

Rezekne to Kaunas

Warren: Within 4 kilometres of Rezekne, the Itala gives up the ghost completely. It was running rough until we pulled up at the side of the road, where the car dies. After some hours of the usual magneto ritual performed when the car inexplicably stops, it's hauled onto Anthony's trailer, retiring injured for the day.

We have now crossed the border into Lithuania, a beautiful, lush country dotted with spectacular lakes. Bev and Lynne have found a hotel for us all outside Kaunas, where the car park becomes Grand Central Station for car repairs. This evening while Lang, Anthony and Peter Tombs attempt to get the Itala going again, I'm busy manufacturing — well, forging — numberplates for Grace and Anthony's truck. I knew my cartooning skills would come in handy somewhere between Peking and Paris. When the sun eventually sets, the Itala is fired up one last time. In the darkness, enormous sparks leap out of the magneto like some electrical contraption in Dr Frankenstein's laboratory. That rotten, stinking, mongrel magneto.

Mick: We all leave Rezekne in high spirits but the good cheer doesn't last long for most of us. The Spyker and Contal cruise through the day all the way to Kaunas without any hassles but the other three vehicles have trouble.

LEFT: ANTHONY PUTTING HIS CONSIDERABLE SKILLS TO WORK, FIXING THE FUEL LINE ON KEITH'S DE DION.

BELOW: WARREN BROWN, FORGER EXTRAORDINAIRE, SPRAY-PAINTING HIS *FAUX* NUMBERPLATES.

ABOVE: MICK HARD AT WORK IN THE BEER GARDEN OF THE HOTEL IN KAUNAS.

RIGHT: THE ITALA ON THE TRAILER WITH MAGNETO PROBLEMS.

Just out of town the Itala's ignition decides it won't handle high engine revs. A leaking radiator spilling water onto the magneto seems to be the obvious problem, but even after this is repaired the electrical gremlin is still running amok. After many hours and a couple of false starts, the red machine resorts to the sweep trailer and is hauled to Kaunas.

Keith's De Dion carks it just a little further along from the Itala. There's a fuel leak and Keith manages to clamp the offending section of fuel line and carries on for the day.

Latvia has a law forcing all vehicles to drive with their headlights on — a hard ask for 100-year-old cars with minimal electrics. The blue De Dion's modernised lighting system is usually pretty good but right now it's not working and the police pull John over and show absolutely no leniency towards his antique machine. Rather than stuff around on the roadside trying to sort out the trouble in front of a couple of smugly officious cops, John trailers the De Dion over the border into Lithuania, where the law doesn't apply (at least, not at this time of year) and he's free to travel unhindered. The incident only highlights the arbitrary nature of so many road laws.

The border crossing into Lithuania is little more than a formality for all of us. Our passports are stamped, our registration papers checked and we're waved through by the handful of relaxed guards at the post.

Tonight the Expedition suffers its first major theft. We've already had a number of minor ones: cash and wallets stolen from hotel rooms; two attempts at pickpocketing and a camera stolen after the strap was slashed from around the owner's wrist (all three in St Petersburg); tools and things taken from cars. But this time the thieves break into the blue De Dion's trailer and Henry's Nissan, looting them of most of the contents. Henry loses almost everything; John, Andrew and Robert lose significant amounts of personal effects, and Chris and I are relieved of a couple of things too.

Travellers are soft targets for theft and we can only expect it to get worse from here on. We're insured with Marsh, which is already proving helpful in sorting out our claims, and we're glad of the cover. But we resolve to be far more careful. After all, how does Andrew replace his late father's special bow tie? How do we recover the keepsakes given to us so warmly by Siberia's people? The losses cut deep.

JULY

S	M	T	W	T	F	S
3	4	5	6	7	1	2
10	11	12	13	14	8	9
17	18	19	20	21	15	16
24	25	26	27	28	22	23
31					29	30

DAY 48

Kaunas to Gizysko

Mick: We're shocked as we traverse the high ground while leaving Kaunas via the ring road. Sure, even Borghese saw other cars on the road as he drove through this area. And, yes, we've seen traffic every day from Beijing to Kaunas. But Borghese would never have imagined this and we'd almost forgotten it: the entire visible landscape is a seething mass of cars, buses and trucks eddying around a tangle of highways and roads. A century of motoring has changed the world and you don't need a more potent vision of its impact than this.

We lived with daily exposure to all this before the Expedition, of course. It's been fun living in a forgotten age all these weeks but now we're back in modern society for real and we can't escape it any longer. Trucks and cars growl past at twice the speed of the De Dions and we all feel small, feeble and vulnerable on these major thoroughfares with their twenty-first century bustle. We need to get onto the minor roads instead.

First we must enter Poland, another easy border crossing in the European Union. In 1907 there was no Lithuania, no Latvia, no Poland — just Russia and Germany. Again, we marvel at how much the world has changed. We also realise that, despite the social and political upheaval in the intervening years, some things don't change.

The moment we enter Poland, we see a different kind of Europe to what we've just left. The Russian influence is suddenly almost nonexistent (bar the awful Soviet housing blocks in some towns, but in Poland they've painted them in bright colours and made an effort) while Germany's influence is clear: farmhouses and barns are made from brick or stone, all the paddocks are fenced and almost every square metre of useful land is cultivated.

We turn west at Suwalki and find Nirvana for veteran cars. The route to Gizysko follows winding country lanes that are generally smooth and often enclosed by a tunnel of trees. We trundle through villages where the houses and shops are built right onto the edge of the road, where gardens are fenced and tended, where children and old people peddle around on bicycles, and where even a Contal feels almost right.

There are lakes here, too, and the scenery is stunning. We could drive like this for ever but, like all good things, it ends too soon as we find our hotel in Gizysko. We swap wheels for feet and explore this beautiful town with its canal, lakes, boats and fair. This is a holiday town without too much of a touristy feel and it is perfect for us as we finish off what's turned into one of the most enjoyable days of driving we've experienced. To top it off, as the sun is setting the Itala fires up and roars its pleasure after a complete overhaul of the electrics. We're all set for tomorrow.

Warren: Lang reckons he's sorted out the Itala's problems, but after a few kilometres the car plays up something fierce. We pull over and raise the bonnet. What's that on the inlet manifold? It looks like water. It looks like condensation. I put my hand on the brass manifold. It's frozen! The manifold is freezing up — something that happens regularly with aircraft carburettors, Lang tells me, which have built-in heating devices to avoid the carby icing up and your aircraft ploughing nose-first into the ground. Being a pilot, Lang's only too well aware that this can happen, but it's unusual in a car. It's a warm, sunny day and apparently when the temperature and the humidity are under just the right conditions, the carby will ice up. The Itala is back on the trailer — the plan now is to buy a new ignition coil and the matching condensor. We're out of Lithuania and heading through Poland, one of the most beautiful countries we've seen. We arrive late in the afternoon at the lakeside holiday town of Gizysko, where Anthony and Peter Tombs get cracking with the Itala, fitting the condensor and the coil. It fires up like a beauty — problem solved.

LEFT: LITHUANIAN ROADWORKERS GATHER AROUND THE ITALA.

BELOW: ANTHONY CHECKS THE MAP AS THE EXPEDITIONERS HEAD FOR POLAND.

ABOVE: WARREN AND LANG CONFER.

RIGHT: KEITH'S DE DION LEAVING KAUNAS, HEADING FOR GIZYSKO IN POLAND.

JULY

S	M	T	W	T	F	S
					✗	②
3	4	5	6	7	8	9
10	11	12	13	14	15	16
17	18	19	20	21	22	23
24	25	26	27	28	29	30
31						

DAY 49

Gizysko to Malbork

Mick: John effects his usual early escape in the blue De Dion, hitting the road at 6 a.m. to make the most of the empty roads and the extra hour or two of travelling time. The rest of us have a more leisurely start before heading a short distance up the road to the Wolf's Lair, Hitler's major headquarters during the Second World War. He spent two-fifths of the war secreted away in the bunkers here under a canopy of dense trees where the only threat came from the inside.

We walk through the remains of the complex and stand on the same ground that saw such a central part of history being played out more than 60 years ago. Borghese travelled through this territory at the end of a golden era for Europe. He had no idea that there was half a century of bloodshed and turmoil looming.

The region has scores of small lakes scattered all over and most of us choose one near the village of Lutry for a picnic lunch while a handful of locals inspect the cars. Here we notice people are more respectful, not touching the cars without first asking and rarely climbing into them. Not that we mind so much, and when we give them the nod their faces light up and their cameras flash constantly.

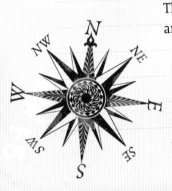

The pretty country roads aren't as smooth and easy as yesterday's and we work a fair bit harder. It's more tiring but beats the hell out of dealing with trucks on the highways. And the route has its rewards, like tunnels of trees that go on for more than a kilometre at a time. Stunning. And eventually they lead us to Malbork, once Marienburg, where we're planning a rest day. John is the first to arrive and it's such a novelty for him that he's not quite sure if he's at the right place.

LEFT: FRIENDLY HOLIDAYMAKERS WAVE TO THE SPYKER CREW AS THEY DRIVE PAST.

BELOW: (L TO R) CHRIS, WARREN, MICK, STIJNUS AND LYNNE AT THE WOLF'S LAIR.

ABOVE: WARREN AND MICK AT THE WOLF'S LAIR.

RIGHT: FOUR CAR CREWS LINE UP – ONLY THE BLUE DE DION IS MISSING. AS HAPPENED OFTEN ON THIS TRIP, THE LITTLE CAR HAS GONE AHEAD OF THE PACK.

Malbork

Warren: Marek Stokowski loves his job. He's a curator at St Mary's Castle in Malbork and his knowledge of the ancient Teutonic Order of Knights is astonishing. Marek lives and breathes the castle — actually, he does live in one part of the castle, an enormous and exquisite red brick structure for which construction commenced in 1276. The Teutonic Knights were a fairly bloodthirsty bunch of German monks who returned from a Crusade in the Holy Land and set up the castle to be the most powerful war machine in Europe. During the fourteenth and fifteenth centuries St Mary's Castle was the biggest castle in the world and one of the most important political and economic centres in Europe. World War II nearly spelt the end for St Mary's when the Nazis and Red Army slugged it out in a violent two-month battle that almost saw the whole place flattened. Sixty years later, the castle is still being reconstructed. It's a monstrous job. Ten years ago, Marek and another curator were given the task of listing every room in this enormous castle — after three months, they gave up.

Mick: First thing today we are treated to a special tour of the incredible Malbork Castle, once the centre of the Teutonic Knights' world. It is Malbork's one claim to fame

LEFT: THE SCENE FROM ST MARY'S CASTLE, ACROSS MALBORK.

BELOW: EXPEDITIONERS CASTING A LONG SHADOW AS THEY TRAVERSE THE CASTLE'S COBBLESTONES.

ABOVE: INTRICATE PAINTWORK ON A CEILING INSIDE THE CASTLE.

RIGHT: THE CHANGING LIGHT CREATES A SPECTACULAR HUE ON THE CASTLE.

Borghese crossed into Germany
south of Kaunas (then named Kovno
— there was no Poland, Latvia,
Lithuania or Estonia in 1907) after
many weeks in the Russian empire.
German motorists greeted them
with a Teutonic 'Hoch, hoch, hoch',
and the authorities gave Borghese a
driver's licence — 'without
examination!' notes Barzini.
They sped on through Königsberg,
Marienburg and Dirschau, finally
stopping in a small town less than
1000 miles (1600 km) from Paris.
The roads were excellent, speeds were
high and the end was within reach.

and tourism, and it's worth the trip. Castle curator Marek Stokowski goes out of his way for us, taking us into areas not yet open to the public and explaining some of the amazing history of the place. It was founded in the thirteenth century, still exhibits fourteenth century murals, was almost destroyed in the twentieth century (the War again) and is now a powerful statement about modern human history; parts of it are original, parts are rebuilt and parts are still in ruin, and no one with any sense of history can go through it without feeling joy, awe, respect, pride, sadness, anger, hopelessness and optimism.

Tonight there's kangaroo on the menu. I have to give it a go, just to say I've eaten roo in Poland. Unfortunately, I can't recommend it — the Poles stewed the meat to death until it was unrecognisable. I should have stuck to the pork knuckle.

DAY 51

From Malbork

Warren: Lang's driving the recovery truck today so that Anthony can have a turn driving the Itala; Bob Barker's riding with us in the red car. It's a beautiful day and I'm up for a water fight with the boys in the Contal. Yes, this is childish; yes, it is stupid — but it's fun. Having no roof or doors on any of the cars means that drivers and passengers are easy targets for a good soaking. In my experience on the Expedition so far, the best ordnance is your 375 ml water bottle which, when squeezed, blasts out water like a fire hose.

Keith's yellow De Dion is always an easy target. It putters along with cranky old Keith hanging onto the steering wheel for grim death and as we overtake I give him a right royal soaking. He just loves it. The Itala speeds off and all I can see is a cursing, soggy Keith chugging away, unable to get his hands around my neck.

Behind us is the Contal, Chris Boyle is sitting in the front seat as if he's being chauffeured around in a Chesterfield armchair. I wave to Mick to drive up closer — I want to tell him something. The Contal whizzes up alongside the Itala ... ready, ready, ready — *bang!* Chris is soaked — I got him a beauty. Mick backs off. I think I've opened a serious can of worms here.

Twenty minutes later the Itala's puttering along, Anthony at the wheel, his wild hair and beard trailing in the wind, when a spidery green contraption roars up alongside and we're pelted with a series of water bombs, thoroughly soaking us. Mick and Chris are cackling like hyenas as the Contal accelerates into the distance and out of sight. Right. The gloves are off. No prisoners.

LEFT: BEFORE THE DAY'S ANTICS BEGIN, WARREN REVELS IN THE FREEDOM OF TRAVEL — AND A DAY WITHOUT RAIN. BOB SAYS IT WAS 'A BEAUTIFUL DAY FOR DRIVING.'

BELOW: SCENES FROM A WATER FIGHT — WARREN'S HAIR TAKES A HIT.

ABOVE: THE CONTAL AND ITALA CREWS ENGAGED IN BATTLE.

RIGHT: ROB SPYKER, AN INNOCENT VICTIM OF THE CONTAL VS ITALA WATER WAR AS WARREN TURNS THE HOSE ON HIM.

We pull into a service station to refuel, and Bob Barker finds a dispenser of disposable plastic gloves. With the precision and dedication of a bomb disposal expert, he prepares a series of fragile water bombs. Back on the road, we continue for a while until Bob spies the rotten Contal hiding amongst some trees, clearly waiting to pounce on us from behind. They realise they've been spotted and are soon alongside us; a huge exchange of water bombs takes place, most of which — including my own — explode on me. Thoroughly drenched, I watch the Contal disappear again into the distance. Right.

We pull into another service station, where someone suggests that condoms would make the best water bombs. Condoms! Of course! According to the *SAS Survival Guide*, condoms can hold 4 litres of water — I think ... something like that, anyway. I approach the service station attendant, who is greatly surprised by three saturated, filthy, bearded men in a century-old car bursting into his shop.

'Ah ... do you sell ... ah ... condoms? You know ...' I make a quick drawing on a piece of paper. His eyebrows lift. 'Yes.' 'Great,' I say. 'We'll need about ten.' He disappears and brings back ten packets, a total of thirty condoms. We look at each other. 'I don't think I'll be needing thirty,' I say.

We're back on the road, the floor of the Itala now an arsenal of water-filled condoms ready to hurl at the Contal. We soon round a bend, where we spy a service station with the Contal, the Spyker, Keith's De Dion and the whole crowd sitting at outdoor tables drinking coffee.

'Right,' I say to Anthony, 'drive in as close as you can and I'll let 'em have it.' Anthony swings the Itala into the service station driveway and I reach for one of the water-filled condom-bombs. Mick and Chris know what is about to happen and leap towards the door of the service station for cover. I hurl one of the water bombs but it goes widely off the mark. 'Turn round again!' I shout to Anthony as he swings the Itala round in full lock. Time for a second go. I pick up a water bomb and it explodes in my hand, absolutely drenching me. 'Turn round again!!' I've got to hit somebody this time. I pick up the water bottle, ready to soak Mick, but inadvertently tip the whole lot over myself. That's enough — let's get out of here.

This evening we're welcomed by a mate of Stijnus's, Dick Bach, who owns a plant machinery hire factory very close to the Polish–German border. The Expedition vehicles will be locked up there overnight. When we arrive, the Spyker is already there and Stijnus, with a very concerned look on his face, drags me back over to the Itala to show me a problem he's noticed with the front right-hand wheel. I can't see anything, so I kneel down for a closer look. *Wham.* Lynne Shaw has dumped an entire bucket of water all over me. Good one. Wait a minute — I can hear the unmistakable sound of Keith's De Dion approaching. There must be a hose around here — I can blast Keith, Peter and Rob in one hit. The De Dion pulls up and I let them have it full bore. Rob leaps out and crash tackles me to the ground — this isn't in my plan. Andrew is in on the act and the hose is now stuffed fair and square down the inside of my shirt at full blast. Wonderful.

Mick: We've got a big day today: more than 350 kilometres to the German border. We settle onto the main road and get into mile-eating mode. John is away at 5.30 a.m., the rest of us two hours later, but Keith loads his De Dion onto the trailer for the first stint — there's no way either De Dion can go the distance comfortably without some fast-paced trailering.

John's day doesn't start well. His De Dion breaks a spring shackle and then the magneto shorts out. Both problems are overcome quickly enough with temporary fixes, the shackle sorted out sufficiently to last the trip and the magneto repaired well enough to complete the day, but Andrew will have to work on it tonight.

Anthony is sharing the drive with Warren in the Itala today. Early in the drive Warren waves to Chris and me to come up beside them. As soon as we're close he showers us with water and the battle is on. Throughout the morning we buzz one another, doing our best to soak the others. Chris and I fill a couple of small plastic bags and score two direct hits with them. Warren tries condoms filled with water but they prove to be useless missiles — allowing us to score more hits at the same time.

This main road isn't as heavily used as we feared and we make good time without an overbearing threat from faster cars and trucks. We pass through some picturesque towns and countless little villages. Near the end of the drive we're amazed to see a sandy beach full of bathers beside a lake, complete with women in bikinis — another first in many, many weeks. It's a hot day, too, and some of us are tempted to swim, but time is getting away from us.

DAY 52

JULY

S	M	T	W	T	F	S
✗	✗	⑤	6	7	✗	✗
10	11	12	13	14	15	16
17	18	19	20	21	22	23
24	25	26	27	28	29	30
31						

To Potsdam

Mick: Last night our cars were left in secure but distant parking and this brings major delays this morning. The last of us don't get away until well after 9 a.m., but luckily the run to Berlin is under 150 kilometres, a short day by any standards. Further west in Europe storms lash the landscape, causing floods and creating havoc on roads, so we watch the skies ahead of us with a wary eye as they darken and begin to drizzle on us.

We cross into Germany within minutes of departing. The border crossing here is slightly more than a formality but not at all problematic, and the only hassle we have is that most of us arrive as a group and have to wait half an hour as the officials process our passports in one hit. Chris and I take advantage of the delay to do the oil change we couldn't do last night — setting a very strange scene for the border guards, who've never witnessed anything quite as unusual as this.

There's no noticeable change as we cross from Poland to Germany at Kustrzyn. Perhaps the change is more remarkable in other regions, but here the only real clues are the different numberplates and the language on the signs.

Again John has left early and makes his way around Berlin to Potsdam, our destination for tonight. He has a slightly damp but trouble-free run and by the time anyone else arrives Andrew has just finished servicing the De Dion and put it away for the evening.

On the eastern outskirts of Berlin the Itala pulls up for lunch, then Keith's De Dion joins it, followed soon after by the

317

Contal and eventually the Spyker. We all have similar plans: to drive through Berlin, see some sights and then make Potsdam by late afternoon. So we form a slow convoy through the German city, swinging past the Reichstag, Brandenburg Gate and other monuments on a whirlwind tour that would have made the impatient Borghese proud.

The rain holds off long enough for us to reach Potsdam with just a splatter of water on our goggles.

Earlier in the day, I managed to make a complete idiot of myself. Out of boredom, stupidity, larrikinism or maybe all of the above, I decided to stand up on the front of the Contal while we were cruising along at about 30 km/h. In front of several Expedition vehicles and the ABC's cameras, I stood tall for a moment then felt the Contal lurch; I lost my balance and stepped forward ... into space.

For one ugly moment I tried to run with it but it was a lost cause. I sprawled down on the road, suffering dreadful damage to my ego but, luckily, almost none to my body. I rolled to my feet and exited stage right with all the calm and dignity I could muster, but when I looked around me all I could see was a dozen laughing Expeditioners who'll be telling this sorry tale tonight to anyone who'd listen, until the beer runs dry ...

Warren: It's hard to believe, but we've just crossed the German border and we're in Berlin. Prince Borghese entered the city escorted by a fleet of other Italas brought by the manufacturers in Turin for use by journalists who were covering the event. No other Italas in sight today, although the cars receive a tremendous response from Berlin motorists. We motor past the Reichstag and then become involved in a traffic jam leading up to the Brandenburg Gate. Keith's little De Dion doesn't like sitting in the traffic — having no radiator fan tends to make the little yellow peril boil. And Keith too. 'I'm not sitting here in this traffic,' says Keith, pouring water over the steaming radiator in an attempt to cool it down. He throws the car into gear and swings the De Dion across the traffic, making a spectacular U-turn. The rest of the cars follow and we're under way, the De Dion — and Keith — happy again.

LEFT: WELL WITHIN GERMANY NOW, THE SPYKER COMPLEMENTS ITS BEAUTIFUL SURROUNDINGS.

BELOW: WARREN ATTEMPTS TO WRENCH MICK HEAD FIRST FROM THE CONTAL'S PASSENGER SEAT.

ABOVE: THE CARS AT THE REICHSTAG IN BERLIN.

RIGHT: STUCK IN A BERLIN TRAFFIC JAM. MEMBERS OF THE ABC CREW CAN BE SEEN SHARING THE 'BARZINI SEAT' IN THE BACK OF THE ITALA.

JULY

S	M	T	W	T	F	S
					X	X
X	X	X	⑥	7	8	9
10	11	12	13	14	15	16
17	18	19	20	21	22	23
24	25	26	27	28	29	30
31						

DAY 53

Potsdam to Braunlage and Gottingen

Warren: It's wet again, of course. We're off early to barrel along through the lush German countryside. The car is running particularly well this morning, and there's only a few hundred kilometres to go before it's all over. It's my turn to drive the Itala today and I can smell Paris from here: the coffee, the baguettes, the dodgy cigarettes, and the poodles smoking the dodgy cigarettes, eating the baguettes and drinking the coffee. This Expedition has been going way too long.

We're driving in the rain through a dark, damp forest when, with no warning, there is a tremendous *bang* from underneath the car, the sound of metal hitting the road, of something spinning below hitting the floorboards and an instant loss of power. I pull the Itala off the road, and the gear lever is shaking wildly — we've finally blown up the gearbox for sure. Lang and I climb out of the car and lie flat on the road to see what's happened. It's a mess. The driveshaft has gone skewwhiff at the differential end and the big brass dust cover has a whopping hole punched through it. I dread to think what's happened inside.

I eventually remove the fifteen or so tiny screws that hold the dust cover on and remove it. The universal joint has completely collapsed; a two-dollar circular clamp that binds the whole assembly together has given up the ghost and the universal joint has decided to completely dismantle. Hang on, one of the two massive steel cross-pins is missing — it's rocketted through the brass dust cover like an intercontinental ballistic missle and must be back up the road somewhere. If that thing had shot out and hit someone, it could have killed them. Lang

and I wander back up the road to look for the steel pin and within minutes, amazingly, Lang's found it. If we can get hold of a new circular clamp, the universal joint can be reassembled.

Only a kilometre up the road is a truck wrecking yard and for an investment of two dollars we're in possession our very own circular clamp. The universal joint is back together — we're on our way.

Mick: More rain. And some of our gear is still wet from yesterday. We're grim-faced as we pull on our driving coats and settle our goggles over our eyes, hoping they won't fog up in the first minute. It's cool, too, the temperature sitting somewhere around 10° Celsius, if last night's weather forecast was correct. We don't have the luxury of wasting time, though, so we venture back out into the greyness and the traffic.

The rain comes and goes throughout the day, and when the sun is out on the odd occasion it's strong enough to make us sweat under all the layers of clothes we wear.

Today we're back onto lesser roads rather than highways. Things are very different because of it. The driving is more varied and less stressful, taking us through small villages and thick forests. But navigation is a bugger. There are so many turn-offs and such short stints between places that none of us goes through the day without one or two moments of geographic embarrassment. The road we intend to take out of Zerbst is so obscure that only the Itala goes that way; not even the sweep truck manages to figure it out.

The alternative road takes the rest of us — in ones and twos — to a ferry crossing over the Elbe River, where there's a café on the opposite bank. Perfect for an idle half-hour break as boats and barges and canoeists glide up and down the waterway.

Soon we reach even prettier roads, winding through narrow valleys and tiny towns whose houses are built right down to the edge of the constricted tarmac. The wet weather brings the dense forests even closer around us before we suddenly pop out into open farmland again.

Somehow today is getting longer and longer. We're not reaching our destination as comfortably as usual, even though it should only be about

LEFT: PETER BROWN GIVES THE THUMBS UP AS KEITH DRIVES HIM AND ROB FROM THE FERRY.

BELOW AND BELOW LEFT: BOB SAYS THEY WERE IN THE 'WITCHES' COUNTRY' THAT DAY AND SNAPPED SOME PROOF.

RIGHT: THE DAMAGE DONE BY THE ITALA'S CROSS-PIN AS IT ZOOMED OUT OF THE ENGINE AND ONTO THE ROAD.

240 kilometres in total. Stijnus stops in Braunlage, about 70 kilometres short of the overnight stop at Gottingen, but the Itala and Grace motor past without pulling in. The Contal and yellow De Dion join Stijnus and we all decide to call it quits for the day when Anthony arrives and tells them he's done over 280 kilometres already just to get here. Someone stuffed up on the day's distance and we're not happy. On these slower roads, with all the delays of difficult navigation, we've spent a full day getting here and now the weather is setting in for heavier rain again. That's enough for us.

The Itala reaches Gottingen but not without drama. Its universal joint explodes, firing one of the pins out through a brass housing and into the forest. The sound is frightening but luckily there's no serious damage and Lang even manages to find the ejected pin! They reassemble the universal, holding it together with a heavy hose clamp, and continue the drive.

John and Andrew are in more difficulty in the blue De Dion, having lost touch with their support crew, and they're also without a phone to reach them. There's no way a humble De Dion can drive all that way in one day, and not even John's super-early start can change that. It's 11 p.m. when they reach Gottingen, well after dark. They're not happy.

1907

HANNOVER, ESSEN

A fleet of cars followed Borghese out of Berlin, but when he put the Itala into top gear he left most behind. Six, including three Italas bearing journalists and the words 'Peking-Matin' (the proprietorial newspaper had decided to rename it), kept up — Barzini was thrilled by the sight of 'seven great motorcars in hot pursuit of one another, going in a line at 40 miles an hour [65 km/h]!' Stopping that night at Bielefeld, just beyond Hannover, they checked their maps, added distances between towns and were thrilled to realise that they were just 680 km from Paris.

JULY

S	M	T	W	T	F	S
				⊗	⊗
✗	✗	✗	⊗	⑦	8	9
10	11	12	13	14	15	16
17	18	19	20	21	22	23
24	25	26	27	28	29	30
31

DAY 54

From Braunlage and Gottingen

Mick: The group splits into three today and won't be complete again until Paris. The main part of it — the Itala, Keith's De Dion, Spyker and support vehicles — aim to reach Maastricht in two days via a route taking them south of the ugly tangle of industrial cities around Essen. While the 1907 trip went to Liege, we're heading for nearby Maastricht in Holland so that we can touch the home country of Stijnus and his Spyker. Besides, Stijnus's mates have promised a party.

John decides to make a break for Paris on the most direct route, but he and Andrew will have to go alone because Henry has to take his Nissan to Maastricht to replace a broken window. John is confident in his car's ability to manage the trip without a mothership, a complete change of attitude compared to the beginning of the Expedition when the little blue machine was utterly untested. It has proven to be incredibly dependable — one of the Expedition's best cars.

Chris and I want a night with locals again, which we only seem to manage when we take off alone, so we plot a northern route and set off, finding the Gasthof Zum Luneborger, a hotel, after crossing the Rhein. The hotelier and his mate challenge us to darts with beer, schnapps and an evil brew called Killepitsch (we call it Kill-A-Bitch because it'd kill a brown dog) at stake. We strut proudly as we win free drinks from the publican, and grimace when we lose. Yes, it's a very messy night.

Everyone else camps in a beautiful spot by a lake near Attendorn. The weather clears and they have a great evening surrounded by a postcard-perfect piece of Europe. The clouds are back next day, drenching the party for most of the day.

LEFT: KEITH IS NOT SCOWLING AT THE BAD WEATHER — HE'S FENDING OFF HAIL BROUGHT ON BY A SUDDEN STORM.

BELOW: SCENES FROM A DAY'S TRAVEL IN GERMANY.

1907

The Sequel: New York to Paris 1908

The Raid of 1907 was such an astonishing worldwide success, the following year Le Matin and the New York Times launched a race from New York to Paris. Despite a massive crowd of 250 000 motor-mad spectators waving the cars off, the incredibly poor state of American roads combined with a harsh winter and unbelievably poor organisation nearly turned the event into a fiasco. Due to blizzards in the US, some cars were placed aboard trains and immediately disqualified, meaning nearly all the field was out of the race before reaching San Francisco. The winning car was an American Thomas Flyer. Neither Le Matin or the New York Times attempted promoting another international race again.

Warren: We're camping again. We don't really need to, but we're all really keen to do it — there's a bit of a collective yearning for the old days in the Gobi, under the stars. We'll be shocking dinner guests when we return — 'Did I ever tell you about the time I was camping in the Gobi under the stars?' 'Only 500 times ... pass the salt.'

Nowadays, I actually sleep better when I'm in the sleeping bag inside the tent than in some hotel. We're all set up in a pristine caravan park in the picturesque German village of Attendorn, where the art of European camping is on display, big time. None of this set-up-a-tent-and-throw-your-sleeping-bag-in stuff like we do. European camping life involves parking a massive white campervan that looks like a giant wheeled refrigerator lying on its side. These things are so big, the entire European Union could hold its Annual General Meeting inside. Attached to these monstrosities are enough satellite dishes to coordinate an entire Martian invasion and on the van in front of me is a radio mast with which you could conduct a clear chinwag with the fellas down at Mawson Antarctic Base.

DAY 55

To Maastricht

Warren: Some of Stijnus's friends in Holland have organised a reception for us in Maastricht. Today we follow the big Dutch bloke in the big Dutch car through the German countryside toward the Netherlands, but all of a sudden the old Spyker comes slowly to a halt.

'It's the silicones,' says Stijnus. Right from Beijing, Stijnus's only ongoing problem has been with the 'silicones', as he puts it. When rebuilding the car for the Expedition, he used silicone sealer for the petrol tank which, once on the road, began to dissolve into the fuel, creating all sorts of blockages. This is the sixtieth blockage he's had. Stijnus has a love-hate relationship with the silicone — sometimes he talks about it almost affectionately. 'Mister Silicones,' he sings gently, 'don't stop the car, Mister Silicones', hoping Mister Silicones won't spoil the day. After removing the fuel bowl from the carburettor and hauling out the goopy silicone, we're all back on the road.

In Maastricht, everyone's waiting under a specially prepared banner, drinking Champagne. Stijnus's mother is here too — it's only a few years since her husband passed away and her son has driven Mr Schotte's car all the way from China to Holland.

Left: The Itala and Spyker mysteriously driving in opposite directions.

Below: The reception in Maastricht for the 'Dutch Rolls-Royce' and its driver, Stijnus.

Above: Stijnus's mother came to meet him in Maastricht.

Right: Stijnus addresses the crowd and shares a joke with Warren.

DAY 56

Maastricht to Bouillon

Mick: We're getting lazy. This is the home stretch and there's not the same pressure to push on, to keep the momentum going. So this morning we take up an invitation to Charlie's place for coffee at 11 a.m., meaning we can sleep in till 9 o'clock if we want! Decadence. And the sun is shining again.

After coffee we drive south through Belgium in convoy till lunchtime, going around in circles and chucking a dizzying number of U-turns as we struggle to navigate through a tangled mess of minor roads. European back roads can be a nightmare.

We have lunch in a beautiful riverside village filled chock-a-block with Belgians out for a Saturday drive. There are cars, motorcycles, pushbikes and walkers everywhere, all having a wonderful day.

John and Andrew carry on along their own route towards Paris. The De Dion is doing them proud, requiring nothing more than the usual top-ups of oils, adjustment of points and attention to the details.

The main group heads straight down to Bouillon for the night, just short of the French border. Chris gets a taste for Belgian beer at lunch, though, and I become his designated driver on a pub crawl for the next 70 kilometres. We stop at every little bar along the way until reaching Bouillon, Chris laughing at his silliness every time but making it to Bouillon with steady feet.

LEFT: MEMBERS OF A LOCAL VINTAGE CAR CLUB (IN THE GREEN CAR) ESCORT THE EXPEDITION VEHICLES.

BELOW: THE ALWAYS-INTERESTING JUXTAPOSITION OF VETERAN CARS WITH MODERN-DAY VEHICLES – ON THIS EXPEDITION, THE OLD CARS HAVE CERTAINLY PROVED THEIR CAPABILITIES.

ABOVE: PETER BROWN WAVES TO STIJNUS AS THE LATTER OVERTAKES THE YELLOW DE DION.

RIGHT: OFTEN THE BEST PART OF THE DAY – SITTING DOWN INSIDE. AROUND THE TABLE SIT (L TO R) KEITH, WARREN, PETER BROWN AND LANG; CHRIS IS AT THE BAR.

DAY 57

JULY

S	M	T	W	T	F	S
~~9~~	~~10~~	~~11~~	~~12~~	~~13~~	~~14~~	~~15~~
(10)	11	12	13	14	15	16
17	18	19	20	21	22	23
24	25	26	27	28	29	30
31						

Bouillon to Verdun

Warren: When leaving Berlin, Prince Borghese encountered massed German army units on manoeuvres — the Kaiser's magnificent horse artillery, infantry, and lance-wielding Uhlans on the march. Barzini was particularly impressed with a stirring war hymn sung in unison, 'the wonderful impact of this forceful, solemn music that was the formidable voice of an army.' Within seven years, this army would be locked in a miserable, unending clash to the death with other armies — many of those troops the Itala's crew observed that day would lie dead or mutilated on a battlefield.

We are at Verdun, the site of one of the most catastrophic battles in history. During World War I, more than half a million French and German soldiers were killed in this one place during a two-year war of attrition. The raw optimism of a new century, the energy and enthusiasm of an era of great Peking to Paris–style adventure, would be blown to pieces and lost for ever in places like Verdun.

LEFT: THE CARS PREPARE TO LEAVE BOUILLON AS CYCLISTS PASS THEM BY.

BELOW: THE CARS ARRIVING IN VERDUN.

ABOVE: LANG AND WARREN AT THE SITE OF A BOMBED VILLAGE IN VERDUN; KEITH IS WITH THEM. LANG AND WARREN MET AND HATCHED THE IDEA OF THE 2005 EXPEDITION AT A WORLD WAR II COMMEMORATION – A D-DAY EVENT IN NORMANDY – AND FITTINGLY THEY PAY TRIBUTE TO THE SOLDIERS OF WORLD WAR I AS THEY NEAR THE END OF THEIR JOURNEY.

RIGHT: THE FRENCH FLAG AT HALF-MAST AT FORT DE DOUAUMONT, NEAR VERDUN.

DAY 58

Verdun to Mary-sur-Marne

Mick: Monday is a gorgeous day and becomes very hot by the standards we've grown used to — the temperature hits the mid-20s. If only there were a beach to go to ...

John and Andrew reach Paris this morning but for the rest of us it's our last full day's drive, to tiny Mary-sur-Marne near Meaux. The run is brilliant — trouble-free and carefree through Champagne country, where the valleys are completely given over to growing grapes. The bright sun brings out the multiple greens of a countryside dotted with villages and cute churches. Keith and Peter stop at a vineyard for a lunch of freshly caught trout, chips and Champagne.

We have a final dinner tonight in Mary-sur-Marne. The trip's not quite over but we know this may be the last time we can get almost all of us together in a place just for us. It's perfect. We toast our success, our friendships and our amazingly capable cars, and finish the evening with a slideshow of Bob Barker's photos that brings back memories from what feels like a lifetime ago. It's amazing how much has been buried in our crowded memories and Bob's images bring it all flooding back.

LEFT: ON THE SECOND-LAST DAY OF THE TRIP, KEITH ENJOYS A RELAXED LUNCH IN CHAMPAGNE COUNTRY.

BELOW: KEITH'S CAR GETS YET ANOTHER PUSH – FROM ANTHONY, ROB, PETER AND ANDREW THIS TIME – AS IT LEAVES A CHAMPAGNE TASTING.

ABOVE: WARREN TRIES TO WREST A VODKA BOTTLE FROM STIJNUS'S CHICKEN.

RIGHT: WARREN MAKING SURE EVERYTHING IS PERFECT FOR THE DRIVE INTO PARIS, AS HE PATCHES UP DAMAGE TO THE ITALA'S PAINTWORK.

DAY 59

JULY

S	M	T	W	T	F	S
☒	☒	☒	☒	☒	☒	☒
☒	☒	☒	⑫	13	14	15	16
17	18	19	20	21	22	23
24	25	26	27	28	29	30
31

Mary~sur~Marne to Paris

Warren: 'A head-on collision?' I ask. 'Is he all right?' It's 6 a.m. and we're preparing for our drive into Paris. The ABC crew left at around 4:30 and only 3 kilometres from our camp site, Mark, one of the English drivers, strayed onto the wrong side of the road, writing off his Land Cruiser and the Seat sedan heading towards him. I feel sick. Our last day, all this way with no serious accidents, and now this. Miraculously, no one is hurt. Mark is okay, but he fell into one of those right-hand drive moments in a left-hand drive country.

Way back in China, Lang and I made a pact that if I drove the Itala out of Beijing, he'd drive it into Paris. Well, the day's arrived, the Itala has made it and Lang's behind the wheel. It's a particularly beautiful, cloudless day — perfect, hopefully, for our arrival at the Eiffel Tower. We drive in convoy to the outskirts of Paris, the beginnings of which look like so many big cities we've driven through: expressways, industrial areas, complex destination signs, serious traffic. We keep the cars together as much as possible.

We are now gridlocked in Paris' heavy traffic, something which Keith's little French car isn't too happy about, and it starts to boil. It's nearly 100 years since the De Dion was last in Paris — you'd think it would be looking forward to it. The cars have travelled such a long way and done so well. As Peter Tombs says, 'It's like asking your granny to run the marathon.' These old grannies have nearly made it across the finish line.

We pull the convoy onto a median strip to wait for Keith to catch us up. 'He's back on the road!' someone yells and we move off. Whoops — we were supposed to turn left there, I realise as I look at the map. We're heading toward Gare du Nord, Paris' whopping equivalent of Grand Central Station and a place we really don't want to go to. I figure out how we can get back on track, but roadworks and policemen blocking off streets only seem to make things worse.

Okay, if we turn right here and follow the railway, we'll be back on track. If we follow this street we should see ... there it is! The Arc de Triomphe in all its glory, the tricolour flag fluttering in the breeze. Lang puts the Itala in first gear, ready to take the plunge into the traffic frenzy that circles the archway.

'Good luck,' I say as he pushes out into the oncoming wave. We're on. I don't believe it. Here we are driving our 100-year-old cars around the Arc de Triomphe. I turn to look behind me — here's Keith firmly gripping the yellow De Dion's steering wheel, the bonnet raised, Anthony on the running board pouring water into the radiator as the little car putters around the circuit. Beside him John Matheson in the blue De Dion; behind is the monstrous Spyker loaded with hangers-on and weaving in and out of the traffic while the Contal zaps between cars, as it has done all the way from Beijing. It is a very emotional sight. I feel so proud to be part of this crazy rag-tag group, people who started off so fresh, clean and naive as to what this Expedition would entail, and here they are, weatherbeaten, filthy and now incredibly experienced — all of us battling the traffic together around the giant arch and onto the Champs Elysées.

Down the Champs Elysées the group of five cars meanders, turning onto a bridge and crossing the Seine; we must be getting close to the Eiffel Tower. Suddenly we see a large crowd of people standing beneath a giant banner declaring 'Pekin-Paris Arrivée'. 'There it is,' I say to Lang, and he swings the Itala under the banner, pulling the handbrake on and switching off the engine.

Lana Hurst, a welcome face I haven't seen since Beijing, races up to me with a glass of Champagne and gives me a kiss. It is all like some dream. I climb out of the Itala and turn around. The enormous frame of the Eiffel Tower right above me knocks me off balance. I don't know why, but I just wasn't expecting it. I never thought we'd ever get here — across China, the stark remoteness of Mongolia, the endless weeks spent crossing Siberia, western Europe taunting us, but still never any closer to our final destination. I feel as though I've been whacked in the face with a cricket bat — so many emotions spewing up in one hit. It is a feeling of happiness, of some sadness and of unbelievable relief. We've made it.

I first knew of the Peking to Paris event as a kid playing a board game in a holiday annual, where you rolled a dice and moved a button or a coin along the route. The winner arrived at a picture of the Eiffel Tower — and here we are. Game over.

We are greeted by the Australian Ambassador to France, Penny Wensley, who toasts us, the Expedition, and what we have achieved. Lang and I make our final speeches, and a tremendous wave of accomplishment washes over everyone who has had anything to do with the Expedition. We have done what we set out to do and arrived seven minutes late. Peter Tombs takes me aside. 'You guys have done it — it's incredible. No one can take that away from you. You can say to people, "Top that", because what you've done is the best there is.' I think he's probably right.

Mick: Dawn on our last day and the camp is already busy. Our support crews take most of the modern vehicles and trailers into Paris at 4.30 a.m. to park at the Australian Embassy before riding the train back out to the ring road, where we'll pick them up on our way past. We don't have to leave Mary-sur-Marne in the veteran cars until 9 a.m. but many us are wide awake before the first spray of light touches the sky.

We all have different thoughts. I'm packing my tent an hour or two after waking up when I hear someone say, 'This is it, our last day. It's all over.' It hasn't occurred to me at all till this moment and when I think harder I realise I'm still not thinking of the end, just of the here-and-now, of leaving on time, of ensuring I've got everything I may need to reach the destination, of which route we'll take. I can't image the end, not even now. Others are ready to shake hands and give a cheer right away. It's funny how differently we all react.

Chris and I head off early to the ring-road meeting point and get hopelessly lost on Paris' nightmare of roads and freeways. We finally find ourselves again, grab a coffee in a café, and when the owner realises what we're doing, he gives us a bottle of 1999 Bordeaux Supérieur. Wow. Right up to the very end, we're being shown so much friendship and goodwill.

We join the support crews down the road and soon the other cars rumble by. John comes into view in the blue De Dion and suddenly we're a convoy of five

Peking to Paris veterans driving triumphantly into Paris after an amazing journey across two continents and ten countries. We're all here — all of us! What are the odds?

The streets are jammed with cars, not lined by spectators as they were back in 1907. The French Automobile Association and traffic authorities have had no interest in us whatsoever so they don't clear our route, but our cars handle the slow and hot conditions pretty well. We take a few scenic detours when our navigational abilities fail us; but as we cruise up Avenue de Friedland, the Arc de Triomphe looms ahead, bringing powerful reality to a moment we've talked about many times over the past weeks.

The great archway vies with the horrendous traffic for our attention. No insurance company will cover any vehicle here and we understand why when we enter the free-for-all chaos of this uncontrollable roundabout. By force and surprise, we manage to barge through without breaking our convoy and continue down the Champs Elysées, cross the Seine on the Alexander III bridge with its golden statues atop massive pillars, then aim for the Eiffel Tower that we can see pointing high above the Parisian skyline.

The Itala leads John's De Dion, the Contal, Keith's De Dion and finally the Spyker anticlockwise past the Tower's northern pylon and around three sides until we see a crowd waiting for us. We swing under the banner and pull up, switch off the cars and ... I sit for a moment, my head lost in another world until Andrew's outstretched hand breaks my reverie. 'Congratulations,' he says with a huge smile and we shake hands. Champagne in hand, everyone in the Expedition congratulates each other on our journey and gratefully accepts the good cheer of those who've come to welcome us. Some are family, some are enthusiasts, some are locals; some are simply tourists who've stumbled across our little ceremony.

The Australian Ambassador welcomes us with a speech. The Eiffel Tower stands right behind her, a stone's throw away, the perfect symbol of our arrival in Paris.

We've made it. Over 13 000 kilometres in the most unlikely of cars, just as it was in 1907. We've seen a world changed by the motorcar and learnt a lot about what it was like in motoring's pioneering days. We've achieved something we were told couldn't be done — just as the knockers said of the 1907 Raid. Most of all, we've had a ball. This has been the experience of a lifetime, one that we'd never trade for anything.